Praise for The A

M000197983

'A fascinating and comprehensive study into the nature of apologies, covering everything from why a supermarket had to apologise 50 times in a day to how refusing to apologise made a company £1 million in four days.' RICHARD SHOTTON, BEHAVIOURAL SCIENTIST AND AUTHOR OF *THE CHOICE FACTORY*

'I make no apologies for saying hurrah for this book. At last, someone has drawn the distinction between being truly sorry and just faking it – in business, in politics and in life.' VIV GROSKOP, AUTHOR OF *HOW TO OWN THE ROOM: WOMEN AND THE ART OF BRILLIANT SPEAKING*

'*The Apology Impulse* is a brilliant overview of the world of fauxpologies and outrage capitalism, with stories of horribly misjudged responses alongside insights into how to hit just the right note. It made me smile and ponder my own spectrum of contrition, but it will – and should – change the way organizations approach the S-word.' NEIL MULLARKEY, CO-FOUNDER OF THE COMEDY STORE PLAYERS AND CHIEF OF IMPROV YOUR BIZ

'A highly relevant and important book. It is both witty and wise.' JULIA HOBSBAWM OBE, HONORARY VISITING PROFESSOR IN WORKPLACE SOCIAL HEALTH, CASS BUSINESS SCHOOL

'How businesses behave and what they say really matters. *The Apology Impulse* explains how companies can do both things better, and comes from authors who know how to do this well.' CHRIS LEWIS, FOUNDER AND CEO OF LEWIS, AUTHOR OF *TOO FAST TO THINK* AND CO-AUTHOR OF *THE LEADERSHIP LAB*

The Apology Impulse

*How the business world ruined sorry
and why we can't stop saying it*

Sean O'Meara

Cary Cooper

KoganPage

Publisher's note

Every possible effort has been made to ensure that the information contained in this book is accurate at the time of going to press, and the publishers and authors cannot accept responsibility for any errors or omissions, however caused. No responsibility for loss or damage occasioned to any person acting, or refraining from action, as a result of the material in this publication can be accepted by the editor, the publisher or the authors.

First published in Great Britain and the United States in 2020 by Kogan Page Limited

2nd Floor, 45 Gee Street	122 W 27th St, 10th Floor	4737/23 Ansari Road
London	New York, NY 10001	Daryaganj
EC1V 3RS	USA	New Delhi 110002
United Kingdom		India

www.koganpage.com

ISBNs

Hardback	978 1 78966 034 0
Paperback	978 0 7494 9320 2
Ebook	978 0 7494 9321 9

British Library Cataloguing-in-Publication Data

A CIP record for this book is available from the British Library.

Library of Congress Cataloging-in-Publication Data

Names: O'Meara, Sean, 1981- author. | Cooper, Cary L., author.
Title: The apology impulse : how the business world ruined sorry and why we can't stop saying it / Sean O'Meara, Cary Cooper.
Description: New York, NY : Kogan Page, 2019. | Includes bibliographical references and index.
Identifiers: LCCN 2019028041 (print) | LCCN 2019028042 (ebook) | ISBN 9780749493202 (paperback) | ISBN 9781789660340 (hardback) | ISBN 9780749493219 (ebook)
Subjects: LCSH: Public relations. | Apologizing. | Corporate image. | Customer relations.
Classification: LCC HD59 .O47 2019 (print) | LCC HD59 (ebook) | DDC 659.2–dc23
LC record available at https://lccn.loc.gov/2019028041
LC ebook record available at https://lccn.loc.gov/2019028042

Typeset by Integra Software Services, Pondicherry
Print production managed by Jellyfish
Printed and bound by CPI Group (UK) Ltd, Croydon, CR0 4YY

Contents

About the authors

Sean O'Meara is a publicist, writer and occasional musician. He founded the public relations and digital communications consultancy Essential Content in 2015. He lives in Manchester, UK.

Professor Sir Cary Cooper CBE is the 50th Anniversary Professor of Organizational Psychology and Health at ALLIANCE Manchester Business School of the University of Manchester, President of the Chartered Institute of Personnel and Development, Immediate Past President of the British Academy of Management and President of the Institute of Welfare. He is the author/editor of over 170 books and over 350 scholarly articles on organizational psychology and HR topics. He has seven Honorary doctorates and is Honorary Fellow of the Royal College of Physicians. He received a CBE from the Queen in 2001 for his contribution to occupational health and was knighted by the Queen in 2014 for his contribution to the social sciences.

Acknowledgements

Sean O'Meara – With sincere thanks to Pauline Johnston, Pat O'Meara, Robert O'Meara, Ryan O'Meara and Kim O'Meara for the many years of inspiration, support and encouragement.

Thanks also to my friend and co-author Professor Cary Cooper, editor Christopher Cudmore and all at Kogan Page for giving me the benefit of their skill and talent (and patience) throughout the process, and to everyone who contributed their experiences and expertise for this book.

Cary Cooper – To all the Comms and PR professionals who did the right thing and owned up to their mistakes/failures.

CHAPTER ONE

Introduction

O n the morning of his wedding in March 1951, Mr R M Hosking of King's Heath in Birmingham realized he'd got an embarrassing problem. Through no fault of his own he was without a morning suit in which to get married. He'd ordered one and paid for it in plenty of time. It just never arrived. As he set off to get married in a pair of his soon-to-be father-in-law's trousers, Hosking would have been entirely unaware that the events leading to his misfortune had been set in motion the previous year. It would be of little comfort when he realized, but he wasn't the only groom without a suit to get married in that year.

A year before Hosking was due to tie the knot, Clement Attlee's Labour Government had made a change to the tax laws that inadvertently provided a hefty tax incentive for engaged couples to get married before the beginning of April, when the UK's fiscal year ends.[1] The advantages – specifically that any married couple could claim the full married man's allowance for the year ahead provided they were married by the end of the previous tax year – were so large that March swiftly overtook

August to become the most popular month for weddings in the UK.[2] It remained the most popular wedding month for almost two decades after Attlee's new rule, despite the obvious disadvantage of the famously bad British weather.

In 1951, the first year in which couples could take advantage of the new rule, the number of March weddings almost doubled on the previous year. Without knowing it, approximately 80,000 happy couples, like Hosking and his wife-to-be, would put an enormous strain on the entire wedding supply chain. And that is why Hosking had to borrow a pair of trousers from his fiancée's dad. The initial and unprecedented spike in March weddings took a lot of people by surprise. Unfortunately for Hosking that included the company from whom he'd ordered his morning suit.

A few weeks after his suitless wedding, he received a letter from the company who'd let him down. The letter said:

Dear Sir,

Words fail me to express the humility in which I stand for the disgraceful way you were let down. This is the first time such a thing has happened in the history of the Firm, and I can only say that the orders received were phenomenal. You are very moderate in your espressions [*sic*].

Your fee for breach of contract is inadequate – I enclose an extra £5 and ask you and your wife to have a bottle or two of wine on my House, to make up in a small way for our lapse. I offer my sincere apologies to you and your wife.

Yours faithfully,
H N Moss
Managing Director

The writer of the letter was Harry Moss, the then managing director of Moss Bros & Co of Covent Garden, now Moss Bros PLC, a global chain with annual revenue in the hundreds of millions.[3] Moss had enclosed two cheques along with his apology: one a refund from the company and a personal cheque from his own account that, in today's money, would be worth a few hundred pounds.

In November 2018, Hosking's son Patrick shared the letter on Twitter, almost 67 years after it had been sent. Citing a 'magnificent grovel', he asked why companies don't apologize like this any more. That's a question lots of us have been asking recently.

Moss's apology was never intended to be public. It was a letter from supplier to customer expressing genuine remorse and seeking to put things right. That it was

'Why can't organizations apologize any more!'

written in such a fantastically grovelling style is merely a bonus. In terms of intent and structure, this apology was almost spot on.

By today's standards especially, the letter could be considered a masterpiece; it is sincere, carrying with it an offer of repair and it's refreshingly free of any corporate equivocation or excuse-making modern consumers have come to accept as standard. It focuses almost entirely on Hosking and not the organization. Compare this letter to any of your favourite shrink-wrapped corporate apologies from the last few years and it becomes very clear very quickly that lots of organizations have forgotten their manners.

What went wrong?

2018 was a good year for bad public behaviour. Facebook and Starbucks set the early pace for corporate contrition. Tesla and Uber ended the year on a rousing crescendo. 2019 wasn't much better. Lots of organizations issued apologies. Very few of them said sorry.

As authors we've been closely monitoring these high-profile public apologies for more than two years. It's been remarkable to see how much effort goes into bad apologies and how skilful public figures and organizations have become in crafting semantically acrobatic statements – calling them apologies would be a category error – to deflect, reframe and evade the misdeeds they find themselves addressing. It's been even more impressive to witness, through the conduct of recently contrite organizations, just how much they didn't mean their apologies.

The lengths organizations will travel linguistically to *not* say sorry while appearing to apologize has been similarly impressive. The highest profile and most eagerly awaited apologies of the past few years have been insincere, passive, self-regarding and, perhaps most unforgivably, they've been far too long.

We've known how to apologize since biblical times. The Bible and the Quran are full of tips on saying sorry and forgiveness. And pretty much the entire point of Yom Kippur, Judaism's highest holiday, is to say sorry.

The current situation has nothing to do with organizations and public figures being unaware of how to say sorry. The world is chock-full of advice on how to do it properly. Two separate 2016 studies of 755 people conducted by Professor Roy J Lewicki, a scholar in the subject of trust development, negotiation and conflict management, identified the six key elements of an apology: regret, explanation, acknowledgement of responsibility, repentance, offer of repair and request for forgiveness.[4] There are more than 1,500 highly-cited studies about saying sorry listed in Google's academic database. There's even one about how to apologize to 'psychologically entitled shoppers'.[5] The lessons are there if we want them.

> *There isn't enough genuine atonement to go round.*

The current mess is a supply and demand problem. There isn't enough genuine atonement to go round. Consumers are demanding accountability, organizations are reluctant to provide it and people are getting short-changed as a result. In the absence of the genuine apologies consumers demand, crude fakes are flooding the market.

If you've been paying attention and looking beyond the headlines, you'll have noticed a worrying countertrend emerging alongside the highly noticeable bad apologies. In the background, partially hidden behind the blockbuster bad mea culpas issued by the likes of United Airlines and Facebook, there's an audible hum of mass apologia emanating from Twitter accounts, Facebook pages and press offices around the world.

Everyone is issuing apologies. Public figures, world leaders, YouTubers, iconic institutions and huge organizations have been busily dishing out high-minded, low-quality apologies at an impressive rate. In fact, in January 2018, the UK media reported on 35 high-profile public apologies. More than one apology per day making the news in that month alone. It was a month in which Virgin, H&M, YouTube, Asda, the *Daily Mail*, Vladimir Putin and even Pope Francis all issued public apologies.

Look past the headlines and you'll see that for every airline apologizing for violently 're-accommodating' a terrified passenger, there's a stationery shop apologizing with comparable vigour for advertising in the wrong newspaper. For every Facebook executive appearing at a government hearing, there's a social media executive desperately attempting to placate a handful of outraged Twitter users. Everyone is apologizing and no one is saying sorry.

So to answer Patrick Hosking's question – 'why can't organizations apologize any more?' – in short, it's the fault of people like us. People who make their living communicating on behalf of organizations, institutions and public figures. The PR people, crisis management consultants, social media account managers and the rest. And we are sorry.

Or rather: 'We regret that our services did not live up to our usual high standards.' And if you think that's not a proper apology, you're in the minority. A 2019 study by YouGov found that only 49 per cent would have a problem with that kind of wording if it were offered to them. The business of saying sorry is in such a crisis that almost half of UK adults think vague waffle about meeting high standards counts as an apology now.

Apologizing has become a public relations exercise and consumers are buying it. Publicists and communications strategists have got into the nasty habit of writing apologies on behalf of their clients with the sole intention of *not* saying sorry. We happily dish out apologies to anyone who demands one, but we are not sorry.

Apologizing has become a public relations exercise.

We might acknowledge an 'upsetting event', as the United Airlines' CEO did after a passenger was dragged from a flight. And yes, we might also concede that 'we are disheartened by the way this situation unfolded' as United's rival Southwest Airlines did following a similar situation on one of their planes. But please don't mistake these boilerplate responses for genuine contrition. In the chapters that follow, it'll become clear that public figures, businesses, politicians, even lifestyle bloggers apologize a lot and that it means little. After all, the word 'apology' derives from *apologia*, Greek for 'defence' not regret.

The inability of organizations and public figures to simply say sorry when they've done something demonstrably bad is not a new phenomenon. It's just getting bigger and more visible. What is new, however, is the parallel and equally pernicious phenomenon – an almost perfect counterweight to the non-apologizers – the eagerness, often desperation, of some organizations and public figures to say sorry when they needn't and shouldn't. This is the Apology Impulse.

Why write this book?

In this book, we'll be exploring the psychology behind the apology impulse and how our instinctive fear of mass disapproval and hypersensitivity to even the smallest criticism, typically driven by social media and, latterly, viral news publishers, causes us to apologize for the most trivial of things and withhold the big apologies when they're actually required. We'll analyse the factors behind our keenness to say sorry and the consequences of dishing out apologies to anyone who demands one.

We'll be also examining some historical apologies, profiling some of today's most prolific apologizers and taking a deep dive into what happens on those rare occasions when apologies are demanded but not given.

We'll be asking why women are considered better apologizers than men, why Spain refused to apologize to Mexico, which British supermarket managed to apologize 50 times in a single day, how one British company banked £1 million in less than a week simply by not saying sorry, why one of the most anticipated apologies in history came with a legal disclaimer, why one beer brand paid good money to deliberately make itself look bad, and how one company's stock value went up by billions of dollars when their CEO said sorry for being what can only be described as a jerk.

The apology... is in grave danger of becoming irrelevant.

Why write it now?

The apology as we used to know it is in grave danger of becoming irrelevant. If we want to rescue it from obscurity and return 'sorry' to its rightful place as a rare and important word, we need a plan. It's imperative for professional communicators, many of whom are privileged to have access to large platforms, to stop abusing the word 'sorry' and return some credibility back to the act of apologizing. We can only do this by taking more care over what we say when we are sorry and by doing our best to give up the bad habits we'll explore in this book.

CHAPTER TWO

Who's been apologizing and what are they sorry about?

If our tweet alienated you, please know that we are deeply sorry, and that we offer our sincerest apologies. If you follow our feed, we often reference popular memes to talk about the ocean. In this case, the memes used had connotations we were unaware of until now.

MONTEREY BAY AQUARIUM, TWITTER, DECEMBER 2019

German essayist and social critic Thomas Mann said: 'A writer is someone for whom writing is more difficult than it is for other people.' Something similar is true for apologizing. The people called upon to do it professionally – the unfortunate CEOs, press officers and anonymous spokespeople we get most of our apologies from – are often the ones who have the most difficulty getting it right. We all know how to say sorry. Yet when saying it is part of the job, it's suddenly almost impossible to do it properly.

Who is actually saying sorry?

You can tell how much trouble an organization thinks it's in by who it selects to deliver an apology. An anonymous apology, for example, either issued via press release, on the phone to a journalist or from a social media account, tells us an organization is not in crisis mode. It has its fingers crossed that this whole thing, whatever it may be, will soon blow over. That's how Paperchase (criticized for advertising in the *Daily Mail*), Zoopla (criticized for an advert) and University College London (in trouble over a tweet) elected to deal with their various reputational scuffles.

When the leader of an organization is the one giving the apology though, you can generally assume one of two things has happened. Either the leaders themselves did something stupid – the CEOs of Papa John's (accused the late KFC founder Colonel Sanders of using a racial slur), Tesla (called Wall Street analysts 'boring') and Qatar Airways (claimed that women couldn't do his job) all fit the bill here.[1] The CEOs were apologizing for their own conduct, not that of their organization. Or, if the CEO hasn't publicly embarrassed him- or herself recently, it's a fairly safe bet that the organization is in, is about to be in, or is scrambling to avoid, a genuine crisis. Merlin Entertainments (Alton Towers' rollercoaster accident), Volkswagen (emissions scandal) and United Airlines (far too many to neatly fit into parenthesis) all put their key executives centre stage when they needed to look properly sorry.[2]

Who says sorry is part of the message: 'We're taking this seriously, here's our CEO...'. When Nick Varney, CEO of Merlin Entertainments, faced the media after an accident at Alton Towers, his very presence on-screen showed that his employers grasped the severity of the situation. He handled almost every public element of the crisis response, from TV appearances to visiting victims. *PR Week* said Varney delivered 'a textbook example of how to handle a crisis'.[3]

It works the other way too. The visible absence of a leader in a crisis rarely goes unnoticed, even if the organization issues an apology. During a scandal-hit 2018 that saw Google and its parent company Alphabet Inc facing allegations of gender discrimination, permitting a culture of sexual harassment and potential culpability in election interference, the firm's co-founder and Alphabet Inc CEO Larry Page was conspicuous by his absence throughout the whole thing.[4, 5, 6] The news media noticed and started asking the quite legitimate question: 'Where *is* Larry Page?'

The visible absence of a leader in a crisis rarely goes unnoticed.

CNBC cited a 'leadership vacuum' at Alphabet.[7] The *Wall Street Journal*'s Andy Kessler wondered out loud: 'Has anyone seen Google founder Larry Page? Me neither.'[8] While Nick Varney's presence during the Alton Towers crisis added credibility to Merlin's crisis response and their claims of being genuinely sorry, Page's no-show did the opposite. His almost total absence from public life was never more obvious than at a September 2018 Senate Intelligence Committee hearing into foreign interference in American elections.[9] Positioned between Twitter's CEO Jack Dorsey and Facebook's COO Sheryl Sandberg – both had attended to answer questions from lawmakers – there was an empty leather seat with a microphone pointed at it. That's where Larry Page would have been sitting if he had shown up.[10] The Senate wanted people to know he hadn't. So they 'empty-chaired' him.

Speaking of that particular Senate hearing, why had Twitter sent their CEO and Facebook their COO, instead of CEO Mark Zuckerberg? For all of her many impressive achievements and unignorable public profile, Sandberg is not the de facto 'face' of Facebook in the way Dorsey is the 'face' of Twitter. Could it have been a deliberate move by Zuckerberg? He might have been rightly concerned that consumers had heard enough of his apologies. Or, perhaps it was a ploy to leverage useful qualities that Sandberg had but he lacked, namely the fact that she is a woman.

A 2017 study called 'Male vs female: How the gender of apologizers influences consumer forgiveness' published in the *Journal of Business Ethics* found that organizations 'must carefully consider the gender of the spokesperson in the wake of transgressions'.[11] The study found that consumers respond to apologies differently, depending on the giver and what they are apologizing for. It boils down to (old-fashioned) gender perceptions. Consumers perceive women as 'warmer' and men as 'more competent' and since consumers were already questioning Zuckerberg's competence after his handling of the Cambridge Analytica scandal, Sandberg could have been considered as a more credible, not to mention palatable, voice than the CEO. Zuckerberg himself had previously remarked that he wasn't always the most qualified person to answer questions about what goes on at Facebook.[12]

How are organizations saying sorry?

The *way* an organization apologizes – as well as the things it will and will not apologize for – is notable too. It affords us a glimpse into an organization's subconscious. Every organizational apology is attended by a unique set of priorities and anxieties. The content and tone of the apology don't merely address the transgression. They instruct consumers on how that organization wishes to be perceived, revealing the values of the people communicating on that organization's behalf. And just like everyone else, the people inside these organizations get anxious, experience pressure, hate being yelled at and, quite understandably, they don't particularly want to feel hated. This is why we see so many eccentric and weird apologies.

People get anxious, experience pressure, hate being yelled at.

For all of the value the communications industry places on crisis planning and strategy, authenticity and transparency, its leaders consistently fail to anticipate the influence that being yelled at can have. No amount of training or experience can prepare a professional communicator to cope with the dawning sensation that a seemingly large portion of the Internet is really mad at them. This is why Paperchase apologized for advertising in the *Daily Mail*. It's why the Twitter CEO apologized for eating at Chick-fil-A. It's why Monterey Bay Aquarium apologized (sincerely) for joking about one of their otters being fat and it's why department store Bloomingdale's apologized for – and swiftly withdrew from sale – a T-shirt that said 'fake news' on it.[13,14]

The ostensibly trivial matter of not wanting to be yelled at or hated is a critically under-acknowledged source of organizational apologia. It's why the founders of Silicon Valley start-up Bodega apologized simply for existing.[15] Bodega, the world's 'most-hated' start-up according to multiple press reports, launched just as the Silicon Valley saviour-in-a-hoodie archetype was wearing thin.[16] It was nothing more than a matter of bad timing. Consumers had grown weary of Ivy League-educated future billionaires seeing something, literally anything, and trying to 'disrupt' it. Bodega got bad press for its plan to disrupt convenience stores, popularly referred to in North America and Spanish-speaking countries as *bodegas*, prompting founder Paul McDonald to write on the company blog: 'Despite our best intentions and our admiration for traditional bodegas, we clearly hit a nerve this morning, we apologize.'[17]

Sure, their idea wasn't groundbreaking; Bodega was essentially a posh vending machine. But their only crime was coming up with an idea that consumers didn't like or want and for that, no apology is ever necessary. To apologize because people don't like your idea is effectively an apology for existing.

The gravity of all these situations and whether an apology was ever due depends entirely on your world view. Lots of people love Paperchase but dislike the *Daily Mail*, so what seems to some people like a run-of-the-mill advertising choice seems to others like an endorsement of the newspaper's entire editorial standpoint. Viewed from one perspective, Jack Dorsey of Twitter was just getting some chicken. But the CEO of the particular restaurant chain he chose is on the record as being against gay marriage.[18] And Dorsey's hankering for chicken came during Pride Month. So to others, his dining choice seemed massively insensitive.

To apologize because people don't like your idea is effectively an apology for existing.

Corporate and public life is now so complicated that the smallest peccadilloes get over-amplified and distorted beyond identification. As a result, consumers are treated to a wide array of odd-sounding apologies. And just as we can tell much about an organization's subconscious by the things it will and will not say sorry for, we can possibly tell more about a society's own preoccupations by the apologies it demands of organizations.

The corporate apology starter pack

Apologies come in an array of formats, each serving specific functions, few of which involve actually saying sorry. Bad apologies are often bad because of how they're delivered. And there's an embarrassing number of ways to get it wrong. Here are a few of the most popular ways organizations mess up their apologies.

Quantum superapology (Schrödinger's apology)

Have you ever heard a company say 'we take the protection of consumer data extremely seriously' when they *haven't* just been hacked? Likewise, have you ever heard a transport provider promise that they are 'committed to meeting punctuality targets' unless they're about to apologize for not meeting punctuality targets? And when was the last time a political party said 'we take all complaints of racism/sexism/bullying seriously and are committed to tackling racism/sexism/bullying in all its forms' when they *weren't* facing credible accusations of not taking it seriously or tackling it?

This rhetorical trick forms the basis of a quantum superapology. The wording deliberately positions an organization slightly, but not totally, above criticism for the transgression they're being asked to say sorry for. They are simultaneously sorry and completely innocent, in the same way Schrödinger's famous hypothetical cat was simultaneously dead and alive.

If an organization can tell you with a straight face that they take the protection of your data very seriously, but that you might want to change all your passwords, that's a quantum superapology. It's another way of saying: 'We did nothing wrong, and here's how we're going to fix it.'

The jargonpology

It's not fair to blame the communications industry for every bad apology. Without the legal industry to lend a helping hand, the world wouldn't have some of its most memorable examples of bad corporate contrition. And lawyers can have an outsized influence on how organizations communicate after they've had to apologize too. For example, in April 2019 Tesla CEO Elon Musk was told by the US Securities and Exchange Commission that he must seek approval from lawyers before tweeting about certain topics.[19]

You can spot when lawyers have had their hands on an apology because trivial inconveniences like facts and reality are so deftly obscured by jargon. These over-cautious legal brains, in their determination to avoid admitting liability, are the reason we get such linguistic elasticity when organizations try to say sorry. Words suddenly don't mean what we think they mean. A jargonpology is a hybrid of a denial and an acceptance – ratios of each may vary – all held together with words that sound made up. The best examples will often contain an intoxicating blend of euphemism and straight-up fibbing.

'Overcharging' becomes 'pricing issues' (Whole Foods);[20] an 'explosion' becomes an 'an overpressurization that was followed by a fire'(seriously, it's in Chapter 7); and a cow on the line becomes a 'bovine incursion' (South West Trains customer e-mail). This approach allows the apologizer, through wilful obfuscation, to set the terms on which they are judged. Jargon acts like a soft-focus camera lens, aberrating the true picture to remove harshness and give it soft edges so we perceive it more favourably. These apologies can often segue nicely into...

Jargon acts like a soft-focus camera lens.

The fauxpology

The first instinct when facing criticism is to reject it, either by denial or demonstrating limited culpability. We all do it and it's OK to admit it. If a flat denial is out of the question, it's normal to draw up a mental list of the list of ways you can prove that actually this isn't as bad as people are making out. A great way of doing this is to shift the burden of responsibility away from yourself or your organization and onto your potential victims.

'I'm sorry you feel that way...' or 'Sorry if anyone was offended...' are two well-used modern examples. The majority of fauxpologies follow the 'sorry if...' format. If you really want to deliver a bad apology that people will cherish for years to come, you can invert that formula, start with 'if...' and work from there.

When the CEO of Volkswagen Herbert Diess (not the same CEO who oversaw and apologized for the diesel emissions scandal) accidentally invoked Nazi terminology during an internal meeting, he gave out an absolute gem of a fauxpology using the 'if you're offended...' approach.

Diess had used the phrase *Ebit macht frei*, 'ebit' referring to 'earnings before interest and taxes' and 'macht frei' roughly translating as 'sets you free'. It was troublingly similar to the infamous *Arbeit macht frei* ('work sets you free') slogan inscribed on the gates of the Auschwitz concentration camp in Nazi-occupied Poland during World War II. Naturally some people thought this was maybe a tiny bit misjudged, especially for Volkswagen. Diess agreed in retrospect.

In a statement, he acknowledged his firm's 'special historical responsibility' – Volkswagen was literally founded by Hitler's German Labour Front (the Nazi labour organization which replaced many German trade unions under Hitler). Diess then went on to say with the exact amount of sincerity you'd expect from an under-fire mechanical engineering PhD who'd grafted his way to become a captain of Germany's car industry: 'If I have unintentionally caused offence, I am extremely sorry. I would like to apologize unreservedly.'[21]

He wasn't done being robotically bad at apologizing though. He topped his statement off by removing himself from the sphere of accountability entirely. 'At no time was it my intention for this statement to be placed in a false context.'[22] This apology, if you were in any doubt about what Diess was getting at, is as much about the context *you* apply to his remarks as it is about the remarks themselves.

The display-only apology

This one is useless for anything other than filling a space. 'XXXX Rail apologizes for the delay and any inconvenience this may cause…'. You hear (or read) this sort of apology every single day. It's a contrition-free allusion to generic regret, a placeholder where the apology should be. These have no specific recipient and are issued only to satisfy some internal rule demanding that when an organization fails it must say sorry to nobody in particular and in the vaguest terms possible. The ubiquity of this apology belies its meagre utility. They are of no use to anybody and yet there are loads of them.

You'll find these apologies on website error pages, locked doors to public buildings and broken-down lifts, but the natural habitat of the display-only apology is the public transport sector. Public transport is an industry that appears to go out of its way to let down its customers, so it makes sense that it issues so many display-only apologies to accompany the disappointment. There's even a website that tracks them – www.sorryfortheinconvenience.co.uk. The site's founder, Manchester-based web developer Omid Kashan, started the site after noticing how many times the operator of Manchester's tram system said sorry:

> The initial idea came about whilst waiting for a Manchester Metrolink tram, and I wondered just how many times in a given day the announcer would say sorry for delays or cancellations. I had a browse through their Twitter feed later that day and was struck by the fact that pretty much every other tweet contained an apology.

Omid's site got a good deal of media coverage when it launched, which had an unusual effect on some of the organizations apologizing. 'In the days after the site launched there was a distinct downturn in the number of apologies coming out of the Metrolink Twitter,' explained Omid. Are display-only apologies so useless that as soon as you pay attention to them, they disappear?

The straw man apology ('strawpology')

Another great way to downplay culpability while *looking* like you're sorry is to construct a rhetorical straw man and apologize to him instead. Using the same logic as the straw man fallacy, in which someone engaged in debate seeks to refute an argument that hasn't been made instead of dealing with the argument put to them, 'strawpologizers' find it far easier to apologize for something other than the thing they ought to be sorry for. United Airlines pulled this trick in 2017 after footage of a passenger being dragged off one of their planes went viral. Instead of addressing and apologizing for the fact that this passenger ended up covered in blood and screaming, CEO Oscar Munoz constructed his straw man out of the situation's more minor details. 'We apologize for the overbook situation,' said Munoz, completely misreading what was about to happen.[23]

The 'overbook situation' was his first straw man. And United later admitted the flight wasn't even overbooked anyway, so it was the flimsiest of straw men to begin with.[24] When this approach didn't work he made another attempt. 'This is an upsetting event to all of us here at United. I apologize for having to re-accommodate these customers.' 'Re-accommodating' the passenger was the second straw man. People still weren't buying it though. United needed three attempts to finally find the correct words for the relevant deed, but not before their share price had dropped and the government had launched an investigation into them.

This type of linguistic sleight-of-hand is predominantly within the purview of individuals and public figures subjected to the most intense public scrutiny, such as politicians, CEOs, journalists and, latterly, social media influencers. These people get used to having apologies demanded of them and respond by dishing out only partially relevant responses. A CEO may apologize for their 'choice of words' when it was actually the content of what they said that drew criticism. They may apologize for 'failing to communicate effectively' when it was actually the content of their message, and not how it was delivered, that upset people. Consumers and critics can now spot these types of apologies a mile off and they inevitably prolong the embarrassment of the organization giving them.

The passive apology

We've all seen this one and it doesn't require much explaining. 'Mistakes were made...', 'offence may have been caused...',

19

'lessons must be learned...' 'terrible apologies must be given...'. When an organization lacks the courage to own its mistakes, the passive voice is there to soften the messaging. Consumers rightly find it hard to trust these apologies.

There are plentiful other ways to mess up an apology, but the highest-profile bad apologies tend to fit one of the definitions above. It's worrying then, that the communications industry appears to have such a well-thumbed playbook for avoiding accountability. And if organizations are treating apologizing as a game – there's ample evidence to suggest many are – then a lot of them are playing it on 'easy mode'. By identifying some of the tricks and habits they use to make life easier for themselves when they've transgressed, we can better scrutinize the content of their messages without being distracted by the format. We can also shine a spotlight on the genuinely good, useful apologies that eschew the templates above.

CHAPTER THREE

The six reasons organizations apologize and the one reason they won't

We would like to take the opportunity to offer our sincere apologies to Mr Bing for publishing disparaging untrue statements about him, and for inappropriately urging our readers to telephone Mr Bing, and to disturb him with derogatory remarks based on our inaccurate reports.
DAILY MIRROR APOLOGY TO STEVE BING, OCTOBER 2002

Before we can really get stuck into some of the 'best' public apologies, it's essential to understand the various factors that influence how, why and when organizations apologize. We're going to be analysing the techniques and tricks of those who give apologies as well as those who demand them. We can't do that fairly without first interrogating the fundamental concept of what it actually means for an organization to be sorry.

In the human world, away from the boardrooms and PR consultancies from which the majority of corporate apologies emanate, 'sorry' comes from a place of mature empathy. The intensity of that empathy can vary from 'sorry I'm late' to 'sorry I ruined our marriage'. In the pathologically apologetic United Kingdom, 'sorry' can even be the conversational lubricant that permits us to break social norms – 'sorry, do you know if this tram goes to the airport?'. It's disproportionately self-effacing, but it's empathy all the same – an acknowledgement of putting a very tiny burden on a stranger.

Dr Guy Winch, author of multiple books on human interaction, describes an apology as 'the antidote to guilt'.[1] We say sorry and we apologize to each other because it's emotionally painful not to and we risk damaging the relationships that our survival instincts compel us to preserve. We accept apologies for the same reason: it's emotionally painful not to. We understand that the people in our lives are fallible and capable of doing bad things, even if they are not bad people. So saying sorry is inherently transactional. The fulfilment of a human-to-human apology is forgiveness.

Organizations, while they are admittedly populated by empathetic humans, are not quite the emotional sum of their human parts. Organizational apology impulses are not powered by pure empathy. The server at the fast-food counter may well say 'sorry for your wait', but it's a transactional lubricant, part of the buying process. The odds of that server genuinely empathizing with you as you stare at the menu are slim to none. As consumers, we understand that completely. 'Sorry for your wait' is not an apology from which they are seeking forgiveness.

Organizational apology impulses are not powered by pure empathy.

When organizations *do* apologize, they apologize only for observable failures. When was the last time an organization confessed to something they could have kept a secret? Whistleblowers, regulators, aggrieved customers and journalists act as proxies for an organization's conscience. As consumers, we accept and understand this too. We hold organizations to certain standards and we accept that they will sometimes fail to meet them. Only when we hear about those failures do the organizations apologize.

How organizations fail

There are two types of failure for which an organization will apologize: **operational** failure and **cultural** failure. Operational failures, those everyday errors like faulty goods, missing deliveries and late departures, are easy to understand and the associated apologies are normally easy to accept – assuming the consequences fall below a certain level of severity. A 1992 study into consumer responses to operational failures found that consumer perceptions of an organization that has committed an operational failure can be restored completely, provided there's an outcome that fosters a sense of 'procedural fairness'.[2] That is to say, if a customer feels an organization has adequately made things right – and it doesn't always need to be financial compensation – then their feelings about that company are as positive as they were before the failure, sometimes better.

Cultural failures are more profound. Problems like insulting or offensive advertising, boardroom inequality, bullying or even just mildly 'tone deaf' social media posts don't reflect on an organization's ability to deliver their product or service; they speak to its core values. This matters more than ever before. Apologizing for a cultural failure is hard; it's far easier to apologize for what you *did* than for what you *are*.

When Arcadia Group chairman Philip Green was revealed in Parliament in 2018 as the previously unnamed businessman behind an injunction to prevent accusations of sexual harassment from being published, it was a huge cultural failure. As soon as consumers knew Philip Green had tried to quash the accusations, that same toxic energy infected his entire organization. Consumer research organization YouGov reported that consumer perceptions of Arcadia's Topshop brand plummeted when the news came out.[3] YouGov CEO Stephan Shakespeare remarked that: 'In the space of a few days Topshop's Impression score among the general public has fallen from +7 to +2. Among women aged 18–34 its score has dropped from +25 to +20.'[4]

The quality of Arcadia's products hadn't changed, the prices hadn't gone up and the stores were still staffed by the same friendly and hardworking people, but consumers were put off all the same. Even Philip Green conceded that the revelations were 'hurting his business'.[5] Perceptions of corporate culture matter. People want to feel good about their consumer choices.

That's why adequately compensating consumers let down by a cultural failure is almost impossible. It's better than doing nothing, but it's an expensive, inexact transaction. What level of compensation would you accept for doing business with some-one accused of sexual harassment? Days before the Philip Green revelation, Topshop had already experienced a cultural failure, receiving broad criticism for taking down a pro-feminism book display in its flagship London store. On that occasion they tried to make it right and donated money to a gender equality charity as an accompaniment to its apology.[6]

The social media response to this move was overwhelmingly negative, but social media, as we'll explore, can be a wickedly unreliable measure of real-world consumer satisfaction. Topshop's perceptions did drop somewhat after the book display episode, but recovered quickly and the dip was nowhere near as pronounced as it would be after the harassment crisis. However, perceptions of Topshop would arguably have suffered less had they simply run out of clothes.

Despite the obvious corporate instinct to separate church (culture) and state (operations), there's an unavoidable overlap between the two. Operational failures can be symptomatic of deeper-lying cultural failures and vice versa. And these serious underlying cultural failures can often present as operational failures in the first instance. The 2015 Alton Towers rollercoaster crash in which 16 people were injured and two suffered life-changing injuries was the result of human error – an operational failure. But that human error came about because staff had stopped following safety protocols and knew how to manually override safety systems.[7] That's an internal cultural failure.

Topshop said the decision to remove the book display came from a 'production and creative standpoint'. That's an operational failure. When it was later revealed that it was CEO Philip Green who'd demanded it be removed, it became a cultural failure. At this point Green might – ironically – have been better served by allowing one of his female executives to take over. The 2017 Wei and Ran study into gender influence on consumer responses to corporate apologies found that consumers responded better to women when the apology was for a transgression related to 'values' (culture), while apologies for 'service' (operational) failures were better received when they came from men.

When KFC ran out of chicken in February 2018 it was a classic operational failure that turned into a 'meme-able' moment that turned into an ad campaign. More than half of its UK stores had to close at short notice, leaving families who'd planned on getting KFC for their dinner inconvenienced. One customer complained of waiting 15 minutes queueing at a drive-thru, only to be told there was no chicken, before queueing twice as long to get back out. People were taking it badly. A police force in London had to send a tweet telling people to stop ringing up about it.[8]

Consumers weren't happy, but they understood. Nobody was accusing Colonel Sanders of inappropriate conduct and there was no suspicion of a culture problem at KFC. They just ran out of chicken for a bit. So when the apology came, it was a simple and clear path to recovery. KFC took out newspaper adverts featuring an empty KFC chicken bucket. The KFC branding had been changed to 'FCK' so it said 'FCK, we're sorry'. They made a thing out of their operational failure and generated enough goodwill from this apology that they were able to use it as a jumping-off point for a new ad campaign.[9]

So why do organizations apologize?

Organizations fail all the time, but they don't always say sorry. Failure alone is not enough to trigger an apology. There has to be something in it for the organization. Apologizing has to offer a better outcome for the organization than saying nothing; whether that's repairing their reputation, quelling a social media backlash or avoiding litigation. And while consumers can accept apologies from organizations, this is not the same as forgiveness. The bonds that facilitate human forgiveness don't exist between consumers and organizations. You only have one spouse, one mother and a few friends. But there's always a different supermarket, airline or Internet provider if you really need one. Our social hard-wiring doesn't push us to make peace with supermarket chains in the way it pushes us to make peace with our family and friends.

Failure alone is not enough to trigger an apology.

Consumers don't forgive, they simply decide how much corporate failure they're prepared to accept before it becomes too much hassle. That's why boycotts happen. It's also why boycotts fail. We accept operational and cultural failure as part of the deal. It's why people still wear Boss suits and drive Volkswagen vehicles despite the obvious reasons not to (Hugo Boss joined the Nazi party before Adolf Hitler and Volkswagen used forced labour during the Holocaust).[10,11] Consumers make a moral and emotional compromise every time they buy a T-shirt or get on a plane. Although not every consumer can afford to be picky about where they spend their money. Only the most privileged consumers can shop with their conscience every time. Organizations know this.

Even in the most extreme cases of corporate failure, businesses have gone on to thrive without saying sorry. Grünenthal, makers of the infamous sedative Thalidomide, still has customers. It survived for decades without saying sorry for the Thalidomide controversy. Their drug was responsible for thousands of miscarriages and birth deformities and consumers knew about it for years. It took Grünenthal 50 years to say sorry, but while we were waiting for the apology, the company carried on making drugs and making money. So if organizations can thrive commercially without saying sorry, why do they do it? There are six main reasons for an organization to say sorry when they've failed and one main reason why they won't.

1 Customer satisfaction and the cost of doing business

[Twitter] Good morning Natalie, I am sorry to see the lack of chocolate on your 'chocolate' digestive. If you can provide the product barcode and your e-mail address I will be able to feed this back to our supplier.[12]

The majority of customer satisfaction apologies pass us by. And it's a good job too. They're boring and painfully insincere, a function of the 'display-only' apology and its enduring uselessness. But if you are interested, take a quick glance at the Twitter replies of any retailer you fancy and you'll see that their social media team spend most of their time saying sorry. For example, on 5 October 2018, the same day Topshop made their sexism apology, Sainsbury's, Tesco, Asda and Morrisons – four of the UK's largest retailers – made a total of 151 customer service apologies between them. Sainsbury's apologized 31 times, Tesco 29 times, Morrisons apologized 41 times and Asda apologized 50 times.

Almost all of these apologies were accompanied by offers of refunds, replacements, compensation or, at the very least, an offer from the retailer to investigate further. These kinds of apologies are embedded into an organization's communications model.

The funny thing with these customer satisfaction apologies though is that they make no difference. The organizations might as well not bother. When it comes to minor operational failures, it's not giving an apology that matters; it's the compensation. Sorry is just a word to signal 'we've heard you'.

A 2018 study involving 1.5 million Uber customers found that 'the most effective apology was the provision of a $5 coupon, with or without any accompanying apology text'. The study also found that 'apologizing without offering a coupon has a potentially negative effect on future spending'.[13] For minor operational failures, sorry on its own can actually make things worse.

Thankfully, consumers are good at managing their own expectations. The concept of 'acceptable loss', a military euphemism for 'collateral damage' that's become popular in commerce, works both ways. Retailers put expensive items on display fully knowing they can be stolen. If they didn't display them, people would be less likely to buy them. So the few items that do get stolen in service of this pursuit are deemed acceptable losses. Consumers are prepared for acceptable losses too; they factor into their buying preferences the understanding that sometimes they will be let down. An international commuter that couldn't deal with being delayed would never get on a plane. And the only guaranteed way to avoid getting a mouldy strawberry is to not buy strawberries. So consumers accept the risk of being disappointed. It's the price of doing business.

To that end there's actually very little reputational damage to an organization when it experiences a basic operational failure. Consumers have already accounted for it. They were never expecting perfection. Provided there is some degree of procedural fairness after the failure, an organization's reputation will remain intact. It's not a big deal because nobody cares if someone else got a mouldy strawberry.

There are two factors that do move the needle on public perceptions of an organization dealing with an operational failure: either the degree of loss escalates – be that inconvenience, disappointment, the financial burden; or the operational failure has some sort of entertainment value – maggots in your salad or glass in your crisps will do it. But most of the time, a minor operational failure is entirely unremarkable. Cultural failure is different. We might not care about your mouldy strawberries, but we do care if you are treated unfairly by the shop manager.

2 Problem solving and service recovery – why empathy is overvalued

If an airline has ever lost your bags, or a burst pipe has left your home without water, the amount of empathy displayed by the person dealing with your situation was probably lower down on your list of priorities than you might remember. No amount of empathy will mitigate the inconvenience of being without your luggage or having no running water. When consumers face genuine inconvenience or loss, they really don't want to hear how sorry someone is.

When operational failures are moderate to severe, consumers focus on an organization's ability to solve their problem. Given a choice, most consumers would rather deal with an abrupt pragmatist than an empathetic scatterbrain. A study of operational failures in airports in which researchers filmed customer reactions (as part of the UK TV show *Airline*, the customers gave consent to be included in the study after filming) found that they reacted more positively to displays of competence and creativity than they did towards displays of empathy. In fact, displays of warmth from the service personnel lowered the consumer's perception of their competence, perhaps also explaining why participants in Wei and Ran's 2017 study into gender perceptions of apologies viewed stereotypical female warmth as a sign of lower competence. [14,15]

Study lead Jagdip Singh says that in a service recovery scenario, apologizing has a negative impact: 'Saying "I'm sorry for this – the same thing happened to my sister" makes the customer feel that the employee is not really paying attention to the problem, and customers see it as a distraction.'[16] The more severe and far-reaching an operational failure, the more crucial the perception of competence becomes.

3 Customer retention, restoring trust and apology dividends

Sometimes an organization will apologize for the simple reason that it risks losing customers if it doesn't. These customer retention apologies are typically associated with moderate to severe operational failures that suggest an organization doesn't really have its act together and people are paying a high price for that fact. This is where operational failure becomes an *unacceptable* loss, a matter of trust. A customer retention apology has a different dynamic to a service recovery apology. Service recovery is designed to resolve a problem mid-transaction. Customer retention apologies can become due at any point during the customer life cycle, from online checkout abandonment to product recall. And they are time sensitive.

During an operational crisis, an organization needs to communicate to its customers that it is safe to resume the relationship. The best way of doing that is acknowledging the failure, explaining it and illustrating how customers will receive procedural fairness. The interesting thing about customer retention apologies is that they can sometimes enhance an organization's reputation beyond its original level. It happened with KFC and it happened with the toy retailer Build-A-Bear too.

When the Build-A-Bear Workshop launched its 'pay your age' discount campaign in 2018, the whole promotion collapsed under the weight of its own popularity. Queues were up to seven hours long at some locations and social media complaints about the general chaos escalated quickly.[17] Police were called to some locations after reports of assaults. The toy retailer cited crowd safety concerns, shut down the promotion and closed stores, leaving thousands of young children disappointed and their parents angry.

The following day, Build-A-Bear CEO Sharon Price John went on NBC's *Today* show to say sorry. It was a solid apology too: she explained what went wrong and how her company were going to put it right. The impact was immediate, Build-A-Bear shares jumped from $7.80 on the day of the promotion to $8.15 on the day of the apology.[18] Not bad for a failed marketing campaign. What was that about men being best at apologizing for operational failures?

KFC also benefited from the 'good apology dividend'. Parent company Yum! Brands' share price snuck up a bit on the day of the apology, but the apology generated its own legacy. The apology advert was *AdAge*'s editor's pick. It was popular enough that KFC were able to use it as an excuse to bring Colonel Sanders out of retirement.

The same dynamic can be seen in even the most extreme examples of failure, even when people have suffered at the hands of their own government. The infamous Tuskegee Study of Untreated Syphilis in which African–American men with the disease were not told their diagnosis or offered treatment remains one of the most controversial medical experiments in American history. In 2007 then President Bill Clinton apologized, calling the study 'deeply, profoundly, morally wrong'.[19] A 2008 study found that African–Americans who were aware of the Tuskegee experiment and also aware of the apology had more trust in medical research than those who knew about the Tuskegee experiment but did not know about the apology.[20, 21]

4 Organizational panic, stress and fatigue

Before social media, it wasn't particularly easy for organizations to accurately understand how their customers felt about them, especially at short notice. Sales dips would be a tip-off and bad press coverage would be cause for concern, but it wouldn't be until the data from a round of focus group sessions arrived that they would be able to identify their customers' precise grievances. The Internet changed that forever. Review websites, blogs and of course social media have made it possible for organizations to find out in real time how people feel about them. This will not always be a pleasant experience. Especially since by far the biggest trigger for these unexpected waves of critical feedback come from perceived cultural failures. H&M, Prada, Topman and Marks & Spencer are all examples we'll explore. And it really doesn't take much for a backlash to happen. M&S found itself in receipt of a social backlash because of a pattern on their toilet paper.

The sheer volume and speed of customer feedback can force organizations into intense and unplanned periods of self-examination. These are highly stressful and unpleasant scenarios that put genuine stress on those involved, especially those on the front line like social media managers and PR folk. If that organization doesn't have a solid plan for handling criticism, it can lead to panic and hasty decision-making. Nobody enjoys getting criticized or being told in a hundred different ways that their organization is terrible and should be boycotted. Even the most resilient organizations are prone to abandoning logic in these circumstances and previously clear-sighted communications teams suddenly see risks everywhere they look. And when all you've got is 'sorry', everything starts to look like a crisis.

Consumers have the option of logging off and going for a walk when social media engagement becomes too intense or unpleasant. Professional communicators have no such luxury. They have to sit there and come up with a response. When forced into these reputational crisis situations, organizations frequently decide that they disapprove of themselves as much, if not more, than the shouty consumers berating them. That's often a false conclusion, but it doesn't matter. Apologizing feels like the only way out of an unpleasant situation. So organizations, even really big and powerful ones, just say sorry.

Paperchase, University College London, Sofitel, Tesco, Sony Pictures – these are just some of the organizations who have given apologies for perceived cultural failures and they gave them purely because they were demanded. Corporate Twitter is a target-rich environment for apology-hunting.

5 Regulatory and legal compliance

Do you remember just before the European-wide General Data Protection Regulation (GDPR) came into force in May 2018, and you kept getting e-mails from the owners of every single mailing list you'd ever been on telling you how much they cared about your privacy and asking if it would be OK if they could keep sending you e-mails? It probably didn't take you long to realize this wasn't due to a moment of collective soul-searching from the marketing industry. It was 100 per cent to do with regulatory compliance.

We're sorry to tell you this, but a lot of corporate apologies come from the same place. As authentic as some apologies might seem on the surface, they simply wouldn't happen without the influence of industry regulators. This is all to do with the concept of 'corrective advertising'. Trade regulators around the world, including the Federal Trade Commission in the United States and the Office of Fair Trading in the UK, have the power to force organizations to take corrective steps if they've breached any of their rules. These regulator-mandated correctives often require organizations to spend a set amount of money on advertising and to place adverts in a set amount of publications. So if an organization is compelled into taking out advertising, they may as well make the most of it.

When Wells Fargo Bank launched their 'Re-established' ad campaign in 2018, there were multiple ads targeted at different local markets throughout the United States, all artfully produced and all conveying roughly the same theme: 'We're sorry (sort of) and we've changed (kind of).' Wells Fargo never explicitly said 'sorry', but the messaging was sufficiently contrite that you could tell Wells Fargo wanted you to forgive them. The entire campaign invited consumers to accept Wells Fargo back into their hearts because Wells Fargo had remembered – at the most commercially convenient time possible – to tell consumers all about their founding values, a very American brand of 'down-home' trustworthiness.

Their advert was heavy with visual metaphors. Picture the visuals. Six horses pull a 19th-century stagecoach across a quintessentially rugged American landscape – all in slow motion. It's a Wells Fargo stagecoach, a nod to the humble, earthy beginnings of what is now the world's fourth largest bank by market capitalization. A piano plays, the ethereal twinkling melody is melancholy yet somehow hopeful. The horses gather pace, their glistening muscularity powered seemingly by nothing but sheer brand authenticity. A trustworthy-sounding lady starts speaking. She wants you to know that Wells Fargo has changed. Wells Fargo is making 'a complete recommitment to you, fixing what went wrong, making things right'. A close-up lingers on a horse's mane, he gallops onward, presumably towards a future where banking is fairer, more transparent and crucially, according to the voice-over, where 'product sales goals are eliminated'.

A cynic might think that last line about eliminating product sales goals had something to do with Wells Fargo getting sued for $185 million by regulators in 2016 after staff were discovered to be fraudulently opening accounts for customers who didn't want them because Wells Fargo had set product sales goals that incentivized that exact behaviour.[22] And that cynic would of course be correct. Wells Fargo had been well and truly shamed by lawmakers and regulators. This ad campaign was their way of saying sorry. Not to their customers though; they were saying sorry to their regulator.

Court-ordered apologies tend to be similarly insincere. There are two types: apologies that come as part of a legal settlement, typically for libel; and court-mandated apologies as part of restorative justice. Both are ultimately useless in conveying genuine remorse and fostering reparation, but they can be entertaining. In October 2002, while facing a $40 million lawsuit, then-editor of *The Mirror* newspaper Piers Morgan published an utterly terrible apology to American businessman Steve Bing.[23,24] Having been backed into a corner by Bing's lawyers, Morgan made his apology so fawning and over the top that virtually nobody who read it could take it seriously. Morgan had weaponized the language of contrition to ensure anyone who read it knew this was not a sincere apology. On the page opposite to the apology, *The Mirror* ran a story about why Americans don't understand sarcasm.

6 Because they're sorry

This one is as obvious as it is rare. Professional apologizing is a cynical game. Communications teams must appear simultaneously contrite and in control when delivering an apology. The value of their company often depends on it. This is a hard balance to strike and consumers can be forgiven for doubting the sincerity of any corporate apology they hear.

Although, every now and then, organizations take us by surprise and say sorry because they *are* sorry and because saying sorry is the right thing to do. General Motors CEO Mary Barra gave a famously effective and sincere apology for their 2014 ignition switch recall scandal. This was a huge crisis for the firm. GM eventually paid compensation for 124 deaths related to the problem.[25] Barra's response was widely praised for its sincerity and lack of equivocation, with Barra telling Congress in 2014: 'My sincere apologies to everyone who has been affected by this recall, especially to the families and friends of those who lost their lives or were injured. I am deeply sorry.'

Fortune magazine was the most lavish with its praise, remarking how Barra, who took the helm at GM just months after the

Professional apologizing is a cynical game.

scandal emerged: 'Ignored the GM template for handling these situations – minimize their importance, fight them, drag them out, settle grudgingly.' She didn't just apologize though; *Fortune* noted that Barra had used the scandal as the driver behind a complete corporate culture change at GM, noting her remarks at a GM 'town hall' meeting to assembled employees: 'I never want to put this behind us.'

Merlin Entertainments, which owns the Staffordshire theme park Alton Towers, is another organization who were genuinely sorry and showed it. The organization experienced a truly horrible communications crisis. CEO Nick Varney had the unenviable task of facing the media after the 2015 accident. The accident was obviously a reputational disaster and Merlin were completely to blame. They were found the following year to have breached the Health & Safety Act and fined £5 million.[26] In a perverse way, the magnitude of the situation made Varney's task easier. How could he do anything other than just say sorry?

There are so many ways crisis management can go wrong and this was by no means a perfect performance. But the organization's first big decision, to put their CEO out as the face of the company, was important. It set the right tone. There's no doubt Varney would have been assisted by a team, but it was a symbolic and important gesture that the CEO was taking the heat in person, instead of hiding behind lawyer-approved statements.

Varney did the media rounds, most notably appearing in a tense exchange with Kay Burley of Sky News, who appeared more interested in extracting a punchy headline than finding out what was going on. Varney's choice of words during the interview were deliberate and important. After Burley's opening gambit, Varney referred immediately to the situation as a 'tragic accident', affording it the gravitas that most would agree it deserved.

Varney was clear in how Merlin were going to address the problem. Within the first five seconds of his interview, he'd set out two things he was working on: helping the victims and their families; and identifying the causes of the accident. His interview was notable too, for its use of relatable language. Varney resisted the temptation to fluff and bluff his way through the gruelling 13-minute showdown, eschewing jargon and instead speaking in human terms. He referred to 'the accident', rather than the temptingly vague 'an incident'. He spoke of feeling 'dreadful' about what had happened and reiterated that Merlin Entertainments were 'deeply, deeply sorry' before adding: 'I'm not going to make excuses. We've had an accident, it's been a terrible accident and we have to make sure we do the right thing.'

It wasn't a perfect performance. The combative nature of a live television interview demands that subjects are pushed into uncomfortable corners and Varney did venture uncomfortably close to giving a quantum super-apology by talking about his organization's own 'high standards', which Burley rightly pointed out weren't high enough. Though he did voluntarily concede that their safety measures 'clearly weren't adequate'.

And that was brave. The second the words left his lips, they appeared on the ticker at the bottom of the screen and became the headline shortly after. The most resonant remark Varney made, and the one that really distils the messaging, was when he was asked by the BBC's *Today* programme if the accident would affect Merlin Entertainments' share price. Varney said: 'You'll forgive me if I'm not really focused on the share price at the moment.'

He might not have been focused on the share price, but his demeanour might actually have been influencing it. A 2015 study found that the markets react more favourably to apologetic CEOs when their facial expressions communicate obvious contrition.[27] As an exercise in crisis communications, there's much to learn from Nick Varney. Cleary an experienced communicator, he favoured the frustratingly rare strategy of telling the truth, saying sorry and refusing to evade tough questions. Also notable was his ability to assert key points while under pressure from the interviewer.

Varney made sure that the loudest message, the only message that mattered, was that Merlin Entertainments and he were sorry. We've seen before, and will continue to see, so many examples of organizations apologizing not only for their part in a crisis, but also for how they handled themselves during that crisis. Varney didn't have to do that.

Alton Towers visitor numbers have actually increased each year since the accident, albeit from a significant drop during the year of the accident.[28] But more interestingly, according to online statistics and market research company Statista, 69.3 per cent of UK adults said the likelihood of them visiting a theme park was not affected by the Alton Towers crash.[29] This says a lot. A bad crisis response has the capacity to impact entire industries, not just organizations.

Support for Nick Varney was high too. He was widely praised in the trade press for his handling of the crisis and consumers noticed too. A Change.org petition for Kay Burley to be sacked for her harsh treatment of Varney received almost 58,000 signatures.[30]

Why organizations won't say sorry

The most common but rarely given answer to 'why won't you just apologize?' is typically 'our lawyers won't let us'. The prevailing corporate orthodoxy is to not say sorry when doing so could be taken as an admission of liability for something really bad. This produces an odd dichotomy: organizations become socialized into apologizing for trivialities that pose no risk of inviting litigation while withholding the box office mea culpas from the people that genuinely need them. This is misguided for a number of reasons, not least because it doesn't seem to work. Studies into US medical malpractice lawsuits found that apologies can actually mitigate litigation and in some cases, the absence of an apology will increase the chances of a healthcare provider getting sued because the patient is angry that nobody said sorry for what went wrong.[31] UK organizations too are labouring under the misapprehension that saying sorry could get them sued. The Compensation Act (2006) is very clear that this isn't the case, stating: 'An apology, an offer of treatment or other redress, shall not of itself amount to an admission of negligence or breach of statutory duty.'[32] There's even a campaign to raise awareness of this misconception and clarify the Compensation Act led by communications professionals (search online for 'The Apology Clause campaign' for more information).[33]

There's another reason organizations won't say sorry when it looks like they should. The organization simply doesn't know if it's at fault or not. After the August 2018 Morandi Bridge collapse disaster in Genoa in which 43 people died, Giovanni Castellucci, the chief executive of Italian toll-road operator Autostrade per l'Italia who were responsible for the bridge, expressed regret and sympathy, but held back from explicitly giving a formal apology, saying at a press conference: 'Apologies and responsibilities are things that are interconnected. You apologize if you feel you are responsible.'[34] It might seem cold to take that approach, but at least it's honest and it may also preserve the integrity of any future apologies an organization needs to give.

UK organizations are labouring under the misapprehension that saying sorry could get them sued.

Of course, sometimes organizations just aren't sorry. And that's fair enough too. But in the age of performative atonement and online 'cancel culture', not *being* sorry isn't necessarily a barrier to *saying* sorry – plenty of organizations will apologize just to make criticism go away. So it's notable when organizations do stand their ground in the face of criticism. Protein World, Poundland and Marks & Spencer have provided us with three examples of how to not say sorry with style, which we'll explore later on in this book.

CHAPTER FOUR

Culture, values and consumer expectations

*Why 'sorry' means different things
to different industries*

*We're overhauling our cultural values to reward collaboration and
to foster a workplace that is inclusive rather than contentious.*
UBER E-MAIL TO CUSTOMERS, JUNE 2017

There's no guarantee that organizations, if left to their own devices, would behave particularly well at all. So we have legislation and regulation to ensure things like health and safety, fair trading, pollution, discrimination and the important nuts and bolts of doing business are handled properly. For the cultural stuff that falls outside of regulation and legislation, things like employee well-being, social justice, representation and diversity, there's a social contract. Consumers have specific expectations of the organizations they transact with.

The problem is that these cultural expectations vary massively between industries. Some industries, for example, fashion, cosmetics, gaming, children's toys, music and high-street retail – even coffee shops – are subject to far higher cultural expectations than industries such as banking, insurance, medicine or law.

In fact, we can categorize our expectations of organizations in the same way we categorize their failure: consumer expectations are either cultural or operational. We want our fashion brands and coffee chains to be diverse, representative and kind to their employees. We want our Silicon Valley start-ups to be idealistic, purpose-driven and committed to social justice. We want our food brands to be Fairtrade and sustainably sourced. Yet when it comes to banks, municipal services, mobile phone providers and insurance companies, most consumers just want them to be good value, efficient and to stick to the law.

The burden of over-delivery falls on those organizations for whom there is a cultural benchmark. Those organizations can of course benefit from living up to the various cultural expectations. For example, organizations that have embraced diversity, body positivity and employee well-being have been able to market themselves around meeting those expectations. Brands like Dove and Body Shop have even become advocates for progressive causes, to the delight of their consumers.

But – and it's a really big but – it's frighteningly easy for these organizations to fall short of the consumer's ever-evolving cultural expectations. Diverse advertising campaigns aren't diverse enough. Advocacy isn't inclusive enough. And when this happens, things go very wrong very quickly. That's why some organizations end up grovelling for seemingly trivial transgressions like eating in the wrong restaurant (Jack Dorsey of Twitter), while others just don't have to worry about it. You'd have to look pretty hard to find a bank or pension provider on their industry's naughty step for anything remotely cultural. Yes, they apologize too, but almost exclusively for

Cultural failures are difficult to forgive.

operational failures. Consumers aren't expecting their bank or pension provider to reflect their cultural preoccupations (yet).

Cultural failures are difficult to forgive because they mess with the comforting delusion that organizations really care about our specific anxieties and aspirations. Operational failures are easier to stomach and are forgivable to a point, even entertaining. We can laugh about KFC running out of chicken, even though selling chicken is literally their one job. But even operational failure has its limits. We lose our sense of humour pretty quickly when we think it's our privacy or our safety that's at stake, rather than our ability purchase chicken. So operational failure apologies vary in proportion to the consequences of their failure, not the degree to which they failed.

When a pharmacist gives out the wrong medication to a customer (something the industry calls a 'dispensing error' or a 'selection error'), the outcome is a lot more significant than if the same pharmacist had given a customer the wrong flavour mouthwash. Both are operational failures, but the difference in customer impact is massive; one is a minor inconvenience, the other is a potential medical emergency. They require two entirely different responses.

Of course, some industries are just more prone to major operational failure than others. Airlines are a great example. There's no such thing as a 'small problem' in the airline industry. Airline customers are by necessity in a heightened state of anxiety. This means any glitches, clangers, gaffes – all accepted media euphemisms for operational failures when the stakes are low – become significantly less easy to forgive. If a baggage handler experiences a 'selection error', the outcome is obvious. If a pilot experiences one, it would be headline news. Perhaps that's why, according to a 2014 study by Unmetric, 15 of the world's largest airlines published 52,239 social media apologies between them in the space of just over three months.[1]

There's no such thing as a 'small problem' in the airline industry.

Friction – and why your buying habits influence your chances of getting an apology

The biggest influence on how earnestly and how often an organization apologizes has surprisingly little correlation with its conduct. Far more relevant is the behaviour of that organization's own consumers and the market conditions in which they consume. The best-behaved fashion brands and coffee chains are more apologetic than the worst-behaved banks and insurance companies. Why? It's all to do with friction, or lack of it.

Market friction describes the ease with which consumers can switch from one brand to a competitor. Churches, banks, mobile phone providers and professional football clubs – in fact any organization you care to think of where the hassle of finding an alternative provider is greater than the moral satisfaction of doing so – all benefit from the high friction in their respective markets. It's hard and unpleasant for consumers of certain products and services to switch. Organizations know this and are therefore less anxious about receiving criticism because it's less likely to be a precursor to customer attrition. So they apologize less.

The Pope is not losing sleep over Catholics switching to Buddhism because he won't say sorry for all the things people want him to say sorry for. And banks are entirely relaxed about retaining your custom regardless of how many bail-outs they need or arms manufacturers they invest in because they know full well how much of a pain it can be to switch current account.[2] After all, even after the global financial crisis, only 6 per cent of current account customers switched banks.[3] You're more likely to get divorced than change your bank.

You're more likely to get divorced than change your bank.

Low-friction markets work the other way around and organizations in these sectors need to be on their very best behaviour or else. These organizations rely on perceptions. They need to be liked to retain customers because they are far more exposed to the threat of customer attrition. Fashion, fast-food, take-away coffee, cosmetics – in fact any sector where competition is healthy and switching supplier is relatively painless – these are the sectors where minor transgressions lead to grovelling apologies. Annoyed with Starbucks? If you're in North America, go to Dunkin Donuts, or if you're in the UK, you could go to Costa Coffee if they don't apologize, or at least threaten to go. Offended by an H&M advert? Go to Primark. Outraged by Pizza Hut for some reason nobody really understands? Order a Domino's and wait for them to tweet that they're sorry.

Organizations in low-friction industries know how easy it is for their customers to shop elsewhere, so they practically fall over themselves to say sorry when an apology is demanded of them. Organizations in high-friction industries still say sorry, but they hold back their atonement for demonstrable failings. Banks will apologize for technical problems all day long, but you'll barely hear a peep from them about culture, values, mission or any of the other things those in low-friction industries have to apologize for.

How market friction affects Uber's conscience

In June 2017, Uber sent an apology e-mail to a cohort of people it referred to as 'ex-riders'.[4] These were former Uber customers whose usage of the ridesharing app had dropped off significantly. In the e-mail, Uber claimed to have 'faced some hard truths' and made various weak concessions to 'falling short'. This apology was specifically about Uber's cultural failures. 'We're overhauling our cultural values to reward collaboration and to foster a workplace that is inclusive rather than contentious' said the e-mail. This was not a 'sorry your driver was late' e-mail nor was it an unprompted confession. Uber's culture problems had been well publicized; a sexual harassment and a gender bias scandal had made global news around the same time.[5, 6]

Although Uber's declining reputation was a global problem, it kept this apology local, sending it only to customers in New York. Uber operates in 70 countries, but focused its apology on users in one state. Why only the United States and why specifically New York?

Organizations in low-friction industries... practically fall over themselves to say sorry.

The answer was Lyft. In 69 of the 70 countries in which it operates, Uber has a near monopoly on ridesharing. Boycott Uber in the UK and your alternative is a black cab or private taxi, removing you entirely from the ridesharing model. Boycott Uber in America, and a Lyft driver will be happy to give you a ride. So why only New York?

At the time of Uber's apology e-mail, Lyft operated in all 50 states, but it was taking a big slice of Uber's business in New York because of a local boycott. Uber had upset a lot of New York customers after implementing surge pricing during a taxi protest at JFK Airport. The United States was where the friction for Uber's customers was lowest and New York was where Lyft was picking up business, so New York is where Uber apologized.

The apology did little to stem the flow of customers deserting Uber. Former engineer Susan Fowler, the whistleblower who drew attention to the sexual harassment problems at the company, said the apology was 'all optics' and it didn't work anyway. Uber CEO Travis Kalanick resigned a few days later.[7]

Uber's selective atonement demonstrates an important point. Apologies are, among other things, time-consuming, humiliating and stressful. Organizations will issue apologies of varying quality and sincerity, but there are myriad other factors aside from their own conscience that determine how and when they do it. When an organization faces criticism, it asks itself two questions: 'how badly did we mess up?' and 'what can people do about it?' If the answers are 'very badly' and 'ditch you in a heartbeat', your chances of hearing an apology improve.

CHAPTER FIVE

The definitive modern apology and why everyone ignored it

We are sorry and embarrassed. But most of all, we are deeply sorry. DAVID NEELEMAN, CEO AND FOUNDER, JETBLUE, FEBRUARY 2007

David Neeleman cried when Herb Kelleher sacked him.[1] Kelleher, the founder of Southwest Airlines, got rid of Neeleman just five months after acquiring Morris Air, the small charter airline Neeleman had founded in 1992. Neeleman had idolized Kelleher and when Southwest Airlines acquired Morris Air in 1993, the young Neeleman admitted he'd have sold Morris Air for less, just for the chance to work with his hero.

It's easy to forget that air travel was once a luxury few could afford. We take it for granted now that airlines can transport us from one part of the world to another for about the price of a posh haircut. It's a triumph of human progress and we have Southwest Airlines to thank for it. The Texas-based carrier pioneered the concept of no-frills low-cost air travel in the early 70s, launching with services out of Dallas Love Field airport for as little as $15.[2]

According to his obituary in the *New York Times*, Southwest's New Jersey-born founder Herb Kelleher was a 'fun-loving, chain-smoking, hard-drinking' sort of CEO.[3] He was also a man with an astoundingly tunnel-vision approach to running his airline. He explained Southwest's simple credo in the book *Buck Up, Suck Up … and Come Back When You Foul Up: 12 winning secrets from the war room*:

> I can teach you the secret to running this airline in 30 seconds. This is it: we are THE low-cost airline. Once you understand that fact, you can make any decision about this company's future as well as I can.[4]

Southwest was and still is about being cheapest, to the exclusion of everything else. They don't aspire to be the best, the fastest or the airline with the happiest customers. Southwest wants to be the cheapest. Every decision they make has to support that ambition.

This could be why they apologize a lot. According to research by social media analytics provider Unmetric, published in DigiDay, 64 per cent of Southwest's tweets are customer apologies.[5] In terms of apologies as a proportion of their total social media output, they are the most apologetic airline. They don't make the most apologies in their industry: Delta, Virgin, American and United – the latter we'll be hearing a lot about later – have all apologized more. But these airlines use social media for other stuff too. On the sorry:not-sorry ratio, nobody beats Southwest.

Southwest's apologies are very much a customer service function

Isn't it weird then that Southwest also ranks consistently near the top of the JD Power customer satisfaction survey? Well, actually no. They apologize a lot, but they're not actually sorry. Southwest's apologies are very much a customer service function, a transactional lubricant for the operational friction of running an airline. They're still cheap and that's all that matters.

One of Southwest's biggest rivals for the crown of best airline is JetBlue. It was founded in 1998 by David Neeleman, the Brazilian–American businessman sacked by Southwest just five years earlier. Neeleman too has a laser-guided focus on how he wants his airline to run. In contrast to Southwest's 'we're the cheapest' credo, JetBlue was founded on the principle of bringing humanity back to air travel. It's a customer service airline. The two airlines now regularly tussle for top spot on the JD Power survey, but the firms and their respective founders couldn't be more different. JetBlue and Southwest are popular airlines but for completely different reasons.

JetBlue don't appear in Unmetric's list of most apology-prone airlines, but they do have the distinction of having given what is now considered to be the definitive corporate apology. There's a right way to be sorry, and apologizing frequently is not the same as apologizing *well*. As we explore the various ways organizations say sorry to people, we'll see how these different corporate credos drive crisis communications across different sectors. It's safe to say though that JetBlue's fellow low-cost carriers have very different approaches to addressing customer dissatisfaction.

Valentine's Day crisis

When freezing rain hit the Atlantic coast of North America on Valentine's Day 2007, it triggered an operational meltdown that lasted for five days. More than a thousand JetBlue flights were cancelled, affecting more than 130,000 customers. JetBlue didn't have a contingency for such a large backlog and failed to communicate properly with customers. JetBlue has three founding principles, the third of which is: 'Make it right with the customer.'[6] If their claims about being a customer service airline were credible, now was the time to prove it.

What they did next went on to form a template for the modern corporate apology.

The JetBlue apology came in three waves, in three different formats. It started with a letter from their CEO David Neeleman published on JetBlue's website and shared with the press. The letter is still available on the JetBlue website and it's worth reading every one of the 364 words to understand how good it was, and how bad some apologies can be by comparison.

'Dear JetBlue Customers' started the letter. 'We are sorry and embarrassed. But most of all, we are deeply sorry.' It couldn't have set a more appropriate tone for the entire response. David Neeleman's handling of this crisis was characterized by his honesty and humility.

A reader of the letter might have expected to stumble over some now-familiar corporate apology clichés: 'challenging circumstances', 'factors out of our control', 'mistakes were made' – there were none of these. Neeleman was telling it how it was: 'We subjected you to unacceptable delays, flight cancellations, lost baggage and other major inconveniences.' It would have been so easy for him to phrase that differently by flipping the pronouns around and distancing JetBlue from the problem: 'You experienced unacceptable delays...'. Neeleman was clearly not prepared to minimize his company's role in the situation.

He was sincere and human, but he wasn't grovelling.

He was sincere and human, but he wasn't grovelling. Of the 364 words in his letter, Neeleman used the word 'sorry' three times. And three times was enough. He used the word 'you' 11 times and the word 'I' once. That's an important ratio. It tells us a lot about the balance of the message. As we'll discover, apology statements are very often biased in the opposite direction, their givers preoccupied with saving face and deflecting liability.

The world's first corporate social media apology

At the end of his letter, Neeleman mentions a video. This is where JetBlue's crisis response and apology elevates itself above the merely adequate or good apologies. They were about to take a step into the unknown. YouTube had been around for just two years and Twitter had just had its first birthday when JetBlue posted the clip. Brands hadn't yet figured out the power of social media for managing (or mismanaging) their crises.

David Neeleman probably didn't realize either that he was setting a new standard for crisis communications when he posted a video entitled 'Our Promise To You'. The 'contrite CEO addresses his customers' video is a now ubiquitous template – everyone from BP to Uber has used it. At the time though, it was completely unprecedented for a company CEO to stake the reputation of his organization on a two-year-old video platform mostly used for sharing clips of teenagers backflipping off their parents' roofs.[7] It was a huge risk and it paid off.

JetBlue posted the three-minute clip five days after the initial operational failure, an age by today's apology-on-demand standards. But back in 2007, this was considered a rapid response and the reaction was surprisingly positive. Marty St George, vice president of planning at JetBlue, said:

> Some of this feedback was 'I can't believe you guys let us down like this.' Some of the feedback was 'I still love you and it's OK.'[8]

The video was authentic in the real sense of the word, as distinct from the contrived vision of 'authenticity' that blights modern corporate communications. There was no background music to subliminally tug at your emotions, no fancy editing, no slow-motion shots of Neeleman speaking to customers in stage-managed set pieces. As far as production values went, the JetBlue logo hanging in the background and some very basic title wipes were about it.

Neeleman, sitting a bit too close to the camera, occasionally stumbled over his words. At one point he picked up an official staff badge he referred to as part of JetBlue's process improvements and waved it clumsily at the camera in a way so you couldn't even see it. In other words, 3/10 for presentation and 10/10 for impact. This felt like a real apology. Neeleman was either the world's biggest con artist, or he'd accidentally nailed the kind of authenticity brands pay millions to emulate.

JetBlue didn't bring in a crisis management specialist to assist.

The amateurish presentation didn't matter. In fact, one notable fact about this entire episode is that JetBlue didn't bring in a crisis management specialist to assist. It was Neeleman's company and he was determined to clean up the mess himself. Jonathan Bernstein, founder of Bernstein Crisis Management told *Forbes* in 2007: 'If he called me for advice, I couldn't have done it any better.'[9] The human element of what Neeleman said is what marks this out as a textbook corporate apology.

He started with 'sorry' then went on to explain in plain English what had happened and how JetBlue was working to put it right. Absent from his apology were equivocations and appeals to vagueness. His customers appreciated that. *Adweek* said JetBlue had 'nailed the transparency game'.[10] As the article's author David Gianatasio noted at the time, as well as knowing what to say and how to say it, JetBlue also 'knows when to shut up'. Not every brand does.

An offer of repair

Perhaps the most crucial part of the crisis response was the 'customer bill of rights'. In his YouTube clip, Neeleman told viewers he was introducing the bill of rights to set out exactly what they were entitled to in the event of future delays and cancellations. This was crucial to the success of the apology. A concrete offer of repair is the fifth of six key elements of a credible and useful apology, according to the conflict management specialist Professor Roy J Lewicki. The offer comes before the request for forgiveness.

Instead of only paying the required compensation to the customers affected by this situation, JetBlue used their crisis to establish a new set of customer rights that would apply to all customers from that point on. JetBlue understood that the affected customers were not the only ones whose trust they risked losing. Their other customers were watching how they handled the situation. The bill of rights set out exactly what customers could expect should they encounter problems, right down to the specific amounts of compensation that applied to delays of different lengths. By introducing their bill of rights, JetBlue made the unusual move of putting in writing that they expected problems to happen. They sort of guaranteed it and, without qualification, told customers what to expect when it happened. In doing this, they treated their customers as adults. Everyone knows flights get delayed and cancelled and most people accept that this isn't always the airline's fault. The inconvenience to the customer is the cost of doing business with an airline. The alternative is getting the bus.

The response to the response

In an article published the week after the Valentine's Day crisis, *Forbes*' Tara Weiss said JetBlue's response had been 'the textbook version of how to handle the aftermath'. Crisis management consultant Jim Lukaszewski told Weiss he thought Neeleman had 'set the standard for dealing with these situations'. David Neeleman and JetBlue had given the communications industry a valuable lesson. They'd done for corporate apologies what McDonald's did for fast food and what Stock, Aitken and

Waterman did for pop songs – provided a template. The communications profession was gifted a definitive, simple formula for success. Any organization in a crisis could now look to JetBlue's response and with a few tweaks, create a reliable and tested path to recovery. The JetBlue corporate apology template has been around since 2007. So why hasn't the communications profession been using it? If they had, this book wouldn't exist.

The communications profession was gifted a definitive, simple formula for success.

Looking back on JetBlue's own experience of its crisis, there was a warning that an entire generation of communications professionals were at risk of ignoring. Speaking to *Adweek*, Marty St George admitted the decision to use social media had a profound impact on him. He told *Adweek,* 'This is like crack' and St George appeared to know why he was hooked. 'I spent a lot of money and waited a long time to get feedback like this via traditional market research. [Now] I'm getting instantaneous feedback. To me, that was the power of it.'[11]

And that's the problem. The addictive quality of social media engagement will be a defining feature – and in some cases, the cause – of subsequent crisis management failures for hundreds of organizations, including many of JetBlue's industry peers. It's one of the reasons that this book *does* exist.

JetBlue's video was a social media apology delivered at the dawn of outrage culture. Twitter was in its infancy when JetBlue set the standard for crisis management and the new norms of consumer–brand interactions hadn't yet been established. The digital infrastructure was there, but organizations didn't yet have the techniques for the kind of real-time crisis management social media would demand of them. And consumers hadn't quite discovered the immense power they were about to wield.

CHAPTER SIX

If everyone's sorry, nobody is sorry

Are we all apologizing too much?

*We are sorry that you are disappointed with the range
of shoes on offer for your daughter and that you feel
she is limited in her choice of active shoe wear.*
CLARKS SHOES, AUGUST 2017

There are two notable dates for anyone interested in the apology impulse: 4th and 20th January 2018. They were the only two days in the first month of 2018 on which the media *didn't* report on an organization or high-profile figure issuing a public apology. The rest of January 2018 had an average of 1.2 notable apologies per day.

In the first week of January 2018 alone, YouTube personality Logan Paul apologized for a bad taste video, Virgin Trains and Northumbria Police both apologized for bad taste tweets and book publisher AllSorted apologized for a bad taste joke. As the month progressed, the flow of apologies grew stronger. Two different professional football coaches – Phil Neville and Darren Ferguson – apologized for dodgy remarks about women and referees respectively, YouTube apologized for what Logan Paul did the week before, pop singer Lily Allen apologized for spreading fake news and Asda said sorry for not carrying someone's shopping upstairs – a misdemeanour they will repeat and apologize for again in September the same year.

In addition, three MPs (two of whom apologized within 24 hours of one another), one footballer, Delta Airlines, Marriott Hotels, Highways England, Donald Trump and the actual Pope all apologized for something in the 31 days of January 2018. What a month.

Everyone was apologizing. Tesco, the UK's largest retailer, is a good example of an organization struggling with a reflexively apologetic communications strategy. In 2017, its official spokespeople made 13 high-profile public apologies, either via social media or to the press. That's one public apology every four weeks on average. Many of these apologies were boilerplated statements related to product recalls and payment glitches. The supermarket chain sought forgiveness for an impressive range of trivialities too, including a grammatical error on an in-store chicken display and an Easter beer advert that offended Christians.

Tesco spent a significant portion of 2017 saying sorry, so we might assume they'd experienced a catalogue of operational and service failures. Compared to five years prior, their apology output had increased six-fold. But was Tesco's behaviour six times worse? Probably not. In 2012, they were impressively frugal with their high-profile public apologies, issuing just two: one for a pricing error and one for a translation mix-up that resulted in some mildly saucy Italian slogans finding their way onto a pasta packet. That's one boring apology and one 'funny' apology over the course of a year. Yet by the end of July 2017, they'd made more apologies than in 2012 and 2013 combined.

That's quite a feat of atonement when you consider that 2013 was the year of the horsemeat scandal, one of Tesco's largest ever reputational crises. But here they were, sorrier than ever about packaging and in-store posters.

If we were to plot a trend of the amount of times Tesco said sorry between 2012 to 2018, we'd reasonably assume that the retail giant had gone completely off the rails at some point around 2016, well after the horsemeat scandal. But Tesco was behaving no worse in 2017 and 2018 than it was in 2012 and 2013. And we were still shopping there in record numbers too.

In fact, since the scandal-hit years of 2012 and 2013 (horsemeat burgers and an accounting disaster that wiped £2 billion off their share price), consumer perceptions of Tesco have *improved* significantly. In 2016, Tesco reported that brand trust was at a four-year high. They weren't just the UK's largest retailer; they were also the fastest growing supermarket. Tesco were doing great.

This morass of public contrition has to be a sign that apologies are losing their punch.

But Tesco were not only saying sorry more often, they were saying it more intensely too. They were 'extremely' sorry about many things. In some cases, 'extremely' was appropriate. Such as when they dispensed the wrong medication to a customer who ended up in hospital as a result in December 2017. In some cases it was overkill. When they were 'extremely sorry' for mislabelling some fancy dress costumes – they called them 'Dark Panther' instead of 'Black Panther', upsetting some social media users – we might wonder whether Tesco were just phoning it in. They rendered the far extremity of contrition so meaningless it became a rhetorical dead end. If the horsemeat scandal happened in 2020, Tesco wouldn't have the emotional headroom to express the sort of regret their customers would expect.

This morass of public contrition has to be a sign that apologies are losing their punch. If everyone is sorry, is anyone sorry?

Social anthropologist Kate Fox, speaking of the British tendency to over-apologize, highlights the risk of doing so: 'Our excessive, often inappropriate and sometimes downright misleading use of this word devalues it.'[1]

She's right. It's confusing and misleading to apologize so often. But it's not just British people. All over the world apologies have been demanded, given and amplified to such volume that they seem to just linger there in the public consciousness, not really doing much. 'Sorry' and its semantic poor relations 'apologize' and 'regret' have become like the hum of an old fridge: a mildly annoying but ultimately meaningless sound that we eventually learn to ignore.

Are we really apologizing too much?

Yes. We're all definitely apologizing a lot more than we used to and have been since around 1999. According to Google's Ngram Viewer database of five million books, use of the word 'sorry' increased significantly around the turn of the Millennium.[2]

As of 2008, the last year for which Google holds data, published instances of 'sorry' were at their highest level since 1629, around the same time as the Huguenot rebellions.

After a steady climb in popularity from the mid-17th century, 'sorry' declined significantly from the start of the 20th century. For the first half of the century, there was a clear downward trend in recorded instances of 'sorry'. People were just saying it less often. Then in 1953, just as the UK and USA were experiencing unprecedented economic prosperity and high employment, 'sorry' dropped off a cliff edge completely to its lowest level since the middle of the 18th century. In the 1950s when people were apparently busier, richer and – according to a 2017 study by the Social Market Foundation and the Centre for Competitive Advantage in the Global Economy – when they were happier, they said sorry less.[3]

'Sorry' remained relatively low throughout the 60s and the first half of the 70s. From the late 70s through the 80s and 90s 'sorry' made a come-back, creeping back up steadily before spiking – tellingly – just around the time we all got on the Internet. By the time Twitter had launched, 'sorry' was resurgent, trending higher than it had done for almost 400 years.

This might explain Tesco's impressive apology output. The flurry of apologies we saw in 2017 were not a result of Tesco becoming aware of its own depravity and seeking forgiveness. It was simply part of a commitment to a new style of customer engagement. In 2016, CEO Dave Lewis revealed that Tesco, like many other organizations with a reputation to protect, had moved its focus towards social media:

> We made a decision 18 months ago to redirect our investment and engagement with customers, so you saw us change from traditional above-the-line into more personalized social media.[4]

Social media gives Tesco a platform on which to engage with its customers. A study – albeit conducted by Twitter so take it with a pinch of salt – found that companies who respond to customer complaints on social media tend to enjoy enhanced perceptions and increased customer spend.[5] But as Tesco and organizations like them are now finding out, when you commit to social media, you commit to saying sorry.

Broadcasting our apologies far and wide

As well as saying sorry more often, our apologies now travel further. The media's appetite for reporting our apologies is stronger than ever. Google's search data bears this out. Web pages containing the phrase 'retailer apologizes' – a handy example due to its present-day ubiquity – was until recently, entirely obscure.

Between 2000 and 2008, the search engine had indexed just two pages containing the phrase 'retailer apologizes' (or 'apologises');

Walmart was sorry about a T-shirt with a Nazi skull; and Wisconsin retailer Land's End was sorry for publishing in their brochure an interview that upset some customers. That's not to say other retailers were not making public apologies during that time because they were, but to point out that the phrase 'retailer apologizes' was vanishingly rare until only recently. And if any retailers were apologizing, the media weren't interested in reporting it.

The media's appetite for reporting our apologies is stronger than ever.

Things changed significantly in 2009. Hundreds of news stories containing the phrase 'retailer apologizes' started popping up online. Marks & Spencer, Ann Summers, Primark and Poundland all appeared in news pages containing the phrase. From then on 'retailer apologizes' has become ubiquitous. As of August 2018, Google has indexed more than 7,000 pages containing the exact phrase and around 34 million pages containing semantic variants, such as 'retailer issues apology' or 'retailer sorry'.

We might naturally attribute a trend like this to one of two things: either retailers, like the rest of us, are suddenly apologizing more, or online media outlets are more likely to tell us about it when they do. But the truth is somewhere in the middle. It's a combination of these two things, rapidly accelerated by the advent of 'viral news' – social media-driven trending 'news' content served up by the likes of The Huffington Post and Buzzfeed. So how did a new trend in online publishing force us all into saying sorry?

Outrage capitalism and the plummeting value of 'sorry'

To understand why apologies are in such high demand, we need to understand how viral news publishers can make money from them. The viral news revenue model is quick and dirty. Nobody would pay for a subscription to a viral news website. The content is too easily reproduced for that to be sustainable. Viral sites typically make most of their money from ad impressions (when the advert displays on a user's screen, an impression is not the same as someone clicking it). This model demands high volumes of traffic. This is why a lot of online journalists receive compensation linked directly to how many people read a particular article. Terms and compensation models vary, but generally work on the theory that equates page views to income.

The now defunct viral publisher Gawker Media group, for example, paid some of its journalists on a stipend-payback model. 'The recruits receive a stipend of $1,500 a month, and pay back that amount at a rate of $5 for every 1,000 unique visitors they attract. They then get to keep anything above the amount of the stipend, up to $6,000.'[6]

The economic reality of viral news – and we're including mainstream publishers who've adopted the viral news model, such as UK publishers Indy 100 and Metro in this definition – incentivizes the kind of cheaply produced stories that require minimal reporting and can be repeated and scaled with ease. Although cheaper to produce than in-depth reporting, these stories are meticulously road-tested and optimized before they reach their final iteration.

It's a complex dance of offence-taking, recreational outrage and perceived injustice.

Viral news website Upworthy – which at its peak had around 90 million readers per month but has since significantly dropped in popularity – used to test 25 versions of each headline during its publishing process to identify the variant that generated the most engagement within a specific demographic.[7,8] For a story to go viral, publishers need us to share it. One way viral news publishers promote sharing, aside from road-tested headlines, is to make us angry.

Alex Abad-Santos, senior culture reporter at Vox.com – themselves no strangers to profiting from the clicks of the righteously outraged – explained how it works:

The shameful truth of journalism is that every news outlet thrives on clicks. In recent years, those clicks have dovetailed with the prominence of social media — especially Facebook — so most news outlets (Vox.com included) began to regularly cover stuff that people will want to share on those platforms. Part of that strategy means fuelling outrage, because it's so powerful.[9]

Former Upworthy editor-at-large Adam Mordecai underscored their approach to generating anger-clicks, explaining that his writers are encouraged to include a hero and villain in the headline for higher engagement.[10]

This hero/villain dynamic isn't confined to the newsroom either. Upworthy's own advertising sales page plays on this assumption, inviting potential advertisers to help them right some wrongs and 'pick a fight with the status quo'.[11] Potential advertisers are encouraged to see the world as an unjust place that only viral news can fix: 'Look around: The world is full of wrongs. Happily, there's a right for every one of them, if you have the courage to jump in.'[12]

This supports Mordecai's theory that the hero/villain headline format drives us to share. We're hard-wired to enjoy someone else's comeuppance, especially when it's delivered by a perceived underdog.

In 2017 an anonymous viral news journalist revealed to Wired.com the types of news stories that get the most readers: 'Another type of story we love to share is someone fighting against society's ills.'[13] The anonymous reporter added: 'We also enjoy reading about women shutting down sexist tweets, a celebrity "hilariously owning" someone who left a racist comment, or the heartbroken-turned-angry getting revenge on cheating partners.'[14]

In other words, viral news found a way through 'outrage capitalism' to monetize 'call-out' culture. So we get the headlines we ask for, without knowing we even asked for them. But there's only so much comeuppance-getting to go around before we run out of stories, and a lot of competition for page views. So the viral news media has the perverse incentive of seeking out, and even creating, these hero/villain scenarios.

What better way to do this than by celebrating and amplifying the 'call-out' – the act of drawing critical attention to someone's unacceptable actions or behaviour.[15] And what better source of villains being called out by those heroes is there than businesses and their customers? Businesses and public organizations make the perfect out-of-the-box villain: powerful, faceless and highly visible.

Customers make the perfect heroes too: plucky, powerless and relatable. Brands and organizations, in their commitment to social media accountability, have sleep-walked right into the firing line. The viral news sites were quick to take advantage. That's why we see so many headlines like 'This mum has called out Clarks over the difference in its shoes for girls and boys' and 'I'm the woman who called out United and I'm sick of sexism'.[16,17]

Brand strategist at social media agency Sprout Social, Liz Kannenberg has first-hand experience of dealing with the fallout of this dynamic:

> If anything is crystal clear to me, it's that call-outs don't happen in a vacuum. The impact of call-out culture echoes to every aspect of a business, from consumer sentiment to revenue. A single negative post has the potential to reach thousands of people in a matter of seconds, on a truly global scale.[18]

Kannenberg adds: 'A single call-out can snowball into a reputation crisis for a brand that isn't prepared.'[19]

So the more we read their call-out/apology stories, the more we incentivize viral news outlets to publish more of them. It's not quite clickbait, but it's in the same neighbourhood. In order to ensure a high supply of call-out/apology stories to write about, the viral news media rewards those who extract an apology with increased social clout – a little Twitter fame normally does the trick. This is just one economic driver of outrage capitalism.

What happens next involves the cooperation of the media, their audience and the organizations they write about. It's a complex dance of offence-taking, recreational outrage and perceived injustice. As we'll see, most organizations tend to reflexively apologize when an apology is demanded. Some don't, but the media is playing the percentages. They'll get a result most of the time.

The social clout earned by the original instigator can be anything from a favourable mention in the story, a brief taste of social media popularity or even online fame in its own right. The lady who called out United got her own column in *Time* magazine, for example.

As an anonymous communications undergraduate student observed to *The Atlantic* in 2017: 'In our day and age, going viral or gaining widespread Internet fame is something of legend, a social conquest achieved by only those with a rare knack for cultural phenomena or those merely blessed by fate.'[20]

It's no surprise then that organizations are already deciding that social media might not be worth the hassle. In April 2019 cosmetics retailer Lush announced it was shutting down some of its UK brand social accounts on Twitter, Facebook and Instagram. The retailer, who famously refused to say sorry for its bizarre anti-police window displays despite a social media backlash and boycott threats, attributed its decision to the disconnect between brands and their audiences on social media. 'Increasingly, social media is making it harder and harder for us to talk to each other directly. We are tired of fighting with algorithms and we do not want to pay to appear in your newsfeed.'[21] When the Wetherspoons pub chain removed all of its social media accounts in 2018, CEO Tim Martin said in a tweet (now deleted, obviously): 'We are going against conventional wisdom that these platforms are a vital component of a successful business.'[22]

Organizations have chosen to invest in using a platform where people love to get angry. Multiple studies have found that outrage is the most commonly shared emotion on social media, especially on Twitter.[23,24] And a study by Sprout Social found that 55 per cent of consumers who call out organizations hope to receive an apology.[25] So what do the other 45 per cent want to achieve if they don't want an apology? The study found that 70 per cent of call-outs are done to raise awareness. Of whom though? The organization's apparent transgression, or themselves?

The viral news media also applies its own influence to the process, while presenting itself as a disinterested witness. Everyone knows media attention influences outcomes. So by writing about the demand for the apology, they confer increased social status on the instigator by writing about them, increasing the pressure on the organization or individual to deliver to them the apology they demand.

But the media can often go one step further than simply reporting by 'reaching out' to the organization that has been called on to apologize. This is ostensibly the fair media practice of offering a right to reply, but the reality is different. Not many organizations have the resources to respond to every trivial complaint raised on Twitter.

The media knows as much and wins either way. If the organization does provide a response, the media get to update their story or publish a new one, prolonging the outrage cycle and getting more website traffic. If the organization doesn't provide comment, all is not lost. 'We reached out to a spokesperson for comment, but they didn't get back to us' can be just as damning.

However, there may be a monumentally ironic twist to all of this. The media, often the enthusiastic ringleader, can sometimes become the victim of outrage capitalism and when it does, its appetite for encouraging recreational outrage is miraculously slaked. One such incident is not only indicative of the media's selective discomfort with call-out culture; it also suggests the media may be harbouring individuals prepared and equipped to guide us out of this moral maze.

After Australian cartoonist Mark Knight refused to apologize for a cartoon of tennis star Serena Williams many found to be racist, he received death threats and shut down his social media. Without an outlet through which to vent, his detractors turned their ire on his employer the *Herald Sun*, their publisher News Corp Australia (which owns multiple media brands including Sky News Australia) and eventually, after News Corp Australia stood firmly behind Knight, they zeroed in on its advertisers.

As Knight's *Herald Sun* colleague Rita Panahi revealed, prominent corporate call-outs can produce more heat than light:

> In a 6-week period just 10 accounts sent 4,500 tweets to Sky News' advertisers... the majority of all the tweets sent to Sky News' advertisers came from fewer than 200 Twitter accounts, more than 70 per cent of which were anonymous.[26]

There's a long-tail/short-tail dichotomy at play here with heat and light in unequal measures. The noise we're hearing is often amplified by an army of nobodies, literal nobodies in the form of anonymous Twitter accounts in this case.

Panahi asserts that companies are increasingly intimidated into making stupid decisions, but commends Sky News' CEO Angelos Frangopoulos, who stood firm, saying about those making the most noise: 'Hiding behind "social value", they carry out a commercial terrorist campaign by confecting consumer outrage.' Hyperbole aside, she makes a solid point. The lesson here is quite simple: don't (always) believe the hype. Before organizations make reflexive decisions, they'd be well served to take a breath and audit the dynamics of the situation. A handful of people can make a lot of noise. It doesn't necessarily mean anything.

All apologies become newsworthy, attract clicks and generate money.

Ignoring the hype might be the best advice, but it's not exactly easy. Powerful human emotions like anxiety, panic and shame – all linked to survival to varying extents – can often cause us to reflexively apologize without really needing to. And when our increased appetite for saying sorry is driven by those who stand to profit most from it, it's hard to ignore our survival instincts. This is the media's fault. There's a difference between reporting on genuinely newsworthy incidents, like plane crashes and oil spills and unforgivable corporate misconduct that happen to involve a public apology, and amplifying trivial squabbles between customers and brands. The increase in public apologies we're seeing is down to the latter. All apologies become newsworthy, attract clicks and generate money. So yes, we are apologizing more and we're doing so because the perverse incentives to demand, give and report on an apology are too powerful to resist.

CHAPTER SEVEN

How the experts apologize without saying sorry

'Runway excursion incidents', 're-accommodating passengers' and 'overpressurization'

> *It's misleading to say it was an explosion. It was an overpressurization that was followed by a fire.*
> ARKEMA INC SPOKESPERSON, 31 AUGUST 2017

During a crisis, there's a temptation for communicators to deploy linguistic tricks in an attempt to distance themselves and their organizations from the failings the rest of us have observed in plain sight. The goal isn't necessarily to conceal reality – although some might try that too – but to persuade consumers and media to view it in a more favourable light than it deserves.

It never works because a corporate crisis is never a single big event; it's always a chain of interlocking mini events. The PR response should never be the weak link in this chain.

If communicators eschew clarity in favour of jargon, the response becomes part of the story and the communications team become part of the event.

When is a plane crash not a plane crash?

In January 2017, while attempting to land at Trabzon, a small clifftop airfield on Turkey's Black Sea coast, Pegasus Airlines flight PC8622 from Ankara encountered some problems. It skidded off the runway, plunged down a cliff and came to a terrifying stop just a few metres above the Black Sea. There was panic and shouting as the smell of aviation fuel flooded the cabin. Fire crews had to douse the Boeing 737–800 aircraft with water to stop it catching fire.

Passenger Yuksel Gordu told Reuters: 'It was a miracle. We could have burned, we could have exploded or we could have gone into the sea.'[1] Although terrifying for the passengers and a major headache for the airline, as plane crashes go, this one was minor; no fatalities, no major injuries and the plane appeared recoverable. But it was still a plane crash and the public were entitled to an explanation.

Pegasus Airlines didn't necessarily see it that way. In fact, they didn't necessarily see this as a minor plane crash. So the answer to the question 'when is a minor plane crash like this not a minor plane crash?' is – when it's a 'runway excursion incident' as described by Pegasus Airlines. It doesn't matter if the passengers thought they might be about to die. Pegasus Airlines were going to jargon this one out.

If you search online for 'runway excursion incident' you'll find more than 8,000 pages containing the phrase. If you limit your search to just news articles, there's almost 300. A 'runway excursion incident' is not some obscure, rarely used term to describe a freak set of circumstances. It's part of established and legitimate aviation terminology, describing a situation in which a plane leaves the runway when it's not supposed to leave the runway, for example, when trying to land.

And here's the issue. The term refers as equally to a plane overshooting the runway by a few yards without passengers noticing, as it does to a plane plunging down a cliff toward the sea. It's a term used for recording and monitoring accidents. It should not be used to describe an unfolding situation to the media. The phrase does a disservice to the experience of the passengers.

Of course, it is technically true to describe the Pegasus Airlines situation as a 'runway excursion incident'. In the same way it's technically true to describe Albert Einstein as a patent office clerk, Paul McCartney as the bass player from Wings and George Foreman as a grill salesman. As statements of fact, they are accurate. But the omission of context makes them misleading.

This is a dangerous habit to get into for organizations that need to communicate effectively during a crisis. The temptation to deploy oblique waffle is ever present. It's why inaccessible language so often pollutes corporate crisis communications and it's why we get 'jargonpologies'. The job of professional communicators should be to centre the customers' experience, communicating consistently and clearly. When this fails, when the corporate line is unrecognizable to those who were there, then that's a problem, a jargon incursion incident. Professional communicators should be committed to avoiding this.

This doesn't mean using abrupt or coarse language. It means eschewing jargon in favour of accessible speech that anyone can understand. A good jargon-proofing method is to imagine a 90-year-old reading your statement to a 10-year-old: would both people understand what's happening? If not, then try again.

'A disappointing event for our company'

Although clarity is key when a crisis is unfolding, discretion may also be required to protect people's privacy and, as was the case with the 2017 Equifax data breach, to make sure you don't alert an army of cyber-criminals to a potentially unguarded cache of sensitive consumer data. It's possible to be discreet without being evasive though.

It's possible to be discreet without being evasive.

Equifax, who had 143 million potentially affected customers to apologize to, couldn't manage it. The firm was widely criticized for delaying its response to the hack, issuing confusing information and completely ignoring customer anxiety; they asked customers to provide their social security numbers in order to check if their data had been compromised. The messaging was off and the timeline of events was all messed up. *PR Week* put it best, saying: 'Equifax botched its breach.'[2]

Chairman and chief executive officer, Richard F Smith said in a company statement: 'This is clearly a disappointing event for our company and one that strikes at the heart of who we are and what we do. I apologize to consumers and our business customers for the concern and frustration this causes.'[3,4]

'Disappointing' is inherently misleading in its failure to express the extent to which customers were affected. Missing sales targets is disappointing. Losing to Lidl in a Christmas pudding taste test is disappointing. Potentially exposing 143 million customers to identity theft is catastrophic. Equifax's biggest sin here is talking about how this situation affects Equifax, before addressing the needs of their customers. The statement goes on to talk up the company's record in doing the very thing they're apologizing for not doing – managing and protecting data. (we'll cover this particular habit in more detail in Chapter 8):

> We pride ourselves on being a leader in managing and protecting data, and we are conducting a thorough review of our overall security operations. We also are focused on consumer protection and have developed a comprehensive portfolio of services to support all US consumers, regardless of whether they were impacted by this incident.[5]

The second part of the apology does the heavy lifting where the first part didn't. It addresses safeguards and next steps – key ingredients of a crisis response. But it's disappointing that the opener set the tone for a weak apology and a crisis management disaster class.

Unauthorized takeoff

It probably feels like we're picking on airlines in this book. We're really not. It's just that when your business model involves hurtling through the sky in a metal tube, customer anxiety is baked into the way you operate. There's rarely such thing as a 'minor problem', so jargon is particularly unhelpful at any time. Baffling technical waffle is far from unique to the aviation sector, but the aviation sector is the undisputed champion of the tactical understatement. For the purposes of this chapter, they are the gift that keeps on giving.

Here's a quick thought experiment: if you saw a tweet, posted from the official Twitter account of the United States' ninth-busiest airport, that said an 'airline employee conducted an unauthorized takeoff without passengers', you'd be forgiven for thinking this was some sort of administrative oversight; someone didn't fill out the correct paperwork or wait for air traffic control to give the go-ahead.

That would be to vastly understate the situation. The truth, as it would be told by the man or woman in the street, was that a mechanic at Seattle-Tacoma International Airport stole a plane, flew it for approximately one hour and performed some barrel rolls before fatally crashing onto a remote island. The Air National Guard from two different states sent up F-15 fighter jets and the airport was on lockdown for the duration of the flight. Like 'runway excursion incident',' a classic of the evasive understatement genre, 'unauthorized takeoff' does nothing to cut through the noise.

We're not asking these organizations to rip up their style guides and talk like they're chatting in a bar. But is it too much to ask that they think twice before reaching for the Glossary of Obscure Aviation Terminology? This was a terrible situation completely downplayed by inaccessible corporate language. It was tone-deaf. This isn't to suggest Seattle-Tacoma Airport necessarily owes anyone an apology, but like Pegasus Airlines, they do owe people an explanation and that explanation should be easy for everyone to understand.

This was a terrible situation completely downplayed by inaccessible corporate language.

'Unauthorized takeoff' leaves so many questions unanswered. How was the employee able to steal the plane? What measures were in place to prevent this happening? Language this vague is useless. Spokespeople might think it distances them from accountability, gives them room to fill in the blanks later and eliminates the need for 'sorry'. That's a dangerous assumption. Vagueness so often does the opposite. Weak and evasive messaging has the capacity to turn a bad situation into scandal of historic significance.

Re-accommodating passengers

The *Merriam-Webster Dictionary* website has a neat little feature. Beneath the definition of every word, readers are prompted to share the reason they looked it up. These comment sections are as civilized as you'd expect from a community of dictionary enthusiasts. The exchanges often open up into illuminating conversations about people's own lives and interests, language and etymology.

Under the definition for 're-accommodate' in Merriam-Webster, the tone of the responses is different to the rest of the website.[6] People are angry. One of the most prominent replies under the 're-accommodate' entry begins with 'Oscar "asshole" Munoz, CEO, United Airlines...' and it gets steadily worse from there. The vast majority of comments on this dictionary entry are dedicated to trashing one man. Oscar Munoz. Who knew the Merriam-Webster community could be so brutal?

Oscar Munoz would already have suspected the magnitude of his reputational problems when an apology he gave some days before the dictionary comments were published become a meme. Munoz, CEO of United Airlines – if you'll allow us to stick with the airline industry a little longer – gifted us one of the most insincere and bizarre attempts at an apology of recent times. It must have felt like the whole Internet was laughing at him. (It wasn't United's only 'meme-able' crisis either): 'This is an upsetting event to all of us here at United. I apologize for having to re-accommodate these customers.'[7]

It all came down to that one word: 're-accommodate'. Again, like 'runway excursion incident', this is a legitimate aviation term. It typically refers to the process of moving passengers to another flight if the airline can't offer them the seat they booked. It wasn't the word per se that caused the fuss, but Munoz' devious attempt to shoehorn it into a context where it didn't belong.

The scandal began in April 2017 after a particularly shocking incident. Video footage had emerged of a passenger being dragged, bloodied and screaming, by aviation security from a United Airlines flight waiting to take off from Chicago O'Hare International Airport.

The flight was busy, but not overbooked. The passenger, Dr David Dao, was selected to give up his seat and take a later flight so a member of stand-by crew could take his place. He protested that he was scheduled to see patients in the morning. News media reported that he'd threatened to call his lawyers before the incident turned violent.[8] The video went viral and United Airlines had a crisis on their hands.

United handled it badly from the start. What did it actually mean when Munoz talked about 're-accommodating' passengers?

With impressive audacity, during his initial apology Munoz used the term 're-accommodate' to describe a situation which bore such scant resemblance to the accepted definition that the Internet had no other option but to respond immediately with parodies. His evasiveness and vagueness really upset people.

Not a single media outlet could find a sympathetic angle. CNBC suggested it 'may be time to "re-accommodate" CEO Munoz' and the satirical website Urban Dictionary posted an entry defining the term as: 'To beat up and violently drag paying passengers off an airplane in order to make room for airline crew on stand-by.'[9,10]

It wasn't just the Internet that was angry. Passengers were threatening to boycott, late-night TV host Jimmy Kimmel delivered a monologue about the incident, and the United States Senate demanded an investigation from the Chicago Department of Aviation.[11] Perhaps inspired by Munoz' appetite for understating the obvious, the CDA said dragging the bloodied passenger off the plane was 'not in accordance with our standard operating procedure'. That's good to know.

2017 was a bad year for United Airlines and a bad year for aviation generally. This particular crisis became the definitive airline scandal of our time. All because Oscar Munoz couldn't say sorry properly. If there's one thing worse than having to apologize for what you did, it's having to apologize for how you apologized. Here was another instructive example of an organization prolonging its own embarrassment, harming its share price, damaging its reputation and causing anguish to those involved.

If there's one thing worse than having to apologize for what you did, it's having to apologize for how you apologized.

Oscar Munoz' attempted apology was so bad, so deserving of the immediate ridicule it received, that he, and United Airlines, have now become synonymous with the concept of 're-accommodating'. The United Express Flight 3411 incident even has its own Wikipedia page.[12] The Internet never forgets.

'Overpressurization... followed by a fire'

The conduct of chemicals giant Arkema Inc after an explosion at their plant in Crosby, Texas, makes Munoz an exemplar of crisis communications by comparison. In the immediate aftermath of what local media were rightly calling an explosion, Arkema's press office moved to redefine the terms of the conversation. Their spokesperson literally contested the definition of an explosion irrespective of what physics and chemistry say.

A *Houston Chronicle* reporter tweeted: '#arkema spox says: 'It's misleading to say it was an explosion. It was an overpressurizatiom [*sic*] that was followed by a fire.'[13]

There's evasive corporate speak, and there's whatever this is. It should be funny. The audacity and silliness of what this spokesperson did should have had the Internet pumping out memes in short order. Arkema should have been getting the United Airlines treatment at the very least.

But their specific choice of words endangered lives. As well as playing down the severity of the situation to the media, lawyers for the first-responders said: 'Although the explosions had occurred, no one from Arkema alerted the first-responders who were manning the perimeter of the arbitrary mandatory evacuation area.'[14]

Lawyers? Yes, lawyers. And lots of them. At the time of writing this book, Arkema Inc is subject to lawsuits from two Texas counties, multiple residents and seven emergency first-responders. They variously allege that Arkema Inc is responsible for personal injury and contamination.[15]

Arkema's communications team were so determined for this not to be reported as an explosion, they withheld vital safety information and people ended up hurt. Not only did they push their own narrative, they discouraged the media from calling it an explosion. 'Arkema's response to the explosions at its Crosby facilities' said the *Washington Post*, 'will become a textbook case of how not to communicate during a crisis.'[16]

We quite agree. Jargoning your way out of a situation erodes trust and robs people of the accountability they rightly seek from organizations that have let them down. Communications become inaccessible to a significant portion of the audience. This approach also has the disadvantage of making organizations look ridiculous at the very time they want to be taken seriously.

Jargoning your way out of a situation erodes trust.

This sneaky misuse of rhetorical devices, from subtle wordplay and semantic nuances to out-and-out jargon, might fool some of us, some of the time. But much like when a magician has their method revealed, once we know, it's impossible to un-see how the trick works. The misdirection is suddenly so obvious we wonder how we never spotted it before. We look for it next time.

The same is true of PR-speak. When you've heard it once, you can't un-hear it. People become suspicious of what's really happening behind the curtain, they anticipate the deception. They try to figure out where the smokescreen ends and reality starts. So why do it? Why resort to woolly vagueness when customers, stakeholders and media deserve precision, facts and, often, an apology? The linguistically evasive approach rarely works and smokescreen PR damages more reputations than it protects.

CHAPTER EIGHT

Schrödinger's apology, grammatical deflections and evasions

The practices in the Motherisk drug testing laboratory didn't meet the high standard of excellence that we have here.

DR MICHAEL APKON, CEO OF THE HOSPITAL
FOR SICK CHILDREN, TORONTO, 2015

Qualified apologies, or 'fauxpologies', the sort that start off well and take a wrong turn at 'but' or 'however', do little to console or placate the recipient. The very presence of these conjunctions warns of a qualifying clause lurking just around the corner, waiting to water down whatever good intent had existed. This kind of apology is universally disappointing. We're sorry, but it's true.

While disappointing, there's a pernicious subtype of qualified apology that must be even harder to swallow than 'I'm sorry but...'. It's the sort of apology that teems with self-satisfaction, in which the apologizer focuses on their innocence as a counter-weight to their contrition. It's the kind of apology that an Ontario mother-of-four received from the organization that she blames for destroying her family.

The last time the mother saw her two youngest daughters, aged 18 months and 6 months at the time, was in September 2008. The supervised meeting took place in a church basement in the Ontario town of Kitchener, near where the mother lived.

She didn't know this would be the last time she would see her two girls, but by 2009, a judge had made both girls wards of the province of Ontario. They were adopted into separate families, without access to their mother.

The primary basis of the judge's decision was a positive cocaine test result from a strand of hair provided by the mother in 2008.[1] The hair-strand test was conducted at the Motherisk lab at the Hospital for Sick Children in Toronto. This particular test had been used in thousands of cases involving families in Canada. It was accepted without challenge as irrefutable evidence of drug abuse.

There was a problem here though. The test was flawed. Since this mother had her children taken away, journalist Rachel Mendleson revealed that the flawed hair-strand tests conducted at the Motherisk facility 'tainted thousands of child protection cases across Canada'.[2] In fact, prior to the hair-strand test, the mother had herself provided almost 70 negative urine samples.

This was a huge scandal in Canada. A review led by retired provincial court judge Judith Beaman, which concluded in 2017, completely discredited the tests. Beaman said the tests: 'Had a significant impact on the outcome of 56 cases and seven of those families have obtained legal remedies, with four cases involving children being returned to their parents' care.'[3]

After years of denying culpability in the unjust removal of children from their parents, Dr Michael Apkon, CEO of the Hospital for Sick Children eventually issued the following statement:

> We deeply regret that the practices in the Motherisk drug testing laboratory didn't meet the high standard of excellence that we have here at Sick Kids, and we extend our sincere apologies to children, families and organizations who feel that they may have been impacted in some negative way.

What a mess. This is the worst type of quantum superapology. Much like Schrödinger's cat, who occupies two quantum states – remaining both dead and alive until observed – Apkon similarly appears to occupy two conflicting rhetorical states: contrition and innocence.

Let's unpack this a bit more. The first sentence reflects on the 'high standard of excellence' at the organization. This is despite the fact that the CEO is apologizing for a catastrophic operational failure. These two things are mutually exclusive. You don't get to talk about having a 'high standard of excellence' when an independent review has just discredited your methods and attributed the destruction of numerous families specifically to those methods.

By front-loading his statement this way, Motherisk tipped the balance in their favour. It elevated the hospital to a moral plain it had no right to occupy. They were supposed to be apologizing for the discredited test and the ramifications of people using them, but they managed to find time and space to talk about their own virtues.

Victims are encouraged to believe that what happened to them was an exception.

This approach is practically useless as a means of expressing contrition or repairing damage. It forces the victims to view their own situation through the lens of the organization's own inflated self-image. Victims are encouraged to believe that what happened to them was an exception. This is not fair.

How to spot a Schrödinger's apology

These apologies almost always have a familiar formula. They'll typically feature a signature blend of moral licensing and what might be called 'organizational exceptionalism'. First, the moral licensing: look out for phrases like 'we are committed to...', 'we care deeply about...', 'we have the highest standards of...'. By using this set-up, Schrödinger's apologizer predicates what they just said or are about to say next on their own self-image. The recipient of the apology doesn't necessarily consent to viewing it in those terms, but the person giving the apology makes them.

Moral licensing almost always precedes a confession. If your favourite restaurant has to say 'we are committed to the highest standards of food hygiene...' you probably know what's coming. Moral licensing should always make us suspicious.

After the moral licensing comes the organizational exceptionalism: 'we fell short of our usual high standards' or 'we didn't live up to our customers' expectations on this occasion'. This is a way for Schrödinger's apologizers to pat themselves on the back and frame what happened as an unfortunate one-off. It rarely is. But that's not the point. The recipient of the apology does not benefit from knowing that their rotten luck was the exception, not the rule. It minimizes their experience. This isn't a new trick either. Even the viral Moss Bros apology we celebrated in the introduction to this book does it: 'This is the first time such a thing has happened in the history of the Firm,' wrote Mr Moss. We've learned to forgive moral licensing because we're just grateful to get the apology.

Moral licensing almost always precedes a confession.

When a food retailer was found to have breached its regulator's own supply code rules and received heavy criticism for how it had been treating its suppliers, the organization issued a classic example of Schrödinger's apology.

A spokesperson for Co-op Food, said in a statement (authors' emphasis):

We care deeply about our relationships with our suppliers and we are very sorry that **in these two areas we have failed to live up to our usual high standards.** We are already addressing the issues with the GCA and our suppliers and we hope the investigation will help bring to light any additional cases so that we can put these right as quickly as possible.[4]

That's not the apology the Co-op thinks it is.

In the context of crisis management, this kind of statement points to profoundly misplaced priorities. While it may be true that an organization 'cares deeply', caring is not the same as doing. It is not what matters to the recipient of an apology. Caring deeply clearly isn't enough to have prevented whatever it is the Co-op is apologizing for. And it is demonstrably irrelevant to the specific situation for which they are trying – and failing – to adequately say sorry.

Would any of the affected suppliers be comforted that the Co-op 'care deeply' about the relationship? Probably not. They more likely just want to be treated properly, as per the industry regulations that were ignored.

Similarly, would any of the Sri Lankan sweatshop workers who were earning 64 cents an hour in cramped conditions making garments for Ivy Park, the fashion label owned by pop superstar Beyoncé Knowles, be compensated by the knowledge that Ivy Park has a 'rigorous ethical trading programme' or 'sustained efforts in terms of factory inspections and audits' of which they are 'proud' despite their obvious failures?[5]

This almost Trumpian self-regard is of use to nobody. It's just noise. It's what Michael Shank, PhD and Maxine Bedat refer to in their Huffington Post article on Ivy Park's labour practices as 'a consistent and characteristic drumbeat by almost every major brand's corporate social responsibility desk', dismissing the entire corporate response as 'a complete abdication of responsibility'.[6]

In isolation, these evasions might seem innocuous, even trivial. But when you put a few of them together, they collectively beclown the entire communications profession. Here are five examples of linguistically shifty PR twaddle, accompanied by media descriptions of what actually happened (again, authors' emphasis):

> **'We pride ourselves on being a leader in managing and protecting data'** – Equifax chairman, after a data breach potentially affecting 143 million customers which 'could turn out to be the most costly hack in corporate history'.[7,8]

> **'Most importantly, safety remains our top priority'** – Samsung advert, after recalling millions of Note 7 devices that were found to 'catch fire and combust'.[9]

> **'We take hygiene extremely seriously'** – KFC spokesperson after inspectors 'found a mice infestation and the kitchen and serving area covered in dirt, grime and grease'.[10]

> **'Passenger and staff safety is our number one priority and is at the forefront of everything that we do'** – A spokesperson for First Bus 'after a bus burst into flames outside a quiet Scottish village'.[11]

> **'We are committed to protecting women's health and to always sharing information about a person's care with them'** – A spokesperson for Irish cervical screening programme CervicalCheck after 'the audit found that their (cancer) screening test could have provided a different result and recommended earlier follow-up'.[12]

What can we do better?

It's a natural instinct to want to deflect and reframe when an apology is due. But if organizations are going to deliver meaningful corporate apologies, they have to do so much better. The pattern of Schrödinger's apology is simple: speak to your virtues, then tell us how rare failure is. But this is not an apology; it's an excuse.

Communications professionals are habitually encouraged to draw attention to their virtues to offset their apology. There are even templates online, such as the websites Letters and Templates and Comm100 that encourage apologizers to emphasize how rare and exceptional mistakes are.

Instead of singing their own praises, organizations can communicate a more powerful message by simply pointing their apology in a different direction and recognizing the customer's expectations. For example:

> Privacy is very important **to our customers.** We are sorry we **let them down.** Here's what we are doing to fix it.

By removing themselves and their virtues from the apology, organizations offer the recipient the focus and accountability they deserve. They can assure them that they are understood.

The evasive power of grammar

Moral licensing isn't the only tool apologizers use to let themselves off the hook. Carefully manipulated grammar can do a fine job of distancing agent from transgression. Grammar gives us the power to shape language in any number of ways. In the right hands, sophisticated grammar can be used to add certainty, remove doubt and undergird what we want to say with a robust syntactical structure.

In the wrong hands, grammatical tricks are deployed to add doubt, muddy the messaging and – in some cases – avoid accountability. Here's how communicators abuse language every day when trying to not say sorry.

Modal verbs

In its apology above, Motherisk uses modality as an invisibility cloak. By saying 'may have been impacted' instead of 'were impacted' when referring to the victims, they avoided fully acknowledging their pain. They may as well have said 'sorry if you were upset, but…'. Whether intentional or an involuntary corporate tick, the impact is the same. Modal verbs like 'may' and 'might' are a red flag when used in an apology. They should set your corporate evasion detector immediately aquiver. These verbs are used to communicate a scenario that isn't 100 per cent probable, a thing that hasn't necessarily happened.

It's a really mean-spirited way of robbing the recipient of the acknowledgement they are owed. It's infuriating enough when train operators use them in their 'any delay you *may* experience' display-only apologies when they clearly mean 'the delay you *will* experience'.

So imagine how hurtful it must be to be to have your actual trauma addressed in such theoretical terms, termed as something that 'may have' happened. Motherisk topped its statement off with the churlishly dismissive 'some negative way'. This is just the cherry on top of an absolutely awful apology. It was supposed to be talking to families who've been separated here, not hacked-off rail passengers.

Passive voice

'Mistakes were made and lessons will be learned…'. The passive voice flips a sentence around so the object becomes the subject.

Communications teams are still in love with the passive voice.

'I made a mistake' becomes 'mistakes were made.. 'I ran over your dog' becomes 'your dog was run over' – that sort of thing. It's an easy way out of taking responsibility.

In his essay *The Politics of the English Language*, in which he lists the 'various mental vices' afflicting the English language, George Orwell urges his reader to 'never use the passive where you can use the active'. But he also said 'Never use a foreign phrase, a scientific word, or a jargon word if you can think of an everyday English equivalent', so clearly today's spokespeople aren't familiar with his thoughts on precise communication.[13] Orwell's guidance notwithstanding, communications teams are still in love with the passive voice.

PricewaterhouseCoopers set the gold standard for the passive apology back in February 2017, after they messed up the winners' cards at the Oscars. They gave Warren Beatty the wrong envelope and only after Faye Dunaway had read out the wrong winner did anyone spot the error.

PwC said via social media (authors' emphasis):

> We sincerely apologize to *Moonlight*, *La La Land*, Warren Beatty, Faye Dunaway, and Oscar viewers for **the error that was made** during the award announcement for Best Picture. The presenters **had mistakenly been given** the wrong category envelope and when discovered, **was immediately corrected.** We are currently investigating **how this could have happened,** and deeply regret **that this occurred.**
>
> We appreciate the grace with which the nominees, the Academy, ABC and Jimmy Kimmel handled the situation.

Some 23 per cent of that apology is written in the passive voice. Here's how it could have looked, had PwC had the courage to fully own their mistake:

> We sincerely apologize to *Moonlight*, *La La Land*, Warren Beatty, Faye Dunaway, and Oscar viewers for **our error** during the award announcement for Best Picture. **We mistakenly gave** the presenters the wrong category envelope and when we realized, **we immediately corrected that error.** We are currently investigating **what happened,** and deeply regret **our mistake.**
>
> We appreciate the grace with which the nominees, the Academy, ABC and Jimmy Kimmel handled the situation.

With a basic change of voice, this apology sounds significantly more sincere and, crucially, significantly less slippery. Organizations fear the active voice when apologizing because they think it unduly highlights their mistake. It doesn't at all.

That's not to say all corporate comms should be active. It's quite possible to be evasive in the active voice too, as *The Economist* firmly asserts:

> 'We are forming a committee to investigate these regrettable incidents in order to ascertain their cause so as to avoid them in the future' is weaselly corporate-speak, but it is grammatically active.[14]

In this instance, it was right to harshly judge PwC. Theirs was an egregious deployment of the passive voice apology used only to soft-soap their own culpability. For all the harm it did to their own reputation, they may have been better off not apologizing at all. The University of Pennsylvania Language Log blog said: 'Last night's Oscars debacle has provided us with a clear-cut case of how agentless passives can serve to obfuscate.'[15]

Reuters journalist Gerry Doyle tweeted: 'The award for best use of passive voice in an apology goes to...'[16] While *New York Times* reporter Katie Rosman quipped: 'Have never seen a greater painstaken use of the passive voice in an apology.'[17]

It was a shame really. Other than their use of passive voice, in this context a specific linguistic construct about which American political consultant William Schneider coined the term 'the past exonerative' tense, PwC got their apology mostly right.[18] They apologized swiftly and, in a roundabout sort of way, accepted responsibility. Or should we say, 'responsibility was accepted'? They kept it brief, centred those affected by their mistake and even promised to get to the bottom what happened. So in that spirit, we can afford to be somewhat charitable in our assessment for a moment.

It could simply be that PwC were so embarrassed about the global gaffe and under such pressure to address it, that they hashed something out on the back of a napkin and went with it. We'll never know for sure, but in 76 words PwC taught us a quick but valuable lesson in how to ruin an otherwise half-decent apology.

The indefinite article

The indefinite article, too, can be used to put some distance between an organization and its actions. Instead of saying 'the explosion' or 'the minor plane crash', slippery spokespeople will say 'an explosion' or 'a minor plane crash'. Implying there might have been other explosions worth your attention too. It's a small but important deflection.

When a light fitting fell from the ceiling of a train and struck a passenger on the head in August 2018, the passenger rightly expected an apology. Who wouldn't? What he got instead was a vague acknowledgement that something, we're not sure what, happened and assurances that the company responsible took his safety very seriously, despite allowing a light fitting to fall out and hit him on the head.

A spokesman for Great Western Railway told local press (authors' emphasis):

> We are aware of **an incident** where a lighting grille has come loose and struck a passenger. Fortunately, no injuries were sustained and the customer continued his journey without requiring further assistance from our on-board staff. **We take the safety of our passengers very seriously and are looking into this incident in detail.**[19]

There's something dispiritingly fishy about this statement. The word 'sorry' is notable by its absence, for a start. Secondly, after referring to 'an incident', the spokesperson appears to go to a lot of effort to emphasize, in the passive voice, that the passenger was unhurt. So unhurt in fact, that he managed to continue his journey.

How different it could have been had they said: 'We are aware **that the** lighting grille came loose and struck a passenger…'.

This passenger could be forgiven for thinking Great Western are implying that that he's making a fuss about nothing. And of course, they can't resist telling us and him how seriously they take passenger safety despite – and this bears repeating for a third and final time – a light fitting fell out of the roof of the train and hit him on the head. This isn't supposed to happen on trains.

Stagecoach bus company took the same approach to avoid apologizing after a child trapped his arm in the door of a bus.

A spokeswoman for Stagecoach told local press:

> We are aware of **an incident** on one of our buses on Wednesday as a family alighted from the bus. **Making sure our customers are safe and enjoy a comfortable journey when travelling with us is our highest priority** and we have spoken with the customer to help us investigate this. We are pleased to know that the little boy was not badly injured.[20]

This is a deluxe quantum superapology with passive voice, indefinite article and a dash of jargon (who says 'alighted' outside of the transport industry?)

The child's mother said: 'Really I just want a proper apology from the company.'

We can thank the legal profession for this kind of language.

We can thank the legal profession for this kind of language. Press officers have for years been encouraged by legal teams to keep it vague enough to avoid acknowledging specific fault and as a result, fear of litigation is one the main pollutants of corporate discourse. Once you see it, you can't un-see it. It's everywhere. Organizations that hide behind this kind of vague language really are telling on themselves.

Whether evading blame on behalf of your employer or falling on your own sword, vague and evasive language is the last thing people want to hear. Vacillating in your industry's own language or talking up your virtues makes true accountability almost impossible. It confuses everyone else and leaves you and your organization open to suspicion. An industry-wide commitment to brevity and precision could save everyone a lot of unnecessary headaches.

CHAPTER NINE

Crisis fatigue and the case for rationing apologies

The print on the sock depicting a Lego figure, which looks like 'Allah' in Arabic, is entirely a coincidence, but because our customers have complained, we have chosen to recall the items.
H&M SPOKESPERSON, 27 JANUARY 2018

To a casual observer, the eagerness of so many organizations to apologize might appear to be based simply on a natural instinct to protect their reputation. It's a reflex. Saying sorry absolutely should be a key plank of a crisis communications strategy and is crucial for damage limitation and retaining consumer trust. It matters. Sometimes people deserve an apology and the right thing to do is say sorry. Once that's done, an organization can hopefully take control of the situation and move on.

But sometimes it's not about who deserves an apology and whether they get one. Market forces apply. Who criticizes you is often as important as what you did. In his book, *So You've Been*

Publicly Shamed, Jon Ronson attributes our thirst for calling out large organizations to the inversion of an established power dynamic.[1] Humble consumers now have a platform to take on the big corporations and they're excited to use it. Of course, for some elements of the media, this is their bread and butter. And as we saw in Chapter 7, they're excited to see it too.

Ronson argues that social media and other online platforms have levelled the playing field. Anyone could now stand up to a corporate giant and the social rewards can be huge. Take Shannon Watts, the lady from Chapter 6 who shamed United Airlines and popularized the #leggingsgate hashtag. She got her own column in *Time* magazine. 'These giants were being brought down by people who used to be powerless – bloggers, anyone with a social media account.'[2]

While Ronson is correct that most of us would be relatively powerless in this respect without social media, are we really bringing down 'giants'? Or are the underdogs just taking down people just like them, who simply happen to work for large corporations? From the outside, extracting an apology from a large corporation can seem like a huge victory for the underdog.

Extracting an apology from a large corporation can seem like a huge victory for the underdog.

The reality is often different. When a large organization's social media account is the subject of a consumer backlash – where they're besieged by hundreds, often thousands, of angry messages – it's rare for the heat to rise as high as the boardroom. More often than not, it's a social media executive, or a small team of them, dealing with the fallout and panicking about keeping their jobs.

And here's where the realities of this dynamic become a little clearer. It's not always the underdog demanding the apology. The celebrated critic of United Airlines and their sexist leggings policy was presented to us as the relatable 'every woman' determined to tackle injustice. This is only partly true. She was also an experienced crisis management consultant and political activist with a growing media platform of her own. She was well equipped to take on the fight and she served as a shining example of the potential rewards for being the one to highlight questionable corporate conduct.

When it's not so much David vs Goliath as many Davids vs one or two Davids, the dynamic changes. A communications team can only handle so much negative attention before crisis fatigue sets in. The energy and effort required to solve problems is often under-appreciated.

Preempting the backlash

Lesley Bambridge runs We Mean Business, a London marketing and communications consultancy. Prior to setting up her firm, Lesley worked client-side for a high-profile energy drinks brand that had sponsored the reality TV show *Big Brother*. She had first-hand experience of just how much effort managing the risk of outrage entails, which she described in an interview with the authors:

> Anything has the potential to escalate these days. However we identified and brainstormed the obvious and worst case scenarios that could potentially happen and put a Q&A in place so that customer services and the PR agency were all speaking the same language and were well versed in approved responses for these specific scenarios.

> With the Big Brother and Low Sugar campaigns we had a Q&A for different groups of individuals that we identified as risks; press, influencers, celebrities, pressure groups and vocal social media users with large followings all pose potential risks and if the need for the case to be looked at in a bespoke way was there we had the resources in place and the protocol in place to react quickly.

High-profile social media users aren't just able to influence consumers. As we'll explore later, they can have an astounding amount of influence over large organizations too. This shift in power is having an impact on how organizations prepare for and react to crises. Talking of 'intense' pressure, Lesley describes having processes in place to head off risks:

> We had a twice-daily, weekly and monthly summary from people monitoring social channels and our brand mentions for the duration of CBB [*Celebrity Big Brother*] and the months after the low sugar launch. We had escalation codes and protocols to follow should they be needed. The resource and time that goes into ensuring the business feels confidently safeguarded is huge. It's a financial commitment, but a necessary one.

Unlike the robust but expensive approach that Lesley describes, some of the organizations whose crisis management habits we'll be examining later are reverting to what we might call 'tactical appeasement' instead. When a potential crisis emerges, rather than assessing their own culpability or lack thereof, and then communicating effectively on that basis, organizations appear increasingly willing to symbolically roll over. It's something with which animal behaviourists are very familiar.

Crisis fatigue and tactical appeasement

When a dog rolls onto his back, it doesn't want to be fussed. The dog on his back, exposing his soft underbelly, is sending a clear signal of submission. He's saying: 'I don't want any trouble.' Evolutionary biologist Amotz Zahavi calls this the 'handicap principle'.[3] Zahavi claims that in the natural world – and in our human world – for a signal to be truly trustworthy, it must be costly to the sender. Dogs showing their belly make themselves vulnerable to attack. That's why they curl up to sleep; exposing the belly has enormous potential costs.

It's in the best interests of both dogs and organizations, regardless of size or strength, to avoid unnecessary conflict. Engaging in conflict uses up valuable energy and poses the risk of injury. This risk is heightened by prior injury or fatigue. So both readily deploy tactical appeasement before a paw is raised in anger. It's a costly survival instinct.

Knowing as we do that a poorly navigated crisis can threaten an organization's survival, it's little surprise that some organizations go straight for the tactically submissive approach. In their eagerness to appease what they see as a threat to their reputation – and by extension their continued survival – they admit defeat and hope the threat goes away.

Swedish clothes retailer H&M distilled this concept beautifully in 2018. Why else would the world's second largest fast-fashion retailer, with more than 4,000 stores worldwide and 132,000 employees, remove a product from sale that had no defect, infringed no laws and, as they were told repeatedly, was not offensive?

Their decision to withdraw from sale a pair of Lego-themed socks because a handful of social media users made a fuss provides a number of lessons. When they announced their decision to remove the socks in January 2018, they gave a qualified 'if we offended anyone' apology.[4] They then went several steps further than they needed to and hit themselves in the wallet. They were sending a very costly signal.

A separate statement they gave to Swedish state television was depressing in both its tone and, if you were following the crisis, its inevitability. H&M didn't quite say sorry, but they certainly *sounded* apologetic. We believe that in handling a minor social media crisis in this fashion, they set a quite troubling precedent.

They attributed their decision to recall the socks directly and specifically to customer complaints, rather than to their own provable failings. In doing this they also issued an open invitation to anyone interested to take come and take a swing at them.

Since the sock controversy, fellow clothing retailers Gap (T-shirt offensive to China), Topman (T-shirt offensive to people from Liverpool), Next (accused of racism) and Boohoo.com (accused of sexism) have all had public apologies extracted after facing cultural criticisms online:[5–8]

> The print on the sock depicting a Lego figure, which looks like 'Allah' in Arabic, is entirely a coincidence, but because our customers have complained, we have chosen to recall the items.[9]

The statement merits close scrutiny. It starts off with a soft defence. It references the Lego figure depicted on the sock. It's a Lego-themed sock. So far, so good. But in the second clause of the opening sentence, clearly unsure of their ground, it starts to go wrong.

They concede that the Lego figure resembles the Arabic word for 'Allah'. This is actually debatable. We might admit that if you held the sock upside down and squinted a bit, it bore a passing resemblance. But not everyone saw it like this. In fact, one Arab journalist and researcher attempted to discourage H&M from their course of action:

> Alright, this is getting silly. No, these @hm socks don't look like they have 'Allah' printed on them in Arabic. Take it from me – I'm an Arab. This is literally the dumps of political correctness.[10]

But H&M were already on the back foot. From the position of accepting on very weak evidence that the socks could be offensive, the statement leans even more on appeasement, meekly waving a linguistic white flag: '...but because our customers have complained, we have chosen to recall the items.'

That last part bears repeating: 'Because our customers have complained, we have chosen to recall the items.' Here we have a corporate powerhouse telling its customers that they burdened the cost and embarrassment of recalling merchandise simply because a handful of people complained.

While social media's influence on corporate accountability is in the most part a positive thing, this episode illustrates the trade-off. It's fair for us to expect H&M to have stood firmer. The sheer number of logical left turns necessary for anyone to be concerned by the socks should have given H&M the impetus to back themselves. Unfortunately for H&M, at least one person was prepared to turn off their logical navigation system in order to take offence and complain about the socks. Worth noting too, that this person actually purchased the offending socks.

The great sock controversy of 2018 is what happens when a brand is so hypersensitive to criticism that they're prepared to admit, in public, that because a handful of customers have complained – arguably fewer than those who pointed out the abundant silliness of the complaint – they're happy to bear the cost and trouble of recalling a product.

But why were H&M ready to wave the white flag so quickly? The background is important. H&M were already affected by a reputational crisis that unfolded two weeks prior. Their apology must necessarily be considered in this context.

What did happen two weeks earlier in January 2018? This was the H&M hoodie controversy. H&M had endured a cultural failure that risked permanently damaging its reputation. It was a genuine crisis that had drawn the ire of genuinely world-famous celebrities like basketball star-turned-educational philanthropist LeBron James and rapper Diddy. It culminated in riots in South Africa. It was all about a children's hoodie with the slogan 'cheekiest monkey in the jungle'. Again, ostensibly fine, but when modelled by a black child, fireworks. Even though the child's mother said the hoodie advert wasn't racist, H&M apologized and withdrew.

It's easy to forget that behind corporate social media accounts are real people.

Had they not been reeling from the hoodie crisis, H&M may have stood firmer on the socks. But their communications team were simply not prepared to go another round with the outraged heavyweights of social media and who could really blame them? The brand was on the ropes and the communications leadership moved to protect it from further injury. In this context, there was absolutely no way standing firm on the socks was an option for H&M.

Any reasonable observer, knowing the crisis H&M had faced two weeks before, could forgive them for rolling over. H&M's corporate leaders would have known full well the risks associated with standing firm, especially for those on the front line. It's easy to forget sometimes that behind corporate social media accounts are real people, with mortgages and families and like most of us, an aversion to receiving waves of criticism from people they don't know.

It's up to H&M how they handle their crises, but organizations should be wary of backing down so readily. If you look carefully, you'll see that for every outraged voice going after a company, there's someone else urging them not to back down. Some customers appear to be as sick of hearing corporate apologies as organizations are of giving them. Brands can suffer damage to their reputation when they apologize. In some cases, more damage than had they held firm. H&M took the risk.

The spectrum of contrition

The sheer abundance of apologies is clearly a problem that won't go away until the incentives we've addressed are reconciled. We demand, make and write about too many apologies. But troubling too is the manner in which organizations have ignored the spectrum upon which contrition should exist, completely distorting the meaning of 'sorry'. Some have totally abandoned any notion of proportionality. This points to an underlying corporate anxiety around hearing criticism and addressing failure.

On the one hand, Tesco said they were 'extremely sorry' for upsetting some movie fans after incorrectly marketing *Black Panther* film merchandise as 'Dark Panther' merchandise. But when a Ryanair flight to Croatia emergency-landed in Germany leaving 33 passengers requiring hospital treatment, some of whom suffered bleeding from their ears caused by the sudden descent, and a number of others with no accommodation, the airline issued a statement that was remarkably casual by comparison, saying the airline 'sincerely apologizes for any inconvenience'.

Tesco were too sorry and Ryanair probably could have been a bit sorrier, to be honest. These two examples illustrate the warped perspective of corporate apologies when you compare them to real-world apologies.

Let's imagine the spectrum. At one end is the amount of contrition you'd express for getting in someone's way on the pavement. At the other end, the contrition you might express if you'd run over your neighbour's dog. These are two vastly contrasting emotional states for both transgressor and subject. They require very different responses.

Yet organizations persistently fail to grasp this. And by failing to apply the appropriate degree of empathy and contrition – sometimes too little, often too much – they distort the plane on which apologies can comfortably exist. It can end up being ridiculous:

> Last month, the home of a San Francisco host named EJ was tragically vandalized by a guest.
>
> When we learned of this our hearts sank. We felt paralysed, and over the last four weeks, we have really screwed things up.[11]

Tragically? Paralysed? This is Airbnb responding to a customer's home being vandalized in 2011. They were no doubt going for authentic and sincere, but their apology is significantly over-egged. The problem with hyperbolic statements like this is obvious. They compress the emotional bandwidth available. There are few places left to go linguistically when you've described vandalism as something 'tragic' that left you feeling 'paralysed'.

So when in 2017 an Airbnb customer was murdered by their host in Australia, a scenario that absolutely calls for powerful language, Airbnb's statement, where they describe being 'deeply saddened and outraged', sounds weak by comparison.[12] They peaked too early.

As with real life, corporate apologies should exist on a steady continuum from 'whoops, sorry mate' to 'I hope one day you can forgive me'. But what we have instead, thanks to corporate hypersensitivity, is a perplexing range of emotional peaks and dips. 'Sorry' can now mean anything, from 'please stop tweeting us' to 'yes, we've made a massive mistake'. It'll be unsurprising then, if consumers don't trust corporate apologies.

The case for rationing

A big part of the apology problem is the signal-to-noise ratio. The line between accepting feedback and being sorry is blurring. Too many organizations appear to believe that the only response to negative feedback is to say sorry.

With so many apologies of varying quality floating around, we can no longer hear what's being said. But what incentives are there for organizations to stop? Imagine if there were a tax on corporate apologies. Every organization issuing one would do so in the knowledge that it would cost them. Every spokesperson would live in fear of wasting company money. Organizations would become more resilient and less sensitive to criticism over night.

It's a hard position to argue in 2019, but we need fewer apologies, not more. Quality over quantity. The communications industry delusion of our time is that we should always say sorry. This is demonstrably false, from both a commercial and ethical point of view.

If we're to rescue the apology from the yawning abyss of irrelevance, we all need to stand firmer and be surer of our ground. We must learn to accept criticism without reflexively apologizing and making promises of doing better that we have no intention of keeping. If you're nervous about standing firm, and it's understandable that you might be, consider the downside; apologizing when you didn't need to can completely impact your career. Just ask former British prime minister Gordon Brown.

We must learn to accept criticism without reflexively apologizing.

His hopes of re-election in 2010 took an absolute battering when a private comment he made about a member of the public was picked up on microphone. It wasn't the comment, but the apology, that affected his re-election hopes.

Inside his car, Brown referred to Gillian Duffy, a woman he'd been heckled by minutes earlier, as 'that bigoted woman'. It was an irresistible 'gotcha' moment for the media, despite them being the ones to broadcast what was a private remark. Nevertheless, Brown dutifully apologized.

'Bigotgate' – and you know you're in trouble when your crisis gets the 'gate' suffix – was widely regarded as the turning point in his re-election campaign. Comedian Jon Stewart said of the scandal: 'You actually see the moment when a man's political career leaves his body.'[13]

The thing is though, Brown wasn't really apologizing for what he said. After all, lots of people agreed with him. Brown's problem was that he was simply caught out saying something for which an apology could theoretically be demanded. It was the same media that broadcast his private comments that had then demanded he apologize to the woman he was talking about.

Gordon Brown didn't have a plan B. The woman to whom he apologized, like so many other apology recipients, was rewarded with brief fame, appearing on BBC *Newsnight*, Sky News and even being interviewed about her voting choices in future elections. She became a totemic emblem of early call-out culture. Brown on the other hand, a serving prime minister who months previously had been named World Statesman of the Year, became a political joke; undone by a pensioner from Rochdale.

Being said to owe someone an apology is a peculiar state. It's a type of suspended animation, where you've neither backed down or stood firm. The longer you withhold the expected apology, the more you prolong the talking point. But the moment you give the apology, you create a new headline. This is why you should never apologize unless you actually believe you did something wrong.

The 'Bigotgate' case also illustrates just how drastically our media has changed and how call-out culture – in its infancy in 2010 – could have, in a weird and ironic way, actually saved Brown's campaign. If Gordon Brown made the same remark about the same woman in 2018, it would have been a PR win. The headline would not have been 'PR professionals criticize Gordon Brown's apology following "bigot" slur' but rather 'UK prime minister Gordon Brown called out a woman for being racist – and this is why he's not apologizing'.[14]

Few would have been calling for him to apologize. In the viral news headline paradigm, he was the hero and the woman he called out was the villain. And we don't even need to speculate here. The headline above is not hypothetical. It's a real headline from 2018, with Brown's name swapped for that of Canadian prime minister Justin Trudeau.

Trudeau did a Gordon Brown in August 2018, but he wouldn't say sorry. And this is a leader that doesn't mind dishing out apologies. Thankfully here, he provides us with a real-world example of how powerful not apologizing can be. The set-up was almost identical. A serving prime minister meets the public, a woman in the crowd voices a strong opinion on immigration, and the prime minister calls it how he sees it, resulting in the following headline: 'Canadian prime minister Justin Trudeau called out a woman for being racist – and this is why he's not apologizing.'[15]

Brown's apology was unnecessary. Trudeau's PR win proves it. But worse than that, it was a missed opportunity for cementing his anti-bigotry credentials and an open invitation for renewed focus on what was a distraction from his campaign messaging. Maybe it's a British thing.

Apologies are a bit like single-use plastic bags.

Mic Wright, discussing in the *New European* the public clamour for the newly former British foreign secretary Boris Johnson to apologize for remarks about the burqa in August 2018 pretty much nailed our specific problem. And he could have just as easily been talking about Brown's situation:

> Britain generally has a culture of apology as social lubricant
> rather than genuine contrition. It baffles our continental
> neighbours, especially the French and the Germans for whom
> apologies are something you offer when you actually regret what
> you've done.[16]

Gordon Brown shouldn't have apologized. Eschewing spin was an organizing principle of so-called Brownism. On examining the key differences between Brownism and the preceding prime minister's Blairism, political analyst Nicholas Jones even drew specific attention to Brown's reluctance to spinning his way out of sticky situations four years before 'Bigotgate':

> Just as sharp is the divide over the use of spin doctors such as
> Peter Mandelson and Alastair Campbell. Brownites have detested
> the reliance which Mr Blair has placed on the black arts of media
> manipulation.[17]

Perhaps if Brown had been resourced with his own Peter Mandelson or Alastair Campbell, they would have advised him of the untapped seam of goodwill to be mined from standing firm.

Furthermore, we'd have benefited from having one fewer insincere apology littering our public discourse.

In this regard, apologies are a bit like single-use plastic bags. They serve a purpose, but when we give them out for free, they have a habit of washing up in places they don't belong. We believe that people and organizations should start rationing apologies.

CHAPTER TEN

It's not about you

How CEOs sabotage their own apologies

Nobody wants this over more than I do – I want my life back.
TONY HAYWARD, BP CHIEF EXECUTIVE, JUNE 2010

There are plenty of ways to retrospectively ruin an apology. An absence of restitutions, a lack of transparency, a reluctance or inability to actually put right that which went wrong – take your pick. Embracing just one of these organizational flaws will ensure even the most well-received apology defeats its own purpose eventually. For those in a hurry though, who inexplicably want to see their apology fall flat in real time before their own eyes, there's a quick and easy rhetorical shortcut to failure. Just make your apology about you.

Despite the obvious reputational drawbacks, some organizations seem committed to prolonging their own embarrassment and amplifying their own culpability. In Chapter 8, we examined the phenomenon of Schrödinger's apology, a linguistic tick through which an organization fluffs up its own virtues. It's as a moral counterweight to the transgression for which they are supposed to be sorry. This kind of corporate throat-clearing is endemic in the apologies we've examined and – while damaging to the organization and of no consolation to the subject of the apology – it is at the very least understandable. The organization is giving itself a character reference. It's instinctive for an under-fire organization to seek to qualify its guilt by appealing to its own previous good conduct. Corporate fragility is to blame here. We shouldn't encourage it, but we can at least understand it.

Apologies are about the recipient.

The kind of self-regard we're about to explore is altogether harder to understand. These apologies are bad because the person giving them violated one of the most important rules of saying sorry – apologies are about the recipient. Why would a spokesperson wilfully sabotage their own apology and invite further ridicule and criticism by making it about them? If we're being charitable, we might attribute it to the stress of intense public scrutiny. There's no obvious reputational benefit.

Tony Hayward – BP

The 2010 Deepwater Horizon oil spill, also widely known as the 'BP oil spill', was not just an environmental crisis: 11 people died and 17 were injured on the rig. BP faced numerous communications challenges from the beginning. Every hour the rig continued to leak oil, BP's stock value dropped. The potential ramifications extended far beyond the site of the accident. British pension holders, American coastal communities and animal welfare groups all had reasons to be anxious.

The issue of who 'owned' the disaster provided an extra layer of complexity. US media repeatedly referred to BP as 'British Petroleum', a name the company hadn't used since it merged with US chemical and oil giant Amoco in 1998.[1] BP continually referred to the incident as 'the Gulf of Mexico oil spill'. President Obama referred to it as the 'BP oil spill'. The communications around the spill were a mess from day one.

BP struggled to manage their messaging. Executives gave conflicting accounts of the spill's severity and the estimated clean-up times. At first, it was unclear whether the spill would reach the Florida coast at all, or remain isolated in the Gulf of Mexico. Animal and environmental welfare aside, an accident that impacted US fisheries and tourism would have reputational ramifications several orders of magnitude worse than an isolated spill.

BP's British CEO Tony Hayward, a geologist by trade and well known to his colleagues for a plain-speaking, fact-driven communication style, faced criticism for referring to the spill as 'very, very modest'. He had no business saying that. At least not until he knew for sure. The scope of the spill wasn't clear, but at the time he made this remark, the damaged rig was pumping 3 million litres of oil into the Gulf of Mexico.[2]

Is that a lot for an oil spill? Unless you know about oil spills, it's hard to say. But it sounds like a lot to the man on the street and that's actually what matters here. Speculation to the contrary was unwelcome. Hayward didn't know it yet, but in terms of volume, this would go on to be the largest accidental marine oil spill in the history of petroleum manufacturing.[3] The slick could be seen from space. Modest, it wasn't.

Tony Hayward was failing on a number of levels. He speculated, tried to escape blame, telling the BBC Radio 4 *Today* show 'it wasn't our accident', and he even insulted the United States as a country, implying that businesses there would try to take advantage of BP's situation.[4] He told a reporter who asked about compensation claims: 'This is America – come on. We're going to have lots of illegitimate claims. We all know that.'[5]

He was having a nightmare. Yet for all of his many unforced errors, it was an off-hand remark Hayward made while trying to apologize for everything he'd already said that solidified the BP spill as the definitive public relations disaster. Speaking in front of assembled press, Hayward began to try to say sorry.

'I'm sorry,' he began. So far so good. A strong, simple note of contrition too often absent from corporate apologies.

He continued: 'We're sorry for the massive disruption it's caused their lives.' Again good. Very good. Here Tony is acknowledging the impact the crisis has had on the victims, before adding: 'There's no one who wants this over more than I do.'

Now we're entering dangerous territory. This shouldn't be about what Hayward wants. He should be focusing on the victims and telling them what he's going to do to make things right. Then, possibly sensing he was going off-script, he wrapped his remarks up: 'I'd like my life back.'

This was a disaster. BP's crisis management will always be remembered for their CEO wanting his life back. People died, the environment was damaged, millions of pounds were lost and the entire episode is still characterized eight years later by Hayward's five-word moan. There's even an academic biography called *I'd Like My Life Back: Corporate personhood and the BP oil disaster*.[6]

The next day, Hayward apologized for his apology, saying:

> I made a hurtful and thoughtless comment. I apologize, especially to the families of the 11 men who lost their lives in this tragic accident. Those words don't represent how I feel about this tragedy. My first priority is doing all we can to restore the lives of the people of the Gulf region and their families – to restore their lives, not mine.[7]

Hayward, in his defence, was not an experienced media communicator. He was a media-shy CEO subject to global scrutiny that most people would struggle with. This will be of no comfort to the families of the 11 men who died in the accident. BP eventually brought in the veteran communications strategist, Anne Womack-Kolton, a one-time campaign press aide to former US vice president Dick Cheney. This said a lot about how well BP thought things were going.

Apologizing isn't easy, but it doesn't need to be complicated either.

Ultimately, none of it really helped. Tony would later go on to star in a series of apology adverts. That didn't really help either.

Keep it simple

Apologizing isn't easy, but it doesn't need to be complicated either. When organizations and their spokespeople plan to deliver an apology, they too often forget the core functionality of an apology; to express regret, offer an explanation, accept responsibility, repent, make an offer of repair and finally, request forgiveness – in that order if at all possible.

The temptation for those tasked with saying sorry to reflect inwards on how the situation is affecting their own organization can be more powerful than the will to outwardly empathize. In doing this, organizations inevitably invite more criticism and ridicule.

As well as reflecting inwards on how the crisis was affecting his organization and his leisure time, Hayward attempted to blame others, and came out swinging for the 'people, systems, processes' of the company that owned the well. 'This wasn't our accident' he said.[8]

The 'blame someone else' approach to crisis management inevitably left a sour taste in the mouths of those affected. But it could also have had a material impact on the financial fortunes of both organizations too. A 2015 study published in the *Journal of Corporate Finance* in which researchers analysed 150 press releases distributed between 1993 and 2009 found that organizations that blame others for their failures suffered financial decline shortly after, while those that accept blame experienced financial stability. Sometimes they even improved.[9] It also found that organizations are twice as likely to pass the buck as to accept responsibility when something goes wrong.

If you're going to be self-indulgent with your apology, at least don't be a misery guts.

There's another major downside to the moping 'poor me, it wasn't my fault' apologies of Hayward and others; they convey weakness and rob the giver of much-needed credibility. In times of crisis, regardless of how angry consumers, regulators and politicians may be, the one thing they need is credibility. So if you're going to be self-indulgent with your apology, at least don't be a misery guts.

Stanford professor Larissa Z Tiedens conducted four separate studies on perceptions of credibility. In one of them, participants were asked to rate their perceptions of Bill Clinton's handling of the Monica Lewinsky affair. They watched clips of the different ways Clinton handled criticism of the scandal. Clinton's credibility dropped when he was performatively sad. The study participants didn't necessarily forgive him, but they respected him more when he was angry than when he was moping about.[10] This isn't to say contrition and genuine empathy is bad, but it should never be reflected inward in the way Clinton and Hayward did.

Self-examination, when it accompanies a sincere apology and results in tangible steps toward improvement, is good. It helps an organization identify where things have gone wrong. Self-pity, the sort we've just seen, contributes nothing to the process. Everyone knows it's hard to say sorry. The lesson here is simple. Apologies are not about the giver.

CHAPTER ELEVEN

Keep trying

*Why it took three of the world's biggest brands
three attempts to say sorry*

*This is an upsetting event to all of us here at United.
I apologize for having to re-accommodate these customers.*

OSCAR MUNOZ, CEO, UNITED AIRLINES, 10 APRIL 2017

*The truly horrific event that occurred on this flight has
elicited many responses from all of us: outrage, anger,
disappointment. I share all of those sentiments, and one
above all: my deepest apologies for what happened.*

OSCAR MUNOZ, CEO, UNITED AIRLINES, 11 APRIL 2017

Three experimental studies conducted in 2010 showed that
people consistently overvalue how future apologies will make
them feel. The imagined satisfaction gained from a hypothetical
future apology was significantly higher than the actual satisfaction
of receiving it.[1] These 'forecasting errors' lead to disappointment.

The value we put on the apologies we think we're owed doesn't match up to the reality of receiving them. With that in mind, organizations really ought to do their best to get it right first time. The reputational damage from having multiple bites at the same cherry can be massive.

Facebook

Facebook CEO Mark Zuckerberg's original March 2018 statement on the Cambridge Analytica data breach ran to an exhausting 934 words.[2] The words 'sorry', 'apologize' or even the suspiciously evasive 'regret' were notable by their absence.

Organizations really ought to do their best to get it right first time.

The statement had a distinct feel of damage limitation and liability avoidance to it. Zuckerberg's statement highlighted Facebook's policies and how Cambridge Analytica had breached them. It cited steps they'd already taken to protect user data and concluded on how Facebook would be doing more. At the time of writing the statement, Zuckerberg and Facebook were in the dark about the extent to which their reputations and business would suffer due to the scandal. They also didn't really know where they stood legally or in the eyes of the regulator, so Zuckerberg was deliberately cautious in his assertions.

The following passage toward the end of the statement gives a flavour of how reluctant to admit fault Zuckerberg appeared:

> In 2015, we learned from journalists at the *Guardian* that Kogan had shared data from his app with Cambridge Analytica. It is against our policies for developers to share data without people's consent, so we immediately banned Kogan's app from our

platform, and demanded that Kogan and Cambridge Analytica formally certify that they had deleted all improperly acquired data. They provided these certifications.[3]

Facebook's stock value dropped after he released this statement.[4] So he tried again, this time taking out various full-page newspaper adverts to ask forgiveness, as well as doing the media rounds.[5] In an interview with CNN, Zuckerberg appeared contrite and uttered the magic words: 'I'm really sorry.'

People wanted more. They needed a customer retention apology. Lawmakers and users in both the UK and the United States wanted answers about what had happened. They wanted to know if it was still safe to use Facebook. In the same CNN interview, Zuckerberg explained that he was happy to appear at a congressional hearing if he was the right person to do it, cautioning that there may be other people at Facebook better qualified to answer technical questions.[6] When challenged by Laurie Segall who told him that people wanted to hear from him as the leader and 'brand of Facebook', he countered that he didn't see his potential appearance as a media opportunity.[7]

By April, Zuckerberg was sitting in a congressional hearing being grilled by lawmakers. He was there for 10 hours. And to be fair to Zuckerberg, he did his best not to treat it like a media opportunity. The theme of evasion from the original statement still lingered though; he side-stepped almost a third of the questions by saying he didn't have the information to hand and that he'd reply in writing. But it was an improvement and Facebook's share price began to recover in response. As Reuters reporters put it: 'Mark Zuckerberg fielded 10 hours of questions over two days from nearly 100 US lawmakers and emerged largely unscathed and considerably richer.'[8]

Facebook produced some saccharine TV adverts to recoup some of their lost goodwill. The adverts too were notable by the absence of an apology. The best Facebook could do was admit that 'something went wrong'.

United Airlines

On 16 March 2017, the proud CEO of United Airlines, Oscar Munoz – one of the examples in Chapter 7 – took to the stage at the *PR Week* annual gala ceremony to accept the prize for 'Communicator of the Year'. This prestigious award recognizes professionals from outside of the PR industry who have demonstrated outstanding communication skills in the previous year. Accepting the award on behalf of United's entire workforce at the event, Munoz remarked: 'Communication and communication strategy is not just part of the game, it is the game.'[9]

Announcing their award pick in the run-up to the event in New York City, *PR Week* heaped praise on the airline boss. 'Munoz has shown himself to be a smart, dedicated and excellent leader who understands the value of communications.'[10] Neither Munoz nor *PR Week* could have anticipated what was about to happen. Just 24 days later, there unfolded a sequence of events that *PR Week*, the organization honouring Munoz, would go on to describe as the 'mother of all social media crises'.

The saddest part was that Munoz deserved his award. He'd done a remarkable job since taking over as CEO from Jeff Smisek in 2015. Under Munoz' stewardship, United had its best full-year on-time performance. Its stock price had risen by 27 per cent in the year after Munoz had taken over. A lot of their overall success was down to Munoz being a good communicator. He'd been praised by union bosses for rebuilding employee trust.

PR Week noted that the airline's renewed success was down to its 'ability, led by Munoz, to sign new contracts with all union groups, most well ahead of deadlines, helping to curtail customer service problems.'[11] He'd achieved all of this while recovering from a heart transplant. Knowing what we now know about Oscar Munoz, the *PR Week* accolade seems like a cruel curse.

In the space of three days, Munoz and United suffered untold reputational damage and much of it came from their equivocating apologies and crisis response. It started on Sunday 9 April. United Express Flight 3411 from Chicago to Louisville couldn't take off because there weren't enough seats for standby crew. After nobody volunteered to take a later flight, United commenced what it calls its 'involuntary denial of boarding' process. In plain English, that means they needed to get someone off the flight and pay them up to $1,000 in compensation.

The person they chose for involuntary denial of boarding, Dr David Dao, as we know refused their offer because he had to see patients in the morning and didn't want to reschedule. United insisted he leave the plane. Dao really didn't want to get off and threatened to sue the airline. Then security arrived and tried to physically escort him off the plane, then things went haywire. We've covered the details in Chapter 7 if you want to go back for a refresher on how not to make room on a flight.

Once video footage of the incident made its way onto the Internet, United, led by Munoz, started the long and painful process of completely sabotaging the response. Their first act was to apologize on the evening of the incident for an 'overbook situation'. There are two things wrong here. Firstly, and most obviously, the overbook was not why people were upset. Secondly, it turned out later that the flight wasn't actually overbooked.

The next morning Munoz apologized for what he described as an 'upsetting event'. It was this apology that contained the now infamous and widely ridiculed 're-accommodation' turn of phrase. United received 1.2 million Twitter mentions and 135,000 Facebook interactions.

Instead of continuing with their brinkmanship, it was cheaper for them to say sorry.

And not the good ones. Later on that day, United changed their approach from vague concessions and weird language to blame. A leaked internal memo meant to console anxious staff claimed that Dao had been 'disruptive and belligerent' and that he'd 'defied' airport security. Technically he did defy them, but that's not where the messaging should have been focused. The crisis was spiralling out of control.

By Tuesday (three days later), United and Munoz were ready to take full responsibility. Munoz issued a statement:

> The truly horrific event that occurred on this flight has elicited many responses from all of us: outrage, anger, disappointment. I share all of those sentiments, and one above all: my deepest apologies for what happened. Like you, I continue to be disturbed by what happened on this flight and I deeply apologize to the customer forcibly removed and to all the customers aboard. No one should ever be mistreated this way.[12]

This was the statement United should have led with at the beginning of the crisis. So why didn't they? Like Facebook, they were hedging their bets. United appeared to be pinning their messaging to their stock price. The lower it got, the sorrier they were. But to begin with, they could afford to equivocate on the apology and avoid admitting liability. If it started to plunge, they'd need to decide what would hurt more; the risk of admitting liability and getting sued, or the risk of their reputation becoming so toxic that the price would continue to nosedive. It became a game of chicken and on this occasion, United blinked first. Their stock plunged by $1.4 billion in the days after the incident, so instead of continuing with their brinkmanship, it was cheaper for them to say sorry.[14]

Papa John's – third time lucky

KFC, formerly known as and unofficially still Kentucky Fried Chicken, isn't the Bluegrass State's only major fast-food brand. They have a noisy neighbour just 11 miles across town. Head east from KFC headquarters along Interstate 264 to the suburb of Jeffersontown and you'll find the headquarters of Papa John's Pizza. It's on Papa John's Boulevard.

Founded in 1984, Papa John's is now the United States' fourth largest pizza chain, behind Pizza Hut, Domino's and Little Caesar's, with franchise operations in 45 countries, including the UK, Ireland, Spain, Russia and Belarus.

The similarities between KFC and Papa John's don't end with fast food or Louisville.

Like KFC, Papa John's brand is anchored in the image of its founder. 'Papa' John Schnatter is a real person. His story could almost be the modern retelling of KFC's iconic Colonel Harland Sanders. Schnatter too was a self-made tycoon. He too started out with a single restaurant and just like the Colonel, Papa John added irresistible colour to his public image with a spurious and completely made-up prefix.

The Colonel died in 1980, but 'Papa' John Schnatter is very much alive and kicking and prone to public displays of behaviour of the type that only high-profile billionaires seem capable of making. Schnatter's displays are not of the mild-by-comparison 'embarrassing dad' type made famous by Richard Branson, or even the polarizing Elon Musk type. They're the really bad type.

Schnatter was never really a popular founder figure. He lacked the charisma of a Branson or Musk and with two out-of-court settlements for stalking and sexual misconduct respectively to his name by the turn of the millennium, he has been controversial for a long time.[13] So any public transgression would always leave a sour taste in many an American's mouth. It was therefore solidly unsurprising when he drew widespread criticism and ridicule in 2012 for complaining that insuring Papa John's employees under Barack Obama's Affordable Care Act would put 14 cents on the cost of a large Papa John's pizza. He hired a crisis communications firm to finesse his way out of that situation, but Papa John apparently never missed an opportunity to misread the public mood and in 2017 he found himself struggling to navigate another looming PR crisis.[15]

In November 2017 he'd blamed the NFL, specifically the players who kneeled during the national anthem to protest police mistreatment of black people, for a slump in Papa John's sales, saying: 'NFL leadership has hurt Papa John's shareholders.' The NFL ended its 8-year relationship with Papa John's in February 2018. The firm would no longer be the official pizza chain of the NFL.

Schnatter remained defiant, but the heat was getting too much for the Papa John's board. In May 2018, as an attempt to get their arms around the unfolding crisis, Papa John's hired a Brooklyn-based marketing firm called Laundry Service. The firm had previously worked with major brands like Nike, Fox and Amazon. Their website boasts that they 'make amazing sh!t'. In the case of Papa John's, they certainly did.

The KFC Colonel didn't live to see the golden age of corporate buffoonery, but he did posthumously find his way into the controversy that would mark the end of Schnatter's time at Papa John's. Laundry Service and the Papa John's board had a plan to fortify Schnatter against further public relations calamities. They'd put him through some role-playing interviews, pitching him curveballs and testing his mettle on sensitive issues including race relations, like the ones dogging the NFL that Schnatter had blamed for the sales slump.

On a conference call, in response to a question about how he'd distance himself from associations with racist groups online, Schnatter answered that Colonel Sanders had called black people the n-word and griped that the Colonel never faced the sort of backlash he was facing. Role-playing game over. Laundry Service terminated their contract with Papa John's almost immediately. By July, his remarks had been reported in the press and Schnatter resigned. If he was due any credit at all, it would be that he never denied his remarks and resigned as chairman. Schnatter said in a statement: 'News reports attributing the use of inappropriate and hurtful language to me during a media training session regarding race are true,' adding, 'Regardless of the context, I apologize. Simply stated, racism has no place in our society.'[16]

The Sanders family swiftly denied the accusation in the strongest possible terms, Colonel Sanders' grandson called Schnatter a 'weasel' and his great granddaughter said: 'For Mr Schnatter to use the Colonel as a scapegoat for his own horrible, disgusting mouth and racist beliefs is inexcusable.'[17]

Even in Schnatter's absence, Papa John's had a problem. When a founder is so inextricably linked with his organization, like Richard Branson, Steve Jobs or the KFC Colonel were to theirs, the organization imbibes

When a founder is so inextricably linked with his organization, the organization imbibes their founder's personality.

their founder's personality. That founder *is* their organization. Until his death, Apple *was* Steve Jobs and Apple is a visionary company because Jobs was a visionary leader. Similarly, John Schnatter *was* Papa John's. And because John Schnatter said what he said on that fake phone call, Papa John's was now, unless something drastic was done, a 'racist pizza company'.

There were three attempts at apologies. The first was a saccharine one-minute video. And in a move reminiscent of a famous 2009 Domino's Pizza advert where the firm faced up to their harshest critics, albeit relating to the flavour of their tomato sauce and not the conduct of their founder, Papa John's chose to surface some of the most damaging criticisms about themselves too.

The video had the requisite sombre music, and featured some of the most well-worn corporate clichés like 'we heard you' and 'you expected better'. The text in the video then changes. 'Thank you for your anger', 'Thank you for your criticism', 'Thank you for your honesty', 'It is making us better.' And that was it. No 'sorry'.

The second attempt wasn't much better. Before the actual apology, in an open letter posted to the Papa John's website, new CEO Steve Ritchie had adopted a damage limitation approach. He was desperate to distance Papa John's from Papa John.

He listed lots of things Papa John's the pizza company were going to do differently now that the founder had left the organization: listening sessions, addressing internal culture, 'two-way conversations' were all on offer as reparations. But still no apology. And now people were starting to notice.

'This is not a good response', said PR consultant and crisis management David Oates to The Huffington Post.[18] He went on: 'The fact is that even if the CEO or the Executive Team had nothing to do with the stupidity of its founder and chairman, they are still responsible for all communications – internal and external – that occur under its brand.'

Ritchie had a third attempt and this time, although he didn't hit exactly the right note, he was at least singing in the right key. He essentially revisited his open letter, but added in the crucial missing ingredient: 'I'm sorry.' He positioned his apology early on in the statement, but not before asking for sympathy.

'This past week was the hardest week in my 22 years with Papa John's.' That's how the statement started. And that's after two previous attempts. To be completely fair to Ritchie, this was a prickly situation not of his own doing. His only real option from a strategic point of view was to distance the brand from the founder. So judging his apology with that in mind, we can afford to cut him some slack. But we can also take this as a lesson in why your first apology should be your best apology.

The temptation to appear sorry without saying sorry is strong.

Mark Zuckerberg, United Airlines, Papa John's Pizza all received criticism for issuing weak apologies, before going on to issue fuller and more sincere apologies. For Zuckerberg, he didn't say sorry properly until Facebook's stock dropped. Same for United. For 'Papa' John Schnatter, he couldn't find the right words until he'd had the sack from his own company and it took his successor another three goes to adequately atone for Schnatter.

An organization's initial response to a crisis is often weak and obscure. That's deliberate. The temptation to appear sorry without saying sorry is strong. Organizations issue cautious apologies because they are scared of admitting liability and inviting litigation and hope their silence means the problem will go away. They think they can contain their crisis, so they keep their messaging deliberately vague. Consumers might not immediately understand why the apologies they're expecting to hear aren't forthcoming, but they can spot equivocation and evasion a mile off. Organizations must decide early on in a crisis whether they owe an apology, and if they do, give it without reservation or qualification. Anything else is an invitation to ridicule.

CHAPTER TWELVE

'Forced to apologize'?

Fostering resilience and identifying customer intent

Our film should not have made light of Peter Rabbit's archnemesis, Mr McGregor, being allergic to blackberries, even in a cartoonish slapstick way. We sincerely regret not being more aware and sensitive to this issue, and we truly apologize.
SONY PICTURES, 12 FEBRUARY 2018

If you went near a television set in the UK during the 70s and 80s, you likely heard one of Ronnie Hazlehurst's brilliant theme tunes. Ronnie was the BBC's musical director and set the tone for much of the broadcaster's sitcom output. One of his most memorable works was the opening to *Are You Being Served?* – a campy sitcom set in an upmarket London department store. As the opening titles roll, a cash register dings rhythmically, providing a backbeat for Ronnie's cheesy but brilliant smooth jazz noodlings. The best bit was actress Stephanie Gathercole's vocal, although she didn't really sing anything.

Instead, with impeccably elongated home counties vowels, she sort of crooned out what was for sale on the various floors in the role of 'lift girl'. Listen to it, it's great.

The show left screens in 1985, returning for a very brief revival in 2016, long after the risqué-for-the-70s jokes and Hazlehurst's theme tune had faded into obscurity. It did leave behind a quirky cultural relic though. For a time after, hilarious dads of a certain vintage – and it was always dads – when asked what floor they needed when getting into a lift, might pay a little tribute to Gathercole's vocal and respond with 'ladies underwear please!'

Smartphones have thankfully relieved us of the need for awkward elevator small talk and bawdy sitcom humour. And the occupants of your average lift probably wouldn't get the gag if you tried it today. So when 76-year-old King's College London professor Richard Ned Lebow squeezed into a crowded lift at a 2018 academic convention in San Francisco and asked for 'ladies underwear', he was taking a big punt on lightening the mood in what he described as a 'box full of strangers'.[1]

Lebow didn't know it at the time, but his joke, one he later conceded was 'lame', was about to set off a row that would spread across the academy.[2] Another of the lift's occupants, a fellow academic and someone we can assume had never seen *Are You Being Served?* lodged a formal complaint about Lebow's joke with the convention organizers, the International Studies Association. Upon hearing about the complaint, Lebow wrote to his fellow attendee, calling the complaint 'frivolous' and attempting to resolve the matter informally, per the ISA guidelines.[3] Most would agree that Lebow might want to update his pop culture reference points, but the matter of whether he owed anyone an apology remained contentious.

The matter escaped the confines of academic media shortly after and became a mainstream talking point everywhere from *The Sun* to the *Washington Post*. The predictable arguments about free speech and political correctness set ablaze those corners of the Internet concerned with such things. Think pieces speculated whether his remark was offensive or even amounted to harassment, while others, as expected, took the 'political correctness gone mad' angle in support of Lebow's position.[4,5,6] Nevertheless, the ISA found that Lebow had violated its code of conduct. The Association told Lebow it would take no further action provided he issued an 'unequivocal apology'. He declined.[7] Then he threatened to sue the ISA.

The most interesting narrative to emerge from the affair, and one that was overlooked at the time, came from an opinion poll conducted by YouGov on 15 May, the same day as the deadline for Lebow's apology.[8] The poll asked whether he should be 'made to apologize'. Not 'should he apologize?' – should he be 'made to apologize'. According to the nationally representative sample of 3,317 British adults, 16 per cent said 'yes'. That figure of 16 per cent rises to 29 per cent among 18- to 24-year-olds. Almost a third of young British adults said they believed Lebow should have been *made* to say sorry for his lame joke. Quite how they expected to make him apologize isn't clear, but the very fact that almost a third of young adults were OK with forced apologies puts an entirely new spin on what consumers think apologies are for.

A study published by Wayne State University Press in the same month as the Lebow controversy might have supported Lebow's decision to not say sorry. 'Coerced expressions of remorse', the study found, were viewed with suspicion and were 'less effective at mending a victim's feelings'.[9] Further, the giver of a forced apology was viewed as 'less nice' by the study's recipients.

Forced apologies are useless.

'Less nice' is interesting isn't it? If you think it sounds like a juvenile turn of phrase, you'd be right. This was a study of children. The oldest participants were nine. The study's authors took it as a given that adults could spot a forced apology. They were interested in whether children could. And while almost 3 in 10 young British adults were advocating for a man to be made to apologize for a dad joke, US children, many of whom would still need help putting on their own shoes, had already confirmed empirically that forced apologies are useless.

Lebow never did apologize, but if you search for his name on the Internet, the first things you'll see aside from his Wikipedia profile, are news reports about the controversy. 'All he was asked to do was apologize' said the complainant.[10] Had he done so, it wouldn't have made much difference to his digital footprint. He'd have just been reading slightly different headlines about himself. 'Professor refuses to apologize for sexist joke' simply becomes 'Professor forced to apologize for sexist joke'. He'd still be portrayed as a sexist whether he said sorry or not. Just one with slightly less backbone.

Court-ordered apologies

The court of public opinion isn't the only place where people are coerced into humiliating public apologies. Actual courts, with judges, have been experimenting with forced contrition as a legal remedy. The 'court-ordered apology' is a controversial strain of restorative justice that achieves mixed results at best.

After a hit-and-run driver knocked a 10-year-old boy off his bike, Pittsford Town Court in New York ordered that he write the boy a letter. The apology was an absolute treat for people who like really terrible apologies.

'Dear Julian, I'm very sorry that you rode into the side of the car I was driving on Friday, September 7th' wrote Doug Lamb, the court-ordered apologizer. 'More importantly, I am glad you didn't need to be treated by the attending ambulance on the day of the incident. Wishing you a safe and happy holiday season. Sincerely, Doug Lamb.'[11]

This is an interesting apology: victim blaming, liability evasion, minimizing the severity of the incident by pointing out the boy didn't need medical treatment. It's a genre-defining classic.

In fact, a lawyer seeking to prevent an admission of liability couldn't have written a better apology on behalf of their client, who may or may not have been involved in a hit-and-run and may or not have been called Doug Lamb. Julian said the letter made him angry. His mother called it sickening.[12] We'd call it the obvious and logical conclusion of court-mandated contrition. Forcing people to say sorry doesn't really work.

Demanding an apology is one thing. It's often an act of desperation from a wronged party or a power move for people who lack gravitas. Forcing one is something else. It takes influence and clout to force an apology. Analysis of media coverage relating to notable apologies between January 2018 and January 2019 reveals hundreds of individual news reports of organizations and public figures being 'forced to apologize'. In a lot of those cases, it's just semantics. Organizations have said sorry and journalists have framed it as having been 'forced'.

'Facebook forced to apologize again over abuse posts' wrote the *Financial Times* in July.[13] They weren't really forced. 'Twitter CEO Jack Dorsey forced to apologize for eating Chick-fil-A during Pride Month.'[14] Same again. Asked maybe, encouraged possibly, but not forced.

There are some scenarios though, in which large and powerful organizations have faced such pressure to say sorry, even if they weren't sorry, that 'forced' is the only accurate description. Common to this sort of apology is cooperation between three key players: the low-profile victim, the medium-profile campaigners and advocacy groups, and the media. Examining this pattern of conspiratorial behaviour can hopefully show how under-fire organization succumb to such pressure.

Allergy sufferers vs Sony Pictures

Sony Pictures were 'forced to apologize' for a scene in their 2018 *Peter Rabbit* adaptation in which the anthropomorphized protagonists Cottontail, Flopsy and Mopsy use catapults to fire fruit and vegetables into the mouth of human character and blackberry allergy sufferer Mr McGregor.

The apology came after pressure from American charity Asthma and Allergy Foundation of America (AAFA). The charity, along with the non-profit group Kids With Food Allergies, who have almost 100,000 Facebook followers, took issue with the weaponization of allergens. They published an open letter to Sony Pictures condemning them for the 'joke' which they claimed could put people with food allergies 'in danger'.[15]

What might seem like eccentric hyperbole was actually quite a clever campaigning strategy. By broadening the scope of the perceived offence to include '15 million Americans living with food allergies' they expanded the pool of people who could legitimately be angry with Sony.

Sony had options for explaining their way out of this. They could have pointed out that Peter Rabbit did lots of bad things in their film, but he eventually saw the error of his ways and stopped. They could have pointed out that it was an important portrayal of bullying.

They didn't though and this controversy was just too much to resist for the media, so it became a problem. It had everything the media needed. What had started as a niche complaint about a scene in a movie went on to become a mainstream controversy. It was framed as an attack on all allergy sufferers. In a film featuring talking rabbits wearing raincoats, the sight of a human character using an epipen to treat an allergic reaction was one of the more realistic moments. And in a world where advocacy groups campaign passionately for greater media representation of the causes they care about, Sony might have been surprised by the criticism.

They'd highlighted the seriousness of food allergies, something the Kids With Food Allergies group campaigns for too. A 2016 blog from their website encourages parents of allergy sufferers to 'make sure your teen's friends know what to do in an emergency – ask your teen if they know how to inject in an emergency'.[16]

If extracting a high-profile apology wasn't such fun for their critics and the media, Sony might have expected to get credit and not criticism for increasing media representation, in the way the 2003 film remake of *The Singing Detective* was praised for its realistic portrayal of psoriasis.[17]

Nonetheless, more than 18,000 people signed a petition demanding an apology from Sony and a boycott hashtag emerged in support. Once that happened, headlines appeared in the *New York Times*, the *Guardian*, *Vanity Fair*, CNN – everywhere that matters.

It doesn't matter how big or clever an organization is, this level of criticism is disorientating. Sony, for all of its power and the obvious arguments they could have made in its own defence, just didn't have the appetite for standing its ground. In a statement, Sony said:

> Food allergies are a serious issue. Our film should not have made light of Peter Rabbit's archnemesis, Mr McGregor, being allergic to blackberries, even in a cartoonish, slapstick way.
>
> We sincerely regret not being more aware and sensitive to this issue, and we truly apologize.[18]

This not the reaction of a resilient organization. Nor is it the response of one who is actually sorry. Going by modern standards, the done thing at this stage in the outrage cycle would be to mount a product recall. That's how you *show* that you're sorry. You admit your product has a flaw, then you remove it. Had it been a T-shirt or pair of socks that had caused the controversy, it would have been easy, albeit expensive. Sony said sorry, but it was very much business as usual. The film grossed more than $100 million in its debut weekend, despite the threats of a boycott.

The media is rarely an impartial observer.

In a way, everyone's a winner here. The media had a confected outrage to write about, the film's critics got their apology and Sony didn't really have to much more than issue a statement. As *Forbes* film critic Scott Mendelson put it: 'For better or worse, the studio has apologized, if only because that was the easiest course of action.'[19]

Sometimes events outside an organization's control can conspire to deliver a reputational disaster for them. Tylenol had an entire murder spree named after them through no fault of their own. H&M endured a cultural crisis because of a conspiracy theory about socks. Sometimes life isn't fair.

So it's weird and a touch sinister when the media is so gleeful in reporting on an organization that's been 'forced to apologize', whether due to its own failure or sheer bad luck. It's especially discomforting when you consider the media's own influence on whether or not an organization apologizes. The media is rarely an impartial observer and is often the first to locate the crucial low-level victim and stir up some outrage.

How can organizations be more resilient?

Understanding that it's significantly easier for customers to be outraged than it is for them to follow through with threats of a boycott is a great start. Sony would still be trading today even if it hadn't apologized for *Peter Rabbit*. So would United Airlines and Starbucks. Boycotts are survivable and quite often the threats are nothing but hot air. The NFL has been threatened with boycotts most weeks since players started taking a knee during the national anthem. They're still here. Knowing this is a good step toward achieving reputational resilience.

There's a difference between customers and an audience.

Organizations must understand too that apologies are not the golden bullet for avoiding customer attrition. Customer anger is not the same as customer intent. A significant proportion of the people angry at organizations on social media are not their customers. There's a difference between customers and an audience. And performative social media outrage is not the same actual anger.

As we saw in Chapter 4 the level of friction in a particular industry affects the likelihood of attrition more than the level of outrage does. Banking is a high-friction industry. Changing from one bank to another is not an easy process. Studies show that banking is one of the least popular industries around, but high street banks still have customers despite challenger institutions offering alternatives.[20] The kind of friction that stops people ditching their bank doesn't exist inside the bubble of social media. This isn't to suggest that those organizations should start mistreating their customers, but to demonstrate that threats of a boycott and angry tweets don't necessarily constitute a crisis.

A good way to judge how angry your customers really are is by observing what they do in the real world when they're upset. We understand that the sincerity of an apology is directly correlated to the cost of sending it. Empty statements with no associated actions are practically worthless. The same is true for gestures of anger. When customers take real-world action, there's a cost attached, whether it's time, energy or actual money.

Threats of a boycott and angry tweets don't necessarily constitute a crisis.

Football supporters are an extreme example of why outrage is no guarantee of lost customers. Football supporters are among the most brand-loyal consumers you'll find, willing to pay a premium in advance for the product, even when they anticipate disappointment. They also love to complain and in theory at least, it can be easy to switch. It's a 15-minute train journey between West Bromwich and Wolverhampton in the UK's West Midlands, and both places have football teams. Ticket prices are similar, but that doesn't mean a disgruntled West

Bromwich Albion fan is about to start watching Wolverhampton Wanderers instead, even if the quality of football is superior. As with banks, our parents are the biggest influence on the football team we chose. Football fans are therefore one of the most reliable informal measures of consumer satisfaction we have. It takes a lot for football fans to boycott their team.

A football club's managing director doesn't need to conduct a single survey to measure customer satisfaction. He or she can simply look out of the directors' box on matchday and see how many empty seats there are. Of course, football supporters exist on social media, and like any other consumer demographic, they can produce a lot of hot air. They like to moan and they can be very fickle, but it can be socially costly for them to even express their disapproval. They risk being ridiculed by rival fans and challenged by fellow fans.

In 2016 a disgruntled Newcastle fan threw his season ticket at then manager Steve McClaren in protest at a run of poor performances and results, in effect preventing himself from getting back into the ground for the rest of the season, if ever.[21] That was a protest with a social and financial cost. The Office for National Statistics puts the average 2015 weekly full-time wage for Newcastle at £448.[22] The cheapest adult season ticket at Newcastle United for that season was £525.[23] That fan's sacrifice is significantly more costly than the few seconds it would take him to send an angry tweet. This is disapproval worth listening to. And Newcastle United did listen. McClaren was sacked five days later.

Unlike throwing your season ticket away, social media anger is a consistently bad predictor of customer satisfaction. Remember, 64 per cent of Southwest Airlines' tweets are apologies. So it's safe to assume that they receive a lot of heat on Twitter. Yet they are consistently one of the best-rated airlines on customer satisfaction surveys. Southwest's fellow budget airline Ryanair understand how significant the gap is between angry tweets and customer intent and for that reason, they can provide one of best lessons in resilience we'll ever see.

When Ryanair got rid of its 10kg free baggage allowance in 2018, the social media reaction wasn't great. It was terrible actually. People were threatening to boycott, as expected. But Ryanair appeared to know something the more apologetic organizations did not. They were so confident that these threats were made in a meaningless social media vacuum that they put out a statement effectively daring their customers to boycott them:

> Our flights are full of people who swear frequently they'll never fly with us again, but keep coming back for the lowest fares and better punctuality than any other Irish airline.

> But we recognize it's all about customer choice, so if customers want to choose higher fares and less punctual airlines, then so be it.

> Someone else will take their seat.[24]

We're not advocating organizations adopt Ryanair's entire communications strategy. But this is worth paying attention to. The organizations that comprehend the gulf in meaning between social media criticism and genuine, profit-harming customer anger are the ones best equipped to stay resilient and respond appropriately to problems. The ones that conflate angry tweets and threats of boycotts with potential real-world customer attrition are destined to find themselves issuing a lot of unnecessary, reflexive and meaningless apologies.

CHAPTER THIRTEEN

'We got it wrong'

What to say when you've killed a puppy (and how to fake humility)

As hard as we try, it's obvious we don't always get it right.

OSCAR MUNOZ, CEO, UNITED AIRLINES, 22 MARCH 2018

In 2015 a medical research charity conducted an experiment to discover what type of messaging prompted more people to make a donation. They published two adverts, both identical in their wording: 'Would you give £5 a month to save Harrison from a slow, painful death?'[1] The only difference between the adverts was the picture. In one advert 'Harrison' was a baby boy, in the other, 'Harrison' was a dog.

Harrison the dog received significantly more donations than 'Harrison' the baby. A separate study, in which 240 students were shown fake newspaper reports describing a baseball bat attack that left the victim with lacerations and a broken leg, reached a similar conclusion.[2] The 'victim' in the story varied too. It was either an adult human, a baby, a young child or a dog. The study coordinators filmed the facial expressions of the students to measure their responses. The dog drew more empathy than the adult and the young child. Only the baby evoked more empathy. Both studies came to a conclusion most of us already knew; dogs are too pure for this world.

'We got it wrong'

So you really, really had to feel for United Airlines when Kokito, a 10-month old French bulldog puppy, suffocated in the overhead bin on a United Airlines flight from Houston to New York in March 2018. It must have felt for a moment at United's Chicago headquarters that their run of bad luck would never end. They were barely over their 're-accommodation' crisis. This was a disaster, but what could they really say that would make it better? 'We got it wrong' was about it.[3] They also said sorry, but people wanted more than an apology. They wanted, and deserved, an explanation. And they actually got one. It's just a shame it took the death of a dog for United to realize that they can actually handle a crisis after all.

Speaking to The Executive's Club of Chicago shortly after Kokito had died, Munoz appeared to have at least learned from the BP chief Tony 'I want my life back' Hayward's iconic mistake. Citing the 're-accommodation' incident, Munoz recalled how industry peers assumed he was glad the controversy was over. 'That is the furthest thing from mind' said Munoz, evoking a similar energy to Mary Barra's 'I never want to put this behind us' remark that defined her exemplary handling of the General Motors ignition switch crisis. Munoz added: 'We constantly want to be reminded of how things can go wrong so quickly.'[4]

Munoz was handling this as well as you could hope. And he made another interesting move. He explained how it was company policy, not individual error, that had caused the dog's death.

The cabin crew member made a mistake by placing the dog's crate in the overhead bin. As Munoz explained though, the crew member was following an unclear set of rules.

Again, like the General Motors ignition switch crisis, this was a cultural problem presenting as an operational failure. One of the steps the firm has since taken is to introduce better labelling so animals being transported aren't treated as hand luggage.

This was a cultural problem presenting as an operational failure.

The frequency with which Oscar Munoz has appeared on stage saying sorry is less a reflection on him as a corporate leader and more a reflection of the specific challenges of running an airline. Munoz himself alluded to 'the math', saying:

> at any given moment there are hundreds of United planes in the air carrying tens of thousands of customers, which makes for tens of thousands of opportunities for unforeseen events.[5]

Failures are magnified when they happen at altitude. So when it comes to problems of this magnitude, what an organization says actually matters a lot less than what it does.

In some respects it's actually easier to apologize for catastrophic failures because the temptation to obfuscate and tease out a sympathetic angle disappears. There simply aren't any sympathetic angles to find. When you've killed a puppy, there's really not much else you can say except 'we got it wrong'. It's what you do next that matters.

It's what you do next that matters.

Time will tell if the corrective steps United introduced work and that will be the true measure of how sorry they were. If they're proven to work, 'we got it wrong' will have marked the start of their journey to improvement. If it happens again, history will judge 'we got it wrong' as mere lip service.

Munoz was happy to reflect openly on his organization's various points of failure because 'we got it wrong' was swiftly followed by 'here's what we're doing to put it right'. Other organizations are often happy to speak the language of self-examination without doing any of the all-important self-examining. Without making specific steps toward improvement, these statements risk sounding like nothing more than a cop-out.

'We missed the mark'

On first hearing, It sounds like the same kind of earnest and ultimately welcome admission of failure United made. But does it mean anything? In 2010, when Facebook had its first highly publicized data privacy scandal, they favoured the kind of soft messaging made popular by Silicon Valley to paint their error with the flattering sheen of honest accountability. CEO Mark Zuckerberg authored a letter published in the *Washington Post* full of self-praise and strategic nods to their humble beginnings. 'We built Facebook around a few simple ideas,' the letter began. 'Our intention was to give you lots of granular controls; but that may not have been what many of you wanted. We just missed the mark.'[6]

Zuckerberg promised that Facebook was listening and learning lessons. He promised readers: 'You have control over how your information is shared.'[7] The only thing Facebook had to do was make good on these promises and take actionable steps to protect user data. Could they do it?

Zuckerberg had been apologizing for violating people's privacy since before Facebook existed. In 2003, a site called Facemash – the Facebook precursor – caused havoc on the Harvard University campus for non-consensually publishing students' private pictures and inviting other students to rate them for 'hotness'. A very young Zuckerberg apologized, saying: 'I definitely see how my intentions could be seen in the wrong light.'[8]

Fast forward 15 years to the Cambridge Analytica scandal and we all know that Facebook broke its 2010 promise to do better in how it handled user data. So to answer the question above, in Facebook's case 'we just missed the mark' didn't really mean anything. Unlike United's 'we got it wrong', this was corporate obfuscation, Zuckerberg's tech-for-good persona notwithstanding.

The phrase rarely does mean much at all. In 2015, Anheuser-Busch, who own the Budweiser brand, apologized for their #upforwhatever campaign to promote Bud Light. Critics, including a member of Congress, weren't happy with the label strapline 'removing no from your vocabulary for the night'. Anheuser-Busch said they 'missed the mark' and shelved the campaign.[9]

Dove said they 'missed the mark' too in 2017 with a badly received skincare advert that we'll explore in more detail later.[10] In the same year Pepsi said they 'clearly missed the mark' with a famously ridiculed advert in which they tried to project a 'global message of unity, peace and understanding'. We'll get to that later too. Cosmetics brand Avon claimed to have 'missed the mark' in January 2019.[11] The firm was publicly called out by actress and body positivity activist Jameela Jamil for promoting an anti-cellulite product.

Heineken said they 'missed the mark' – and they really did, by about a thousand miles – with their 'sometimes lighter is better' strapline in an advert that saw a Heineken bottle slide along a bar, past three black people, into the hands of a white person. A spokesperson told the Indy 100 website:

> For decades, Heineken has developed diverse marketing that shows there's more that unites us than divides us. While we feel the ad is referencing our Heineken Light beer, we missed the mark, are taking the feedback to heart and will use this to influence future campaigns.[12]

That is an impressive cop-out and at the same time a classic Schrödinger's apology. Any apology that begins with such a lofty appeal to one's own virtues deserves to be dismissed. The spokesperson references a strapline from a different campaign – 'there's more that unites than divides us' – to mitigate the visual disaster of the advert that was being criticized. Cynical triangulation aside, it really doesn't count as missing the mark when the potential problems with the advert are so obvious. How big does the mark need to be before we stop forgiving brands for missing it?

Any apology that begins with such a lofty appeal to one's own virtues deserves to be dismissed.

Did any of them really miss the mark? The language of humble self-reflection might have worked 10 years ago in Silicon Valley but it doesn't sit quite right when it comes from multi-billion-dollar companies, regardless of whether they learned from their mistake or not.

'We missed the mark' is a corporate affectation, borrowed from the office ping-pong start-up culture most founders grew out of years ago, and upcycled in corporate boardrooms as a post-rationalization exercise. Corporations are outsourcing their internal quality control processes to their critics and reversing out of bad decisions with meek language.

We're being too forgiving. In 2017, Budweiser's parent company generated revenues of $56.44 billion.[13] Dove's owner Unilever posted revenues of $53 billion.[14] PepsiCo did $63 billion, Heineken $24.8 billion and even Avon turned over a respectable $5.7 billion.[15,16,17] These aren't companies experimenting with new campaign ideas in a San Francisco co-working space.

Marketing and advertising has evolved from an art into an impressively exacting science; organizations spend millions split-testing, focus-grouping and tweaking their creative so it hits exactly the right notes with the right customers. Consumer analytics and propensity modelling have enabled organizations to laser-focus their messaging to levels of accuracy that were inconceivable 20 years ago. In 2018, businesses in America spent more than $11 million on marketing data to help them hit the right people with the right message.[18] Make no mistake, advertisers know their audiences. Guesswork, 'taking a punt', seeing what works – these are not the habits of the world's largest organizations. Missing the mark doesn't cut it.

Consumers were far more inclined to forgive the young Mark Zuckerberg – the first time at least – when he was a fresh-faced graduate apologizing in his hoodie. He represented a start-up apparently flying by the seat of its pants and trying new things. His apologies have worn out their welcome though. 'We missed the mark' is corporate PR speak for 'oops!' and it does a constant disservice to the contrition consumers actually want to see.

Cop-out culture

Claiming to have missed some arbitrary mark is not the only way an organization can cop-out while pretending to be sorry. Over recent years organizations have concocted an impressive variety of ways to mimimize, obfuscate and not say sorry while appearing to apologize. These half-baked admissions that 'something went wrong but it wasn't necessarily our fault' have become a reputation management smokescreen. They're just statements of vague regret with all the useful bits taken out.

> 'We missed the mark' is corporate PR speak for 'oops!'

'Sometimes mistakes happen'

There's a restaurant review on the TripAdvisor website that complains of 'mediocre' tapas and 'haphazard' service.[19] In their judiciousness, the reviewer concludes that 'sometimes mistakes happen' and that maybe they'll give the place another try. That's fair enough.

'Sometimes mistakes happen' is also what Adel al-Jubeir, Saudi Arabia's Foreign Minister and chief diplomat, told a group of journalists at the conclusion of an investigation into the 2018 murder of journalist Jamal Khashoggi.[20] Al-Jubeir also threw in a half-price promise that the regime would not 'engage in such acts' again.[21]

This is an archetypal corporate apology dressed up in new clothes. It's remarkably similar to a 2013 remark by Standard Chartered chief executive Sir John Peace.[22] After the bank had been caught and fined for breaking US sanctions by making payments into Iraq and Libya, Peace initially told US regulators: 'We had no wilful act to avoid sanctions. You know, mistakes are made – clerical errors.'

Peace later had to retract his statement when the regulator threatened to revoke Standard Chartered's New York banking licence. He then issued what he thought was a proper apology: 'I made certain statements that I very much regret and that were at best inaccurate. My statement was wrong and directly contradicts [our] acceptance of responsibility.'

In their own obvious comfort with this same strategy, the Saudi regime managed to distil the worst excesses of modern crisis management – the soft messaging, vague equivocations and empty promises – and sharpen them into a pointed implement with which to flick away legitimate international criticism.

We should not be relaxed about this development. Based on what we've seen from Facebook and Uber's attempts to add weight to their initial mea culpas, perhaps the next logical step for the regime, now it has formally acknowledged that 'sometimes mistakes happen', would be the now standard YouTube apology video.

The Saudi Arabia regime (hopefully) won't go on a Facebook- or Uber-style apology tour. And no reasonable person is expecting them to drop to their knees and beg forgiveness for what happened. But they've clearly noticed that large organizations have been letting themselves off the hook by using a certain style of apology, which they've now copied.

And if you run an organization and notice that authoritarian regimes are adopting your crisis management habits, maybe *you're* doing it wrong. Maybe it's time for corporations to refresh their messaging.

CHAPTER FOURTEEN

Self-service apologies

Performative crisis management and teaching consumers to expect too much

Pepsi was trying to project a global message of unity, peace and understanding. Clearly we missed the mark, and we apologize. PEPSI SPOKESPERSON, 2017

It's tough, but comparatively simple to apologize for an operational crisis. Something goes wrong, so you fix it and say sorry. It's not ideal, but life goes on. KFC provide the definitive case in point here. It's worth repeating that for a brief moment in 2018 KFC was famously – and we can't stress this enough – a chain of chicken shops that ran out of chicken.

This highlights an interesting dichotomy. KFC failed to meet minimum expectations and were let off the hook. H&M, whose misdeed was trying to sell socks to LEGO enthusiasts, were not. They were forced to suffer prolonged embarrassment and reputational damage, to the point of being threatened with a boycott.

KFC escaped the naughty step because deep down, consumers don't really care about supply chain logistics. It's just not an axe they want to grind. Only the most committed grudge-holder could stay angry about the time they went out for a Bargain Bucket and came home with a Big Mac.

But a cultural crisis is a different problem with an entirely different set of risks. The impact can be orders of magnitude more damaging to an organization than a simple logistical gaffe and the steps necessary to undo the damage can be significantly more costly.

Cultural hypervigilance

Where is all this outrage coming from? It's not that organizations discovered social media and collectively decided to start taking unnecessary reputational risks. This is a demand-side phenomenon, powered by cultural hypervigilance.

Consumer identity politics, a strand of the consumer culture theory popularized by marketing professors Eric Arnould and Craig Thompson, is dedicated to understanding how consumers achieve a unified and coherent sense of self through their buying choices. 'Consumption can be a self-defining and self-expressive behaviour. People often choose products and brands that are self-relevant and communicate a given identity.'[1] This goes a long way to explain the consumer outrage we see when organizations fail to reflect what consumers wish to see in themselves.

Author and organizational consultant Simon Sinek crystalized the idea in his 2009 Ted Talk 'How Great Leaders Inspire Action' when he told a TedX audience: 'The goal is to do business with people who believe what you believe.'[2]

Organizations are now starting to understand the degree to which modern consumers are emotionally invested in their own consumer choices, but they don't quite know how to handle the information. Their response so far has been to over-promise, assuring customers that their purpose isn't to sell them products and services that improve their lives, but that they exist to uphold the values that consumers aspire to in themselves. On the basis of that promise going unfulfilled, consumers have become hypervigilant to the cultural and moral implications of what organizations do, what they stand for and what they stand against.

Consumers have become hypervigilant to the cultural and moral implications of what organizations do.

Consumers will always be far better equipped to handle the mild inconvenience and disappointment of an operational failure – such as the temporary absence of fried chicken – than they are the emotional gut-punch of an organization that challenges or contradicts the consumer's own view of themselves. So it's easy to imagine how it feels for people when they see their favourite stationery shop getting friendly with what they perceive to be the wrong newspaper. They get upset and stay upset. The stench of a 'culture problem' can take years to wash out.

The burden of corporate innocence

The communications profession is stuck at an impasse of its own making. In 2011, brand consultants Millward Brown and Jim Stengel, the latter being the former global marketing officer of the world's largest advertiser Procter & Gamble, published a study entitled 'Grow: How ideals power growth and profit at the world's greatest companies'.

The 10-year empirical study examined the growth of 50,000 brands and explored the factors most responsible for driving that growth. A central claim of the study was that brands with a social purpose, those that strove for a 'higher good', grew faster and larger than those that didn't. In short, cultural perceptions have an economic impact.

'I have always believed that great brands are built on improving the lives of the people they serve; I wanted to prove that maximum profit and high ideals aren't incompatible but, in fact, inseparable,' said Jim Stengel.

The study singled out 50 brands for specific praise, attributing to their growth such lofty virtues as 'eliciting joy', 'activating experiences of happiness' and 'enabling connection'. The study's conclusions invited the communications profession to view notably 'touchy-feely' brands like Innocent Smoothies, Dove Skincare and Apple as exemplars of how cultural and social purpose fosters growth.

But the conclusions, as well as Brown and Stengel's methodology, were criticized at the time and remain controversial today. Professor Byron Sharp, an Australian marketing science expert well known for his work on loyalty programmes, wrote in 2011 that he believed the study was 'deeply flawed' and that it told marketers 'nothing reliable'.[3] Sharp cites the 'halo effect', a tendency to attribute the characteristics we want to measure to already well-performing subjects, as a key methodology flaw. Richard Shotton, head of behavioural science at award-winning global media agency Manning Gottlieb OMD, and perhaps the most vocal critic of the 'Stengel 50', also doubts the validity of parts of the study:

> The argument was 'Innocent Smoothies has a purpose, and we know it is working because Coca-Cola's holding company has grown so much'... The problem is that Innocent is a tiny per cent of Coca-Cola's revenues so the metric he used and what he proved are two different things.[4]

Brown and Stengel's central thesis, although arguably flawed, has been hard to resist. Marketers were eager to accept the idea that their brands had a purpose above and beyond selling products. They sought to emulate the inherent 'niceness' and cultural palatability of the 'Stengel 50' brands. In doing so, they felt they were absolved of the sin of being in marketing.

Despite early criticisms, the study was hugely influential. Innocent Smoothies, famed for their wacky marketing copy and saccharine social aspirations, attracted an army of twee imitators. All of a sudden our groceries were talking to us, telling us what we wanted to hear. Packaging became the canvas upon which marketers painted grand cultural and social aspirations. Journalist Rebecca Nicholson coined the term 'wackaging' to describe the overly friendly and irritating way brands that sought to convince us they were more than just a product.

Dove's 'Campaign for Real Beauty', now widely criticized by media commentators and consumers for being patronizing and cynical, was hailed at the time for empowering and liberating women from unhealthy standards of beauty.[5-8] It too spawned an army of imitators, keen to profit from the goodwill generated by promoting female empowerment. Pantene shampoo had 'Strong is Beautiful', Always had 'Like A Girl' – each competing to be seen as the brand that cares the most that you feel good in your own skin, regardless of your many imperfections, which of course were fixable with the products these brands were promoting.

Brands were now selling narratives and ideals. Consumers were taught to care about 'look and feel', brand purpose and higher good. They were tricked into thinking brands shared their cultural and social values.

Even as far back as 2008, before the Stengel 50 and before social media truly gave consumers the means to criticize them for it, brands were falling short of their own stated ideals. As a result, the industry tasked with the stewardship of brand perceptions and reputation has spent the last decade needlessly doing its level best to invite as much criticism as possible.

By striving to engage with consumers on a cultural level, organizations set themselves an almost impossible task. Facebook and Uber are just two of the many large organizations that failed to live up to their consumers' cultural expectations and when they said sorry, their apologies were robustly rejected by consumers and the media as a result. The mistrust in these purpose-driven businesses had been building for years.

Innocent Smoothies, who built a brand by tapping into environmental anxieties, promised us their products had a low carbon footprint. The product information on their smoothie bottles reassured us, in their signature tone of voice, that all of the fruit came from 'the countryside'. What the copy omitted to say was which countryside.

A 2006 investigation by the *Telegraph* revealed that it actually came from the countryside just outside Rotterdam, entirely at odds with 'the image of a cottage industry' that Innocent had invested heavily in projecting.[9]

Innocent knew consumers would be happier picturing a generic countryside, no matter where it happened to be and the environmental cost of its location relative to the UK, than a fruit processing facility on an industrial estate somewhere in the UK. So they sold us that idea. Innocent and brands like them had found a way to use the distinctive language of social purpose to conceal the commercial realities of building a smoothie empire.

Sam Chase from the environmental campaign group Rising Tide called it 'greenwashing', adding that: 'People will be happy to pay more for a product if they feel it is environmentally friendly... You pay a premium for feeling good about yourself.'[10]

Consumers are practically daring brands to let them down and will gladly take offence over the way something looks.

For many organizations, purpose, culture, high ethics, whatever we want to call it, was only ever a marketing strategy. Brands had a found way to profit from repackaging our own social and cultural anxieties – carbon footprint and body image to name two – and selling a partial solution back to us at a premium. This audacious deception, coupled with the consumer megaphone of social media, has left these brands frequently and visibly falling short of the expectations they invited their audiences to set. With such high moral and cultural expectations, it's no surprise that consumers are now so vigilant. Consumers are practically daring brands to let them down and will gladly take offence over the way something looks.

Resetting the unrealistic expectations that consumers have of organizations isn't a particularly appetizing task. It would take years to accomplish and cost untold millions of pounds. But saying sorry all the time isn't a great idea either. A near-constant state of corporate contrition does nothing to help organizations protect or improve their reputations and risks further eroding the fragile trust between organizations and consumers.

Expectation management, a chronically overlooked and underused tool in the modern communications toolbox, is just not fashionable any more. Organizations, having promised the earth to their audiences, are now nervous about having their cultures publicly examined. They did what the expensive consultants told them to: they assured their consumers they shared their values, that they too were concerned about social justice, the environment, body image and an entire catalogue of easy-to-market causes. They forgot to remind their consumers that they also exist to sell products, deliver services and make money.

The exceptions that prove the rule

There are a few organizations that got social purpose right first time. These organizations can pursue social goals and sell products at the same time. Since 1985 the outdoor clothing brand Patagonia has donated 1 per cent of sales, more than $89 million in total, to environmental causes. They have a transparent supply chain and create resilient products that last, benefiting the consumer and the environment. In 2016, they closed stores to allow US employees a paid day off to vote in the presidential election.

Patagonia's European marketing director Alex Weller understands the difference between authentic social purpose – the expensive kind that requires dedication and ideas – and the other kind, marketing campaigns dressed up as a social conscience. 'You can't reverse into a mission and values through marketing. The organizations that are struggling with this are probably the ones that are thinking about marketing first.'[11]

Ice cream maker Ben & Jerry's does social purpose properly too. Since 1988 they've been donating to the peace-building initiative 1% For Peace. They even launched the Peace Pop to facilitate this. They've been offsetting their carbon emissions since 2006 and opposing Arctic oil drilling since 2005. They adopt edgier, less mainstream causes too, such as the Occupy movement. They take risks with their brand to support the causes they believe in.

But both Patagonia and Ben & Jerry's built their companies on foundations of transparency and accountability long before the Stengel 50 made it cool. This has permitted them to pursue these ideals authentically, while running hugely successful businesses at the same time. So when they do receive criticism, they have the confidence to explain without apologizing.

When Ben & Jerry's launched a new ice cream flavour called 'Resist' in October 2018, they knew they'd invite criticism. It was essentially an anti-Trump campaign and involved the controversial activist Linda Sarsour. The ice cream maker, founded by Ben Cohen and Jerry Greenfield, both Jewish, was criticized for its partnership with Sarsour, a prominent critic of Israel whose views were described by the Anti-Defamation League as 'problematic'.[12] *The Times of Israel* said 'the flavour gives Israelis brain freeze', Israeli customers threatened to boycott and the Ben & Jerry's Israeli franchise refused to stock the product.[13]

Ben & Jerry's didn't apologize. But they did explain. 'Thanks for the feedback. We may not agree on everything, but the work that Linda has done to promote women's rights is undeniably important and we are proud to join her in that effort.'[14]

How simple was that? Ben & Jerry's were sure of their ground. Years of authentic commitment to social causes empowered them to explain without saying sorry. The organizations Alex Weller describes as 'thinking about marketing first', who conned consumers with an out-of-the-box, social purpose 101 approach, can't do what Ben & Jerry's did.

They don't have the same wiggle room when their commercial realities and cultural preoccupations conflict and they don't have the confidence in their own authenticity to stand firm. These are the organizations that so often find themselves apologizing when what they actually owe is an explanation.

Performative crisis management

For some brands, being sorry has become a form of performance art. After an edited clip of a Dove skincare advert circulated on social media, Unilever, the brand's owner, was criticized for being 'tone deaf'.

The ad featured a sequence of models of various races, removing their T-shirts to reveal the natural complexion of the next model. The edit that circulated made it look, incorrectly, like a classic before and after skincare advert set-up.

People were upset that a black model was used as the 'before' and a white model as the 'after'. *For some brands,* Lola Ogunyemi, the black model who *being sorry has* featured in the advert, defended the campaign, explaining that the clip didn't reflect the *become a form of* context. Dove didn't have the same confidence. Too nervous to explain, they just said *performance art.* sorry. The backlash escalated nonetheless, which led to calls for a Dove boycott, forcing Unilever to abandon the entire campaign. An expensive decision no doubt influenced by the fact that the authenticity of Dove's commitment to social purpose had been scrutinized in the past.

If organizations did commit more to explaining and less to apologizing, they could simultaneously help rescue the word 'sorry' from the dustbin of irrelevance and repair some of the damage their previously eccentric apologizing habits have done to consumer perceptions.

Sometimes though, even a solid history of 'social good' isn't enough to get you out of trouble. University College London calls itself 'London's Global University'. It is one of the most revered academic institutions in the world with a proud history of progressivism, founded on deliberately secular values to make the institution accessible to students of all faiths.

It was also one of the first institutions in the UK to admit women on equal terms to men, back in 1878. These are the sort of solid social and cultural bonafides that should give any organization the confidence to explain rather than apologize.

It doesn't always work that way. Just before Christmas 2017, UCL sensed some anxiety from its students about the bad weather in London. So it sent out a festive tweet to let them know campus was open as usual:

> Dreaming of a white campus? Our campuses will be open and operating fully today, Monday 11 December, so please make your way in as planned. (We can't guarantee snow but we'll try!) #snowday #londonsnow'[15]

For anyone familiar with Irving Berlin's *White Christmas* – and there can't be too many who aren't – this is an obvious if somewhat cheesy joke. For a handful of people, who in that moment seemed unable to recall the best-selling Christmas song of all time, apparently this remark was UCL's way of expressing its commitment to racial purity and white supremacy.

A very tiny social media rumpus unfolded, driven entirely by the few people prepared to misunderstand the joke. By 'very tiny' we are talking about literally a handful of people demonstrating an impressive skill for detached credulity. Even the viral news outlets were staying away from this one for now.

Despite the obvious intention of the message, the university dutifully apologized, 24 hours and 28 minutes after it sent the original tweet:

We chose our words very poorly yesterday when thinking of [Bing Crosby's *White Christmas*]. We're sorry and we'll choose our words more carefully in the future.[16]

Within 24 hours of apologizing, the *Daily Mail*, the *Telegraph* and *Metro* had reported on both the apology and the tweet that caused it, prolonging UCL's embarrassment just long enough for *The Sun* and *The Times* to pile in later in the week. Pretty much all of the UK's mainstream national and local media covered it. The nation rolled its eyes.

All UCL needed to give was an explanation, if anything, and certainly not an apology. People weren't sincerely upset because the university was advancing dangerous ideas about the cultural make-up of its campus. They were upset that, with the right amount of bad faith, it could possibly look like they were. UCL's critics weren't protecting anyone here, they were just pleased to have a 'gotcha' moment. And lacking any plan to react, UCL had to let them have it. They were rhetorically outflanked by people pretending to be upset. They apologized because they didn't know what else to do.

Property website Zoopla found itself dealing with a similar, but even more trivial controversy, issuing a bizarre on-demand apology a few months after the UCL episode. Their blunder involved five talking crabs.

The advert, displayed on the London Underground network, featured a row of crabs, each with a house on its back instead of a shell, discussing how it was planning to sell its 'home'. The first crab says 'I'm selling my house on Zoopla', the second crab says 'me too', as do the third and fourth crab. The fifth crab calls crabs 2, 3 and 4 'copy crabs'. That's it. That's the advert. It appears to be utterly risk-free, almost timid.

But there's a problem just around the corner for Zoopla. Some consumers now expect organizations to anticipate any and all possible interpretation of what they say or do, and the attending cultural sensitivities, in advance. 'Me too', the line repeated by Zoopla's talking crabs, is no longer just an innocuous way of expressing agreement. The #metoo hashtag is a historically signif-icant movement in the fight against sexual harassment. It's the phrase that's given voice to vulnerable people facing sexual oppression around the world. Any advert that attempted to ridi-cule or hijack the term, the movement or its supporters would rightly expect to be criticized. But this wasn't that advert.

A few people sorely wanted it to be, accusing Zoopla of 'hijacking', 'mocking' and 'exploiting' the movement. But there's a world of difference between 'me too' and '#metoo'. The adver-tising industry trade magazine *Campaign* reported that

> consumers took to Twitter to call out what one user described as 'repulsive hijacking' saying 'the people responsible should be held to account and donations made to women's charities. Truly shameful if you profit from this disgusting ad.'[17]

There is no scenario in which a property website profits from mocking the #metoo movement. It's inconceivable that Zoopla had been attempting to 'hijack' anything or wanted to ridicule the movement. But Zoopla's apparent confidence that they were on safe ground with talking crabs was evidently misplaced. They hadn't anticipated the willingness of their audience to assume bad intent.

The Advertising Standards Authority has guidance for adverts that mock or ridicule. The guidance mainly covers protected characteristics like age, gender, race and disability towards which the agency rightly asks advertisers to be sensitive. Aside from these characteristics, the only other thing you're not really supposed to mock is religion. And even then it's sometimes OK:

> Anything that appears to mock a religious belief is also likely to be considered offensive. Incidental references to religion and light-hearted use of humour are, however, likely to be acceptable. The use of humour is an approach that requires advertisers to tread carefully.[18]

The ASA rejected the complaint about Zoopla's advert. A spokesperson said:

> While the ad does use the phrase 'me too' we consider that viewers of the ad are likely to interpret its use as the crabs all agreeing to sell their houses on Zoopla, rather than a reference to recent sexual harassment claims and the resulting #metoo campaign. Therefore, in that context, we consider it unlikely that the ad will cause serious or widespread offence and for that reason, the ad does not break the rules.[19]

The ASA could not have been any clearer. They were telling Zoopla that they understood their advert and its meaning and that they expected others would too. But Zoopla couldn't resist the temptation to apologize.

A spokesperson said:

> The aim of our latest ad campaign is to demonstrate, in our usual light-hearted tone of voice, that Zoopla is a popular and well-known property website when selling or renting a home. In no way was the ad intended to carry any other meaning or allude to any other context and we apologize for any offence it might have caused.[20]

There's a lot to criticize Zoopla's apology for: it is front-loaded with jarring peppiness, it's self-regarding and the tone switches half-way through to weak, vague contrition. The biggest issue with this apology is that it was entirely unnecessary. Zoopla had the perfect opportunity to not apologize. The advertising regulator had just told them their advert was fine.

The danger of giving away free gifts

Stationery and gift shop Paperchase was similarly stung by an advert. In this case though, it wasn't the content of the advert that exposed its audience's reactionary willingness to assume the worst intent. Paperchase's major sin was offering free gifts as part of a national newspaper Christmas promotion. The problem was it chose the wrong newspaper.

Campaign group Stop Funding Hate, who use social media to highlight which companies advertise with newspapers they deem to be spreading hate, tweeted, tagging in Paperchase: 'After a torrid few weeks of divisive stories about trans people, is a Daily Mail promotion what customers want to see from @FromPaperchase?'[21]

Paperchase hadn't been singled out here. Stop Funding Hate do this to every advertiser they can find who spends money with publishers they suspect of spreading hateful messages. Paperchase didn't immediately apologize. They posted a tweet of their own in response:

> Thank you for taking time to share your opinion. We genuinely like to know what customers think about us – even though on this occasion some of your feedback is uncomfortable to hear. We promise to review in detail all customer feedback on this promotion.[22]

Then they waited. They gave it almost a day, and then they apologized, in the style of a freshly reprimanded school child:

> We've listened to you about this weekend's newspaper promotion. We now know we were wrong to do this – we're truly sorry and we won't ever do it again. Thanks for telling us what you really think and we apologize if we have let you down on this one. Lesson learned.[23]

Paperchase are of course perfectly entitled to advertise in the *Daily Mail*. They are also perfectly entitled to apologize for it, if that's what they believe they should do. They were in a difficult situation and decided on balance that they should say sorry.

Paperchase didn't apologize reflexively. They asked Twitter if they should apologize. What they crucially didn't realize is that the people they asked were not entirely representative of the people who buy their wrapping paper. The people they were relying on to tell them honestly if they've made a mistake were followers of Stop Funding Hate. These were precisely the demographic who were angry with them in the first place.

In crowdsourcing their communications strategy to Twitter, Paperchase absolved themselves of the self-reflection required to inform a robust crisis management policy. It bears repeating that Paperchase had done nothing wrong. They did something that looked wrong to some people.

Their decision to say sorry speaks as much to their own anxieties of how they're perceived generally as it does to a desire to retain customers. Every communications decision has a cost, whether that's cash, time or energy. For many organizations, the cost of explaining and setting the record straight is higher than the cost of just saying sorry and hoping the problem goes away. But when there's nothing specific to say sorry for, these apologies ring hollow.

How bad would it really have been for Paperchase to take the Ben & Jerry's approach?: 'We don't agree with everything the *Daily Mail* says, but we wanted to give away some wrapping paper and they've got millions of readers.' And how bad would it have been for Dove to say 'actually that clip makes it look worse than it is. Here's the original...'?

It's a risk, but no more risky than apologizing and unlikely to be more costly. Dove and Paperchase said sorry, but they still ended up binning their campaigns. The current status quo of endless reflexive apologies can't work for ever. Apologizing for how things look rather than defending how things actually are ('we're running a promotion to give away wrapping paper') is entirely performative. There's scant reputational value in it.

So what's the point? It can't be for the benefit of any victim, because there isn't one. It's for the organization's 'audience' – that powerful demographic of loyal customers, non-customers and media influencers who see it as their role to critique and police the content of organizational communications.

Performative crisis management relies heavily on cooperation between audience and organization. Both sides of a cultural crisis, for example, in the UCL case those who didn't get the joke and the university social media team who made it, are required to suspend their disbelief and enter into an undignified public charade.

Those criticizing the joke must ignore the obvious reality that UCL wasn't asking if they dreamed of a 'white campus' in the Jim Crow sense, but in the Bing Crosby sense. UCL is required to ignore the obvious reality that most people know this to be the case.

Self-service apologies

It's impossible for any organization to live up to the standards of moral idealism to which they purport to strive. Especially when they use it to post-rationalize their bad decisions. When Pepsi tried its hand at a bit of 'social good', they ended up producing what *Ad Week* called 'one of the most reviled ads in recent memory'.[24] The ad essentially saw Pepsi attempting to position itself as the official drink of the United States' resistance movement, with television personality Kendall Jenner as its star, dishing out the drink in the middle of what appeared to be a Pepsi-sponsored Black Lives Matter march.

Pepsi's ad backfired, obviously – Martin Luther King's daughter Bernice even mocked it, tweeting a picture of her father being manhandled by police with the caption: 'If only Daddy would have known about the power of #Pepsi.'[25] But more impressive than the distance by which it missed the mark was the speed with which the message sailed past its intended target. The ad was launched, ridiculed, parodied, removed and apologized for all within a single day. A sequence of events that typically takes at least a couple of days unfolded so rapidly that it looked almost as if Pepsi had its apology prepared in advance, just in case. All the rest of us needed to do was press the right buttons and their apology would drop from the vending machine – to people watching it unfold, it must have looked like the world's first self-service apology.

A spokesperson for the drinks company said: 'Pepsi was trying to project a global message of unity, peace and understanding. Clearly we missed the mark, and we apologize.'[26] Pepsi's apology illuminated brilliantly the problem with the new, post-Stengel social contract between organizations and their consumers: organizations contrive to be seen as inherently good, they fail, we complain, they apologize.

The creative cost of reflexive apologies

Giving an apology in the hope that people will leave you alone does nothing to enhance an organization's reputation. It does, however, devalue the word 'sorry' and set unrealistic standards of future conduct. If Zoopla are going to apologize for their talking crabs, what else will they apologize for?

Central to a credible, sincere apology is a demonstrated commitment to doing better in future. By saying sorry and accepting blame when none is due, organizations set themselves an impossible task. An organization cannot sincerely commit to doing better when deep down they don't really think they did anything wrong.

By saying sorry and accepting blame when none is due, organizations set themselves an impossible task.

To what improvement, if anything, could UCL, Zoopla or Paperchase have plausibly committed? That they won't ever again make a joke that some people won't enjoy? That they'll consider every possible interpretation of their messaging and eliminate anything with the potential to offend? The only thing to which they can commit are the woolly and impossible-to-define goals of being more thoughtful or choosing their words more carefully. This isn't a communications strategy. It's a timorous concession to their own corporate anxiety.

Apologizing when you've messed up is good and necessary. It's how organizations repair damage and reassure customers they're being taken seriously. JetBlue, for example, can plausibly commit to improvement through their customer bill of rights. That's a specific commitment to a specific improvement. But when organizations are apologizing simply for how they're perceived by others, not what they've actually done, they can't commit to any sort of improvement because they can't control how they are perceived.

This approach is difficult to sustain and bad for business. Imagine how much extra planning and focus-grouping organizations must have done in the aftermath of the above controversies to avoid a repeat. Worse than any cost to the business, is the cost to creativity. In seeking to avoid criticism, advertisers, marketers and professional communicators will be hamstrung trying not to enter an ever-expanding cultural exclusion zone.

We're lucky to be living in a post-deferential age, free from old-fashioned cultural authoritarianism. If organizations really are about to promise that people will never be offended again, as they appear to be doing, we risk returning to an era of cultural deference. Organizations will find themselves treating even the smallest slips in the same way the clergy, aristocrats, judges and public bodies demanded to be treated before we all outgrew the idea of deference.

The sacrifices required to hit the standards of moral purity organizations are setting themselves will be enormous. No more risks, no more punchy messaging. Everything will be calibrated to cause the least offence. Benetton's 'UNHATE' campaign, Sea Shepherd Conservation Society's 'See a tuna, think panda' – these iconic adverts worked because they challenged cultural and social orthodoxies.

How boring and grey will our communications landscape be if the main goal isn't to delight our customers and attract new ones, but to ensure above all else that we're not required to apologize.

One consolation of this situation is that it may hasten a return to the purifying blandness of brands just trying to sell us products we might like or need. And ironically, that approach might preserve some of the creativity and fun we stand to lose to the threat of moral hypervigilance. In fact, Oasis, the juice brand owned by Pepsi rival Coca-Cola, is already doing this.

Since 2015 Oasis has been running the #refreshingstuff campaign, a series of brutally honest and funny adverts across print, outdoor and broadcast. One billboard featured the strapline: 'It's summer. You're thirsty. We've got sales targets.' Another said: 'Please don't stand in front of this billboard. It cost a lot of money.' In a 2018 video campaign, Oasis appeared to take aim at the likes of Pepsi and others who strive so earnestly to portray a purpose.

The amusing spot featured a 'togetherness bottle', a preposterous double-necked vessel designed for two, drinking from each end to promote 'togetherness', an obvious swipe at, among others, Pepsi for promoting 'unity'. The narration, voiced in a winsome whisper characteristic of all such ads, says 'Harmony – just a few billion sales away'.

Not only has Oasis swum against the tide of brand purpose orthodoxy, it openly mocked it. And people loved it. The campaign won awards. So, it can be done. Brands can be honest about wanting to sell us stuff. This knowledge won't send consumers tumbling onto the fainting couch.

Until organizations stop pretending they want to fix the world's problems, one can of refreshing soft drink at a time, they'll always fall short of their customers' cultural expectations. A commitment to a more honest dialogue that doesn't involve selling impossible social ideals would relieve these organizations of the anxiety and accompanying requirement to apologize more often than they might be equipped to handle.

CHAPTER FIFTEEN

Optics anxiety and apologizing for how things look

Topman apologizes unreservedly for any offence caused by this T-shirt. The design was inspired by a Bob Marley track with the number referring to the year of re-release. The garment has been removed from sale online and in stores.
TOPMAN SPOKESPERSON, 16 MARCH 2018

Some people can easily anticipate the potential magnitude of tiny details. Others can't. University College London and Zoopla found out the hard way that the devil is often in the tiniest of tiny details. And attention to tiny detail is by no means a modern preoccupation.

In his 1782 autobiography, *The Confessions*, the Genevan philosopher Jean-Jacques Rousseau spoke of his anxiety at going into a bakery, fearing he was too extravagantly dressed. Buying bread was a task normally undertaken by his footman, but since Rousseau wanted the bread to accompany a bottle of wine he'd just stolen, he was on a solo mission. 'I could not bear to purchase it myself; how could a fine gentleman, with a sword at his side, enter a baker's shop to buy a small loaf of bread? It was utterly impossible.'[1]

It wasn't that Rousseau felt he was above going into an ordinary bakery. He just didn't want to have a 'let them eat cake' moment by striding into an ordinary bakery dressed in his finery while normal people went hungry. His recollection of this event is the genesis of the 'let them eat cake' remark misattributed to Queen Marie Antoinette. Rousseau wrote: 'At length I recollected the thoughtless saying of a great princess, who, on being informed that the country people had no bread, replied, "Let them eat cake!"' Rousseau clearly understood optics. He knew instinctively that an extravagantly dressed philosopher rocking up in that bakery at that time would be a bad look.

His ability to anticipate the view from every unflattering angle remains rare. In fact, inherited privilege can be a powerful inoculant against the foresight required to sense bad optics. And the British aristocracy are famously blessed in this regard. In early 2019 the Second Earl of Snowdon, fed up at the media portrayal of his late mother Princess Margaret as an out-of-touch socialite, started writing a book to set the record straight. On announcing his intent to write it, he made various attempts to promote her as a woman quite accustomed to the realities of plain living. The Earl recounted, without the slightest sniff of irony, that his mother's domestic qualities included making her own salmon mousse and washing her own chandeliers.[2] To an earl or a princess unburdened by a commoner's self-awareness, to wash one's own chandeliers is to have the common touch. To anyone else, making that point just looks silly.

The extravagantly named Richard Temple-Nugent-Brydges-Chandos-Grenville was the Third Duke of Buckingham and Chandos and lived until 1889. He too had an impressive inability to anticipate optics. In the book *Mad Toffs: The British upper classes at their best and worst*, author Patrick Scrivenor recalls how the Duke, when asked by an advisor if he'd consider dispensing with his personal pastry chef and making do with the other five chefs employed to keep him well fed, famously replied 'can't a chap have a biscuit?'[3]

British elite society might represent the high watermark of slapstick self-unawareness, but it can happen everywhere. And lacking the imagination required to anticipate optics is no barrier to advancement; corporations and their leaders can be equally as adept at missing the bigger picture as British toffs. Just ask BP.

The importance of small details in a crisis

The first time Akio Toyoda spoke publicly about the deadly 'unintended acceleration fault' in Toyota vehicles, caused in part by a design flaw with the floor mat, was at an event in Davos, Switzerland in January 2010. It was more than four months after the high-profile crash that killed a family of four in California, triggering the recall of more than nine million vehicles.[4,5] The Toyota chief executive and grandson of its founder Kiichiro Toyoda told gathered press: 'I am deeply sorry.' He explained that Toyota was still investigating the problem and promised that he guaranteed the safety of all Toyota drivers. A few hours later, he was seen driving from his hotel in a black Audi.[6]

This was a free lesson in bad optics and a classic example of something looking bad, despite not necessarily being bad. Toyoda lives in Japan, so it's fair to assume the car he was driving in Switzerland wasn't his own. Under other circumstances, Toyoda's happiness to drive whichever car his hosts had arranged for him could have been one of those 'everyman authenticity' PR wins heads of industry love. On the other hand, it's also fair to assume that someone might have told him that during such a massive crisis the chief executive of Toyota should not be driving an Audi.

As we saw with Tony Hayward's 'I want my life back' moment, boardroom occupants can become horribly disconnected from the realities of what their organizations do. Such disconnectedness leads to blind spots. How things *look* can be as important as how things *are*, even if every instinct compels us to believe otherwise. It shouldn't be like this but it is. Tiny details become huge visual metaphors. A badly designed floor mat, a black Audi – inconsequential without context, but massive with it. When a crisis unfolds, it's not easy for people watching to compute all the details. So the optics become emotional triggers.

After the 2008 MP expenses scandal, 389 members of the UK Parliament were told to repay money.[7] You might remember some of the names and some of the amounts. A few claims were in the hundreds of thousands of pounds bracket. Yet the one that really made people angry was Sir Peter Viggers' floating duck island.[8] It's the definitive image of the scandal, even though nobody actually saw the thing. It's just easier to picture a floating duck island in an MP's garden pond than to get your head around several sets of complex mortgage arrangements. Ironically, Viggers' claim was probably unsuccessful – paperwork showed that a claims officer had rejected his claim, so it's likely that not a single penny of public money went towards his infamous pond ornament.[9] But that doesn't matter. Viggers quit over his expense claims anyway. In a statement, he said: 'I have made a ridiculous and grave error of judgement. I am ashamed and humiliated and I apologize.'[10]

Politics really is the spiritual home of bad optics. One dubious image can linger forever, haunting careers and undermining credibility. 'How will it look?' is why we never see a British MP without a poppy during the UK's rigorously observed 'poppy watch' season during the first weeks of November. It's why MPs avoid being pictured near an 'exit' sign (imagine the fun picture editors would have with that). It's why former leader of the UK's Labour party Ed Miliband is still laughing off his inability to eat a bacon sandwich without looking weird.

Other industries have massive potential for bad optics too. Take the petrochemicals sector: fires, explosions, waste – all profoundly and immediately uneasy on the eye. Organizations like BP are exposed to acute risks because when they experience operational failures, the consequences can become a visual hellscape. Think of an oil spill. We understand instinctively how the consequences play out. Say 'oil spill' out loud and for most of us, the images of dying sea birds, baby seals with matted fur and formerly pristine beaches turned jet black are impossible to escape. Even if the oil spill is contained far out at sea, the visuals are already there.

It's no use trying to make a statement in front of a burning building.

Chris Lewis has more than 30 years' experience in the field of communications as founder and CEO of strategic communications agency LEWIS. He advises his clients to consider the visual details at all times when addressing a crisis: 'For broadcast TV for instance, consideration needs to be given to the backdrop. It's no use trying to make a statement in front of a burning building. The majority of the message is always visual.'

Optics anxiety

Bad optics is just a new way of describing an old problem. We can trace the origins of today's crisis management preoccupation to a 2011 article in the *Toronto Star*. Specifically to the following paragraph, in an article about the NATO-led military intervention Libya: 'US President Barack Obama temporized for weeks, worrying about the optics of waging war in another Arab state after the Iraq fiasco.'[11]

This was one of the first times 'optics' had been used in the mainstream press in that context. Less than a month after this article was published, the MacMillan dictionary designated 'optics' as its buzzword of the week, saying: 'This trendy new metaphor's journey into popular use has been kick-started by the current conflict in Libya, as for example illustrated by this recent quote from Canada's *Toronto Star*.'[12]

Author Kerry Maxwell concluded in her critique of the buzzword: 'In a nutshell, the use of optics characterizes a situation in which a person or organization worries about the public perception of a decision more than the substance of the decision itself.'[13]

It's a very risky strategy to focus excessively on how things *look*. Mundane operational realities are boring but important and Maxwell's summary of optics neatly distils two important issues affecting modern corporate communications. Organizations and leaders are either ignoring optics completely, or fixating on them too much. There really isn't much of a middle ground. It's why organizations apologize for high-visibility trivialities, but ignore serious but mundane problems that fly under the radar. Tesco was desperate to say sorry for upsetting the fans of the *Black Panther* movie, but when challenged via social media about misleading food packaging, they could barely muster a shrug in the direction of the farmer who'd pointed out the problem. In a world where visuals inform opinions, it sometimes doesn't matter if what you do is good, if it has the potential to look bad. You're only as good as your optics.

> It's a very risky strategy to focus excessively on how things look.

Topman vs the people of Liverpool

Topman have made some humiliating apologies in their time. In 2011 they apologized for selling a T-shirt that appeared to make fun of domestic violence.[14] In 2014 they accidentally included Nazi insignia on a men's jacket.[15] They said sorry for both mistakes. They have form for creating their own problems.

However, in 2018 through very little fault of their own they found themselves in a situation so complex and teeming with bad optics that even their harshest critics might have been lenient with them, had it not been such an irresistible news story. What started as a misunderstanding over a T-shirt rapidly morphed into a major conspiracy theory which at its zenith had some people sincerely believing that Topman was mocking the victims of the worst disaster in British sporting history. A Member of Parliament, a victim's advocacy group, a fashion professor and the national media all piled in and eventually, after a thorough public shaming, Topman issued an apology that did nobody any good at all.

Unsurprisingly, the misunderstanding started on Twitter. To get close to understanding this particular misunderstanding – and it does take some understanding – you need to be familiar with two things: the 1989 Hillsborough disaster, in which 96 Liverpool FC fans tragically died, and Bob Marley's back catalogue, including B-sides and remixes. To understand one without the other will lead to problems, as Topman found out.

The trouble started when a Twitter user spotted a Topman T-shirt featuring the slogan 'what goes around comes around'. That's a Bob Marley song title. It's also an offensive slur expressed by a minority of football fans about the Hillsborough disaster. The T-shirt also featured the number 96. That's the year the definitive remix of Marley's song was released. In a truly horrible coincidence, it's also the number of people who died in the Hillsborough disaster.

These weren't the only problems. The T-shirt was red, the colour in which Liverpool FC play. It featured a rose, the symbol of Yorkshire, where the Hillsborough disaster happened. Roses are often laid at Hillsborough tributes. When you combine all of these elements and look at the T-shirt through the lens of an entire city's legitimate trauma and grief, it's easy to see why people got upset, as many people did. The optics are awful.

If you look at it through the lens of a (presumably) young and potentially non-British fashion designer referencing Bob Marley's back catalogue, it's easy to miss all of these connotations altogether, as many people did.

'Topman apology incoming'

This controversy turned into a cultural tug-of-war. Holding one end of the rope were those who wanted the T-shirt removed immediately and for Topman to apologize. Most of the people affiliated with Liverpool or its football team were on this side. For them, the optics were the most important thing. No amount of explanations would satisfy them that this wasn't a deliberate dig at the city of Liverpool.

Holding the other end of the rope were those happy to put the whole thing down to a coincidence and move on. These were mainly people with no connection to Liverpool who saw the T-shirt as nothing more than the intended tribute to Bob Marley. For them, the operational realities were the important thing. Topman was stuck in the middle, completely paralysed. Almost everyone involved agreed on one thing; it was an unfortunate coincidence that looked a lot worse than it should. The problem was what to do about it and some people just wanted heads on sticks.

We can't fairly attribute the entirety of this cultural crisis to optics. If optics describe how things look, Topman had also to consider who was looking. Within 24 hours of the first tweet about the T-shirt, a Merseyside MP tweeted Topman and without necessarily realizing it, summed up the difficulty for any organization dealing an optics problem: 'No idea what is behind this, but it is very unfortunate. Hope you can discontinue the T-shirt asap please.'[16]

Very unfortunate indeed. Setting aside for a moment the logic and ethics of requesting a retailer removes a product because 'it's unfortunate', this intervention marks a watershed moment in the crisis. Topman's problem is no longer simply a consumer satisfaction issue; it's a political issue.

It's always tricky for an organization to handle social media criticism when politicians involve themselves. Their influence isn't necessarily any greater than that of a normal consumer when confined to Twitter itself. This MP has a modest 40,000 or so followers, but the media spin potential becomes a lot more tasty. The headlines change from 'consumers criticize retailer' to 'MP demands retailer withdraws product'.

The consumers criticizing Topman understood very clearly their role in this situation too. One Twitter user posted on 15 March: 'Topman apology incoming...'. This was rapidly becoming the sort of situation you could only watch through your fingers.

Worse was still to come though. Once the Hillsborough Family Support Group was invited to comment, it really heaped shame onto Topman. In seeking comment from the families of survivors, the media were effectively asking them to revisit their trauma to get a vox-pop. The T-shirt was now being directly associated with the victims of a major tragedy. Topman must have been suffocating under the weight of bad optics. How could they do anything other than say sorry? Even though they hadn't *really* done anything wrong.

Topman wasn't really the villain of this piece. The viral news media and their mainstream colleagues played a crucial role in amplifying the negative optics, quoting the most excitable social media comments in their headlines and portraying Topman from every unflattering angle possible:

Topman under fire after releasing 'insulting Hillsborough disaster T-shirt' – *Metro*.[17]

Topman stops selling red '96' T-shirt after fury from Liverpool fans and Hillsborough survivors – *Independent*.[18]

Topman 96 shirt: Red top which 'inadvertently mocks Hillsborough disaster' with 'what goes around' slogan is slammed – *The Standard* (which seemed unduly alarmist.)[19]

Of course, it's naive to expect headline writers to show restraint when there are outrage clicks to be had, but in centring the most eccentric social media reactions, they went out of their way to make life even harder for Topman. It just seemed a bit mean.

It's naive to expect headline writers to show restraint when there are outrage clicks to be had.

To the dispassionate eye, this was nothing more than an unfortunate coincidence. But optics really do matter. Topman never had a chance to exit the scenario with dignity. Their apology was on the cards before they even knew what was happening. The weight of public expectation and the skew of the narrative made it impossible to do anything else. How can you not apologize when an MP and victim advocacy groups invoke the tragic deaths of 96 football supporters?

Optics aside, Topman's misfortune raises a broader question about an organization's responsibilities to anticipate cultural sensitivity. The critics were right to ask questions. Had Topman known about the potential associations with the disaster and ploughed on anyway? Probably not. Were they morally obliged to avoid offending people? Again probably not. It's far more likely they were in the dark about the whole thing until it was pointed out to them. Why would they subject themselves to such humiliation and expense?

Topman apologized nonetheless and this is one of those rare occasions where you just have to accept that they didn't have a choice. As much as we might want to resist giving impulsive, hollow apologies, there was no crisis management approach available to them that didn't involve saying sorry. The only way Topman could gain permission to explain itself was by leading with an apology:

> Topman apologizes unreservedly for any offence caused by this T-shirt. The design was inspired by a Bob Marley track with the number referring to the year of re-release. The garment has been removed from sale online and in stores.[20]

Despite the heavy turbulence Topman had experienced and the frankness of their apology, it wasn't enough. It was never going to be enough. For a start, people were upset that they'd posted their apology to their customer service account, rather than the more popular main Twitter account. So Topman posted a second, longer apology to their main Twitter account. It read:

> We are sorry. Topman apologizes unreservedly for any offence caused by our 'Goes Around' T-shirt. It was never our intention to cause any offence; the design was inspired by a Bob Marley track with the number referring to the year of re-release. We have removed the item from sale online and in our stores with our sincerest apologies.

In other words, 'you win'. That wasn't enough either. Once Topman had said sorry for a second time, those who'd demanded their contrition moved on to the bonus level of the outrage cycle: calls for sackings. Numerous Twitter users went from demanding an apology to demanding someone, anyone, lose their job. All of this because of how something looked.

The cost of caring about optics

Topman is an extreme example of how optics alone have the potential to trip up any organization going about its business. They fell into this crisis through sheer bad luck. Some organizations actually volunteer themselves for that same level of public scrutiny.

Paperchase asked Twitter to tell them if advertising in the *Daily Mail* was bad, H&M attributed a product withdrawal to optics, saying: 'Because our customers have complained, we have chosen to recall the items.' Dove cancelled an entire advertising campaign because people thought a misleadingly edited version of it looked bad. The centrepiece of each associated apology was acquiescence: 'If you say it's bad, we'll get rid of it.'

Brands are now incorporating hurt feelings and skewed perceptions into their crisis management plans.

When 'how will it look?' becomes a key performance indicator on which organizations consent to be judged, they invite would-be critics to inspect the cultural virtue of everything they do, or don't do, from social media posts to product design. That breeds anxiety at all levels, from social media executive up to CEO.

Brands are now incorporating hurt feelings and skewed perceptions into their crisis management plans.

There's another downside too; caring this much about optics is expensive. Rivals to Paperchase will have been delighted to see the giant of the gift and stationery sector publicly promising it would never advertise to the *Daily Mail*'s 1.4 million daily readers ever again, instantly denying itself an obviously lucrative advertising channel unaffordable to its smaller competitors. The most virtuous thing about the Paperchase apology was the way they generously levelled the marketing playing field for their rivals, cutting themselves off at the knees in the process.

Two important things unite the most apologetic brands: optics anxiety, and the obvious absence of a plan for dealing with criticism. Sometimes organizations have to do things that won't look good, like cancelling flights in bad weather or recalling products that have been tampered with. It doesn't mean they're bad organizations. In those scenarios 'how will it look?' is a potentially catastrophic distraction. To protect how an organization's behaviour, culture and reputation is perceived, it's imperative to have a plan. That plan must promote a willingness to stick up for yourself on the basis of how things actually are. Topman was unlucky. They couldn't reasonably have avoided saying sorry. Paperchase, Tesco, UCL, Zoopla and countless other organizations had the option to show their working and explain, yet they chose to apologize.

Given these potentially enormous costs of being sorry, organizations owe it to themselves and their shareholders to treat contrition as a precious resource, not a hall pass to excuse them from explaining or defending their business decisions. It should take more than a social media frenzy to make an organization say sorry.

CHAPTER SIXTEEN

The true cost of corporate atonement

Why frontline staff pay the price

*We don't want to become a public bathroom,
but we're going to make the right decision 100 per cent
of the time and give people the key.*
HOWARD SCHULTZ, CHAIRMAN, STARBUCKS, MAY 2018

When a manager at a Philadelphia branch of Starbucks called the police on two customers in April 2018, he set off a chain of events that would transform Starbucks' entire corporate culture, cost it millions of dollars and dramatically alter public perceptions of the brand.

The store manager claimed the two men, Rashon Nelson and Donte Robinson, both of whom were black, had refused to leave after being declined access to the bathroom. The two men explained they were waiting for a business associate to arrive before they ordered their coffee and they'd asked to use the bathroom in the meantime.

Other customers reported seeing a white customer use the bathroom without making a purchase. When the police arrived, they arrested both Nelson and Robinson on suspicion of trespassing. For those watching, it looked like the manager and the police had racially discriminated against Nelson and Robinson. It took only a few hours for Starbucks to find itself dealing with a catastrophic cultural crisis that attracted global attention. A customer witnessing the arrest filmed what was happening and posted it to Twitter. The video was viewed more than three million times in the next four days.

It took only a few hours for Starbucks to find itself dealing with a catastrophic cultural crisis that attracted global attention.

After an initial, unsatisfying Twitter apology where Starbucks spoke of 'reviewing our policies', CEO Kevin Johnson tried again. He apologized publicly with a 392-word open letter – a letter that didn't contain the word 'sorry'.[1]

Further criticism came Starbucks' way, both about the original incident and the way they handled it, before the coffee chain vowed to temporarily shut down more than 8,000 of its stores at an estimated cost in lost sales of $16.7 million – and presumably to the delight of its retail competitors – in order to conduct implicit racial bias training.[2] This was a laudable move.

Starbucks was clearly trying to at least be seen to be doing something and the racial bias training was a credible offer of repair to Nelson, Robinson and other customers who were watching the crisis unfold. Starbucks had rightly identified an underlying corporate failure and wanted to put it right. Shortly after announcing the store closures, a third Starbucks' apology emerged, this time with a coupon code for a free coffee:

We're sorry. We know we can do better. Starbucks values all people of color and we are working on employee sensitivity training. The best dialogue starts over a cup of coffee and we'd like to buy you one.

This apology, although bearing all the hallmarks of a PR-approved corporate mea culpa, hadn't come from Starbucks. It was a fake that had gone viral. Internet pranksters, keen to exploit Starbucks' very public displays of contrition, convinced thousands that the store was giving away coffee to black people, as part of its post-crisis PR plan.

Trickle-down anxiety

Before Starbucks had even completed the bias training, their obvious anxiety and sensitivity to criticism became a source of comedy and ridicule. This wasn't going well at all.

Although the coupons were fake, they actually worked. Author and comedian Bryan Sharpe shared a now-deleted video of himself asking a Starbucks cashier for his free coffee. Sharpe, filming on his phone, entered the store and said: 'I heard y'all was racist, so I came to get my free coffee.'

The cashier's response would suggest that she believed the hoax coupons to be real, saying to Sharpe: 'Is that a real thing? I mean, I'll give it to you. Yeah I saw that on my Twitter last night,' before nervously but cheerfully handing over a free coffee over to Sharpe.

The fact that Starbucks' own employees couldn't discern between a real apology and the hoax suggests Starbucks was over-reaching in its attempts to convince the public that it was sorry.

The two victims, largely absent from the dialogue around how Starbucks had messed up so badly, settled with the city of Philadelphia for a symbolic $1 each and a commitment from the city to support young entrepreneurs with a grant of $200,000. Their issue was with the police that arrested them as much as it was with Starbucks.

Sharpe later explained that his prank was designed to mock the type of corporate sensitivity and 'white guilt' Starbucks was displaying.[3]

Nevertheless, Starbucks was praised for how it handled the situation. On paper this was a case study of good crisis management.

Starbucks did a lot of things right. They acted swiftly, made a sincere apology and an offer of repair. Their contrition wasn't in any doubt. Customer service expert Shep Hyken, writing in *Forbes* magazine, called it 'a perfect example of how to manage a brand crisis'.[4] There was something unsettling about the approval-seeking way in which they continued to manage the crisis though. Starbucks knew the world was watching and it over-functioned, clutching for redemptive narratives and putting undue onus on their lowest-paid staff as a result.

Approval-seeking policy changes

As well as shutting down stores, Starbucks introduced a policy that was potentially even more costly and posed more risk to their reputation. They scrapped their previous 'purchase necessary' bathroom policy in favour of allowing anyone to use their bathrooms free of charge, regardless of whether they had made a purchase. The thinking behind this policy was muddled and points to conflicting priorities. In their haste to generate some positive headlines, Starbucks conflated two entirely separate issues – the matter of who is permitted to use their bathroom and the matter of racial bias.

In their haste to generate some positive headlines, Starbucks conflated two entirely separate issues.

Businesses, even ones whose business model is predicated on people taking their time and lingering in-store, are entitled to have a bathroom policy that permits only paying customers using the facilities. Most coffee shops in large US cities have similar policies to prevent lingering from becoming loitering and attracting antisocial behaviour.

This crisis was never about whether the bathroom policy was fair in and of itself. It was about one manager who enforced that policy unfairly and escalated the situation by calling the police. Starbucks would already, in theory at least, be addressing that issue with their bias training.

'Purchase necessary' bathroom policies are controversial because they can exclude the most vulnerable people in society such as homeless people and addicts from accessing a safe, private space. But these were not the issues upon which Starbucks had failed. Rashon Nelson and Donte Robinson were neither homeless nor drug addicts. They just hadn't ordered their coffee yet. It was the biased enforcement of the policy, not the policy itself, that caused the problem.

This additional, unnecessary step of changing their bathroom policy undermines the trauma experienced by Rashon Nelson and Donte Robinson, two businessmen about to have a coffee meeting. Starbucks used the very specific trauma of two of its customers as a jumping-off point to address other areas of corporate policy.

To change their bathroom policy was to attempt to address a very broad church of other social issues from homelessness to addiction, both worthy causes, but categorically not the basis on which Starbucks had failed Nelson and Robinson, or within the scope of their experience of victimization. When the criticism is about fair enforcement of a policy, the answer should never be to be get rid of the policy altogether. That simply hides the symptom without addressing the cause. Starbucks' focus had shifted from managing how they responded, to

When the criticism is about fair enforcement of a policy, the answer should never be to be get rid of the policy altogether.

managing how people *perceived* their response. It should never be about that.

Who is really paying the price for Starbucks' mistake?

On the new policy, Starbucks' chairman Howard Schultz announced: 'We don't want to become a public bathroom, but we're going to make the right decision 100 per cent of the time and give people the key.'[5] In his eagerness to please, Schultz commits the entire Starbucks' workforce to an impossible standard of corporate morality. How can any company promise to make the right decision 100 per cent of the time? Imagine the pressure frontline staff would feel reading that. Especially when they know anyone with a smartphone can expose them to unwanted global media scrutiny.

And this perfectly highlights a major problem with theatrical, performative corporate crisis management. The people responsible for being publicly contrite are rarely the same people charged with implementing the changes.

The people who came up with the new bathroom policy change aren't the ones responsible for the cleaning, ensuring safety, handling the increased flow of foot-traffic into stores, or managing the risk of having an open-house restroom policy. That's a job for the low-paid coffee shop and security workers.

The people responsible for being publicly contrite are rarely... charged with implementing the changes.

To make matters worse, shortly after the bathroom announcement, Starbucks issued further guidelines on dealing with disruptive behaviour caused by the new policy, effectively watering down the original commitment to creating a welcoming, inclusive space by using vague qualifiers that would allow Starbucks to deny people access to their bathrooms anyway.

The 'disruptive behaviours' Starbucks cited included sleeping and talking too loudly, effectively rowing back their original commitment and introducing complexity to a decision-making process they promised their staff would get right '100 per cent of the time'. It was never going to be a completely open policy and Starbucks' management effectively created the exact type of uncertainty the revised policy sought to remove.

Starbucks, like many other organizations, passed the buck. They allowed their lowest-paid and most vulnerable staff to pay the price for failures that started in the boardroom. Starbucks management invited their customers and the media to hold their frontline staff to unfair levels of public scrutiny.

The cashier who was coerced into handing over free coffee, the staff tasked with making the right decision '100 per cent of the time', the staff who are now expected to keep the toilets clean despite them being available to everyone – these are the people paying the price for Starbucks' cultural failings.

Howard Shultz won't be required to meet these ambitious standards himself though. He stepped down as chairman a few weeks after making that promise. In January 2019, he announced that he was considering running for president.[6]

CHAPTER SEVENTEEN

The economics of saying sorry

Why an apology could cost $5 billion

My apologies for not being polite on the prior call.
ELON MUSK, 2018

When organizations do bad things, and sometimes even when they don't, they incur a reputational cost. Starbucks, United Airlines, H&M all saw their reputations set ablaze in trials-by-media. But the actual cost is almost impossible to quantify.

Lost custom might be a relatively safe analogy for reputational damage in some scenarios, but it's by no means a reliable bellwether across all sectors. Reputational damage metastasizes at different rates, depending on the dynamics of the sector. Assuming two organizations were embroiled in identical reputational crises, their respective industry conditions would dictate the rate of consumer attrition. Think of it this way. If your local fashion boutique unveiled an advert you found personally offensive, it would be quite easy for you to vote with your wallet.

If your bank, insurance provider or mobile phone company did it, you'd find it a lot more of a hassle to do the same.

Organizations operating in high-friction industries – where the degree of consumer choice is modulated by the ease with which consumers can exercise it – get away with things that their counterparts in low-friction industries can't. That's why in 2017 Uber sent apology letters only to customers in New York, where its rival Lyft was picking them up. They didn't extend the same courtesy to those without an alternative.

Reputational costs are real, but measuring them is like counting feathers in a pillow fight. You know you're losing them, but it's easier to stop the pillow fight than to measure the damage. Less difficult but by no means easy to measure are the costs associated with being sorry that come directly out of an organization's pocket. This is the actual money, dollars and cents, pounds and pence, that finds its way out of an organization's grasp while it's busy saying sorry.

What does being sorry actually cost?

Being sorry is expensive in two different ways. First, you have the operational costs of fixing whatever it is you're sorry about – plugging oil wells, withdrawing products and changing marketing material – the nuts-and-bolts fixes. And then you have to actually be sorry.

The simple act of apologizing isn't cheap.

Recalling the 31 million bottles of Tylenol on sale in the United States during the 1982 poisoning crisis cost Johnson & Johnson $100 million. It was just two months after the recall that Tylenol capsules were back on sale, this time in tamper-proof packaging. During those two months, Johnson & Johnson offered the pill form of Tylenol for free. In the same period of time, Tylenol went away and developed the tamper-proof packing we still use today. The recall, the free replacements, the lost sales and the rapid research and development of bringing an entirely new type of packaging to the market made this one of the most operationally expensive crises of its era. But it was also one of the best examples of crisis management we have. Johnson & Johnson were widely praised for their swift response and commitment to their consumers' safety.

Once the operational fires have been put out, organizations need to start thinking about the cost of making things right. That might include compensation and additional media spend to tell people how sorry they are. The simple act of apologizing isn't cheap. After the Deepwater Horizon oil spill, BP spent an estimated $50 million on apology adverts across broadcast and print.[1]

According to a YouGov poll of a thousand adults conducted on behalf of The Huffington Post, the impact was far from brilliant.[2] Three years after the spill, 59 per cent of respondents said the ads made no difference to their perceptions of BP; 11 per cent said they actually made their perceptions of BP worse; 28 per cent said the ads improved their view of BP; and 2 per cent didn't know.[3]

If you think that's a high cost to pay for mediocre results, it's pocket change compared to some apology campaigns. Uber splashed out 10 times that amount on their global apology tour after a litany of horrible PR stories and ineffective apologies. Fronted by new CEO Dara Khosrowshahi, their $500 million 'Moving Forward' campaign, incorporating TV ads, billboards and online media, focused around values rather than action.[4] It looked and felt exactly how you'd expect a tech company apology to look and feel. Khosrowshahi promised us that he'd been listening. He promised a new culture, a new direction and better service. Uber failed to mention exactly what they were going to do differently and people noticed.

'Uber is leaning on its "Moving Forward" message without any proof that they're changing the culture in any meaningful way', said Adweek's Bill Bourdon.[5] For all the expense, it felt a bit pointless. Compared with the lukewarm reception to BP's sackcloth and ashes performance, Uber's 'Moving Forward' campaign barely moved the needle. According to a study by on-demand insights platform Alpha, 29 per cent didn't remember seeing the ads, 32 per cent said they were undecided about whether to forgive Uber and 14 per cent said they explicitly did not forgive Uber. Just 31 per cent found it in their hearts to let bygones be bygones.[6] That's a lot of money to spend for not a lot of bridge-building.

Lessons from nature

Meaningful gestures aren't supposed to be cheap though. That's the point. This 'costly signalling' is part of the handicap principle proposed by biologist Amotz Zahavi to explain altruism, submissiveness and other ostensibly counter-evolutionary traits in nature. It's as true in the rainforests of Brazil or the open plains of the Serengeti as it is in the 'money where your mouth is' culture of the boardroom. The more costly a signal is to its sender, the more trustworthy it becomes to the recipient. It's why bowerbirds use precious energy constructing elaborate nests, impressing potential mates with all their spare energy. They're taking risks to prove something important. Nature has made the ability to identify bluffers and frauds an evolutionary imperative.

The more costly a signal is to its sender, the more trustworthy it becomes to the recipient.

Organizational communications work the same way. For a gesture to stand any chance of being trusted, it must come at a cost. Talk is cheap and anyone can say sorry. Being sorry, genuinely and sincerely sorry, *ought* to be more expensive than just saying it and when it is, it tends to be more sincere. So it makes sense that larger organizations issue apologies with eye-watering price tags attached.

This costly signal theory doesn't include the *operational* costs associated with doing something wrong, such as refunds and compensation. Organizations have to incur these costs for legal and regulatory reasons. For that reason, they don't confer high levels of sincerity. Consumers aren't that stupid. (This doesn't mean organizations aren't above passing off regulatory compliance as an act of generosity. How many GDPR compliance requests did you receive in 2018 that said 'we care about your privacy?')

The most serious apologies incur self-imposed costs, like H&M's voluntary product recall, Dove's marketing campaign alterations and the various apology adverts aired recently. 2018 was a particularly big year for apology ads. The breaks during June's NBA basketball finals alone featured apologies from Wells Fargo, Uber and Facebook at an estimated upfront unit cost of $760,243 each, not including the cost of production.[7,8] These were serious gestures of contrition not just because they were costly, but because the costs were voluntary. These are restitutions not compensation.

Restitutions and why 25,000 could be the magic number

In January 2019, after the disastrous PR role-playing exercise foreshadowing 'Papa' John Schnatter's exit from his own pizza company, Papa John's donated $500,000 to Bennett College, a financially struggling historically black college in North Carolina.[9] It was an obvious PR move from the new management, but an apparently small price to pay to start the long rebuilding process promised by new CEO Steve Ritchie in his second of three apologies for the conduct of his predecessor.

Ritchie said of the donation: 'In August 2018, I committed to establishing a corporate foundation, and I'm pleased that its first grant will go to an institution that shares our values of equity, fairness, respect and opportunity.'[10]

The City of Philadelphia, the organization ultimately responsible for the controversial and wrongful arrest at Starbucks of Rashon Nelson and Donte Robinson, found that being sorry left them out of pocket to the tune of $200,002. If the extra two dollars in that figure looks a bit odd, it's because Nelson and Robinson settled their lawsuit with the city for a dollar each on the condition that it donated $200,000 to a charity supporting young entrepreneurs.

Not all restitutions will pass muster. Topshop's 2018 £25,000 apology donation to the Girl Up charity 24 hours after cancelling a planned feminist book promotion seemed too reflexive to be sincere.[11] Polly Curtis, who launched the book display, later explained that the donation would have covered the losses that Girl Up could have expected from the book sales they missed out on.[12]

Earnest acts of restitution aren't a fast-track to forgiveness. A big part of how consumers react to these gestures depends on who is making them, and ultimately who is paying for them. One thing consumers don't want to do is to pay the bill themselves.

When it was revealed that the UK tax authorities had spent more than £10,000 on apology flowers to taxpayers it felt deserved an apology, it was effectively using the taxpayers' own money to placate them. The CEO of the TaxPayers' Alliance, called it a 'ridiculous and woefully inadequate way of apologizing to hard-pressed taxpayers who have been let down by the system'. HMRC said they thought it made for a more 'personal gesture'.[13]

Making a donation has become standard reputation management protocol, especially as a quick way of making amends for hurtful or offensive conduct. And for some reason, twenty-five thousand seems to be a popular amount, whatever the currency. Like Topshop, DKNY donated $25,000 after getting in trouble in 2013. Their apology dividend went to the YMCA charity at the behest of photographer Brandon Stanton after they used his pictures without permission. He initially asked for $100,000. Funding platform Kickstarter donated $25,000 to sexual violence charity RAINN after they featured a dating guide that promoted coercive and violent behaviour toward women.[14] In 2018, Irish airline Aer Lingus apologized for accusing staff of stealing, along with a €25,000 donation split between two charities.[15] Maybe this amount hits the sweet spot – not too big that it'll financially harm the giver, mostly wealthy public figures and organizations, but just big enough to seem meaningful.

What's an apology worth?

Restitutions give us an idea of the *cost* to an organization of apologizing, but tell us little about the *value*. Being sorry cost Topshop £25,000 and it cost Papa John's $500,000 (approximately £386,000). Does that mean that Papa John's apology was more valuable than Topshop's? Were they 15 times more sorry and the recipients of their apology 15 times more satisfied? It's unlikely. Since these are self-inflicted costs completely untouched by market forces, it's impossible to determine their actual value. The costs are arbitrary.

To understand the *value* of an apology, we need to know the theoretical financial cost to the organization in question had they *not* issued one. What was the potential damage? Measuring that is difficult for a variety of reasons, not least because once an apology is given, the potential damage of not apologizing goes away. The organization may still suffer reputational damage, but it can no longer be attributed to the lack of an apology.

One way we can measure the potential damage to an organization of not apologizing is to track their fortunes in the period of time between an apology becoming due and the apology being issued. This is where the stock market becomes useful.

Tesla's five billion dollar apology

In August 2018, Tesla CEO Elon Musk gave what investment bank KeyBanc Capital Markets called 'maybe the most valuable apology of all time' causing Tesla shares to surge 8.5 per cent, adding $4.75 billion to stock values.[16]

Having been rude to Wall Street analysts on a previous call, Musk was reportedly contrite on a subsequent quarterly post-earnings announcement conference call. But his apology wasn't just about soothing some wounded feelings, Musk was repairing his own credibility as a CEO.

CNBC reported that Musk said: 'My apologies for not being polite on the prior call.'[17] Ten words. Each one of them worth £475,000,000 to Tesla's stock value.

The apology has to be good though. A bad one can really damage a company's stock.[18] Netflix owed its customers an apology for around two months in 2011 after they'd raised their prices without explaining why. When CEO Reed Hastings finally did apologize, he glossed over important details, such as why prices had gone up in the first place and he even tried to smuggle in a new product launch with his apology, announcing a game-rental service. Shares fell by 7.4 per cent.[19]

The media and consumers may love an over-the-top emotional gesture of contrition, but the markets do not.

After news of the Facebook and Cambridge Analytica data breach scandal in March 2018, Facebook CEO Mark Zuckerberg apologized during an interview with CNN: 'This was a major breach of trust, and I'm really sorry that this happened.' Facebook stock promptly dropped 2.7 per cent.[20] Even the fortunes of privately held companies can give us a measure of apology value, or lack of. At the peak of their reputational problems, notwithstanding a string of public mea culpas, Uber's valuation dropped by an estimated $10 billion.[21] Saying sorry didn't repair the damage. CEO Travis Kalanick eventually left the company and Uber invested another $500 million in their apology tour.

It's all about credibility. The performance of management and their capacity to convince stakeholders that they can steer the ship in the right direction have a direct influence on stock value. When a CEO seesaws, so does the value of his or her company. United Airlines CEO Oscar Munoz' first attempt at apologizing for the now infamous 're-accommodation' scandal saw the stock of the airline's parent company, United Continental Holdings, drop 4 per cent. This wiped almost $1 billion off its market value. After Munoz's second, slightly better but by no means perfect apology, UCH's market value recovered by approximately $750 million.[22]

Investor confidence during a reputational crisis also depends on responses being proportionate. The media and consumers may love an over-the-top emotional gesture of contrition, but the markets do not. The 2018 study that highlighted the problems with Tesco's disproportionate levels of atonement – namely that apologies should be proportionate to the transgression to keep stock value from twitching – set out an organization's apology obligations very clearly: only do it if the thing you're being criticized for was really your fault. Making an unnecessary apology is just as damaging as withholding a necessary one: 'Both apologizing when the firm is not directly responsible for the crisis and failing to apologize when the firm is directly responsible reduce shareholder wealth.'[23]

Studies have also shown that for listed companies, investor confidence during a crisis is directly affected by whether the CEO or a less senior company representative handles the apology.[24] A good way of telling how seriously an organization is taking a given situation is how quickly they bring out their top executives and how readily they try to avoid doing so. Merlin Entertainments knew to bring out Nick Varney in the first instance. Not everyone does.

And of course, apologies can even be used as leverage in disputes. Many a lawsuit has been withdrawn only once an apology was made. In 2013, singer Bob Dylan was threatened with legal action by a Croatian community group for remarks he made in an interview. Group spokesperson Ivan Jurasinovic told the *Telegraph*: 'If he apologizes we will withdraw the suit. The aim is not to hurt anyone but to hopefully have him say that he didn't mean what he said and that he regrets it.'[25]

Is an apology worth $73,000?

The stock market might be useful for measuring investor confidence in real time, but it only applies to publicly traded businesses and excludes other types of organizations completely. Fortunately (for the purposes of this book at least), the infamously litigious world of US private healthcare is a model system for interrogating the actual value – to both recipient and giver – of an apology. To understand why, we can look to something that happened in Massachusetts in 1986.

For a few years, the state of Massachusetts was a legislative oddity. In 1986 it became the first and only state to introduce a law preventing the use of apologies as evidence of liability in medical malpractice claims.[26] This law made it possible for the state's healthcare providers to say sorry without fear of their apology being used against them as evidence of malpractice. Patients in receipt of an apology were still at liberty to sue – and plenty still did – but the apology itself was inadmissible as evidence of liability. In 2005, Senators Clinton and Obama co-sponsored the National MEDiC Act. This would have implemented apology laws nationally. As of 2018, 36 states had adopted the same or similar laws as Massachusetts.[27]

Outside of Massachusetts, the medical industry's attitude toward saying sorry, at least until around 2009 when the majority of state-level apology laws had been implemented,[28] was to simply never do it. Even if a patient had died. The legal brains advising the industry believed apologizing would invite lawsuits. As a result, families and patients were left without an apology on the assumption that if they got one, they'd use it against their healthcare provider.

Patients were left without an apology on the assumption that if they got one, they'd use it against their healthcare provider.

The fear of litigation wasn't just discouraging healthcare providers from offering words of comfort; it was causing them to avoid notifying patients of unexpected outcomes and medical errors. It fomented a climate of secrecy. Additionally, the anxiety and uncertainty around liability fostered a tendency for medical professionals to practise 'defensive medicine', including the expensive habit of ordering more diagnostic testing than necessary. Providers thought it better to order an extra test than get sued for negligence. This fear of litigation wasn't just reducing apologies; it was driving up the cost of healthcare.[29]

Because of the 1986 Massachusetts state law change, two big assumptions about medical malpractice litigation would eventually be proved to be false: firstly, that apologizing invited lawsuits; and secondly, that not apologizing reduced them. The opposites were true in both cases. A 2018 study led by Dr Michelle Mello, a Stanford University professor of health research and policy and also a professor of law found that 'malpractice claims frequently arise when plaintiffs perceive that the healthcare providers communicated poorly or attempted to cover up negligence'.[30] The study showed that patients were initiating lawsuits out of anger that they *hadn't* received an apology.[31]

With the broad implementation of 'apology laws', it became possible to compare the generalized difference in cost for organizations that say sorry and those that don't. A 2010 study into the efficacy of the state-level apology laws, entitled 'Does Sorry Work?' examined average payouts for claims made before and after the implementation of the laws.[32] The study found that these laws 'reduce the settlement of the most severe cases by $58,000–$73,000 per case and "somewhat" severe cases by $7,000~$14,000 per case'.

The study's authors Benjamin Ho, now associate professor of behavioural economics at Vassar, and Elaine Liu, now associate professor of economics at the University of Houston, concluded that the laws 'at least in the short run, induce faster settlements and lower payments for the malpractice cases with the most severe outcomes'. The authors also assert that patient anger is a motivator of litigation and that apologizing can reduce the number of lawsuits a healthcare provider faces, as well as the size of the payout.

The introduction of apology laws didn't just mean more patients received apologies when they deserved them. Healthcare providers benefited from lower settlement claims and everyone else benefited from the lower cost of healthcare insurance as a result.

CHAPTER EIGHTEEN

Crisis communications and the potential for mischief

How organizations profit from their rivals' apologies

*Creating an inclusive environment for everyone
is not just a goal; it's a big part of our culture.
Please send your record locator via DM.*
AMERICAN AIRLINES, NOVEMBER 2018

Considering all that it can cost an organization to apologize and put things right, the potential for mischief is obvious. And this mischief isn't just limited to Internet pranksters creating fake vouchers. Large businesses stand to profit directly from a rival's public embarrassment and many are prepared to invest time, money and creativity in doing so.

Burger King spotted the opportunity presented by KFC's 2018 chicken crisis and were quick to cash in with a marketing campaign offering discounted chicken to disgruntled KFC customers.

They even tracked down one particularly angry customer and offered her a year's supply of Burger King chicken 'King Boxes' for her troubles.

Similarly, when Ryanair had to apologize for cancellations and disruption caused by industrial action in the summer of 2018, it was rival carrier EasyJet who profited, posting a bumper £100 million boost in annual profits that it attributed to the 'one-off events' its rival was struggling with.

Operational crises present a window of opportunity in which organizations can and do exploit their rivals.

Operational crises like these present a window of opportunity in which organizations can and do exploit their rivals. But that window of opportunity is small. Once the chance is gone, it's gone. Cultural crises, though, present a much longer-standing opportunity and reward organizations prepared to play the long game, waiting for their chance to exploit the misfortune – or stupidity – of their competitors.

At least we're not Uber...

In 2017, such an opportunity came the way of US ridesharing app Lyft, who was ideally positioned to benefit hugely and publicly from rival Uber's cultural problems and the associated apologies.

Uber lost 200,000 users in January alone of that year after it was accused of undermining a protest and a New York City Taxi strike at JFK Airport. While unionized cab drivers were striking in solidarity with the protesters, Uber posted a tweet promoting their JFK Airport fares. They got the expected backlash and quickly apologized, but it didn't help. For many, this was the final straw and Uber's platform started leaking users. Lyft subsequently inherited a large chunk of Uber's unhappy customers. The exodus from Uber to Lyft was rapid. Once the

#deleteUber hashtag began trending, Lyft shot to the top of Apple app store.

It wasn't that Lyft had suddenly started offering a superior or cheaper service to Uber. Uber's mistake meant Lyft had simply become more culturally palatable by comparison, something they'd been banking on happening all along. Uber shooting itself in the foot was part of Lyft's growth strategy.

As political commentator and Vox.com editor-at-large Ezra Klein noted shortly after the zenith of Uber's cultural crisis, Lyft had always been happy to let their competitor take the risk of being the controversial pioneer, allowing them to battle the regulators, before Lyft then 'rolled behind with its dumb moustaches and friendly PR operation and did much of what Uber did without incurring the reputational cost'.[1] The 'dumb moustaches' Klein talks about are an integral part of Lyft's brand identity; friendly and quirky in contrast to Uber's slick, union-busting monochrome minimalism.

'For a competitor to benefit from that stumble,' concluded Klein, 'it would have to be able to give anxious riders what they wanted: a ride-hailing company that really did seem nice enough, an Uber alternative you could actually trust.'[2]

Brands can only apologize a finite number of times before consumers get sick of hearing them. Trust erodes quite quickly when consumers realize the apologies aren't accompanied by an overall improvement in conduct. In fact, according to a study by a team of economists examining the absolute cost of Uber's many apologies: 'Consumers who receive an apology hold firms to a higher standard in the future. If that future standard is violated, apologies backfire.'

'In some cases sending an apology is worse than sending nothing at all, particularly for repeated apologies.'[3] Uber's customers didn't just complain or demand more apologies, they voted with their feet. Uber, like Ryanair and the many other prolific apologizers, had used up their apology quota. 'Sorry' was no longer cutting it.

On-demand criticism – an $81 billion market that's ready to destroy your reputation

When consumers lose trust in a brand's values, it presents a potentially enormous dividend to its rivals, who are viewed more favourably solely by comparison. This is where things get very risky, especially for organizations in low-friction markets where it's easy for consumers to switch from one supplier to another, such as air travel or ridesharing.

When consumers lose trust in a brand's values, it presents a potentially enormous dividend to its rivals.

It doesn't take an enormous cognitive leap to imagine a world where organizations deliberately trigger a reputational crisis for a rival, subjecting them to a higher degree of public scrutiny than they are prepared for or equipped to handle. In fact, something similar has been happening for years.

In 2014, 11 of the world's top PR firms signed a joint letter promising not to edit their client's Wikipedia pages to hide criticism and promote positive stories. Katie Richards of Business Insider called this move for what it was – an amnesty:

> The statement is essentially an admission that for years PR agencies edited Wikipedia pages on their clients' behalf, ostensibly to remove 'errors' but also to delete negative information about companies and to add fluffy 'good news' points.[4]

Although these PR firms promised to leave their client pages alone, they never promised they wouldn't edit pages belonging to their clients' rivals. Although there's no evidence that any of the firms who signed the letter have indulged in this practice, it does happen.

So-called 'black PR', the dark art of using the Internet to smear an opponent or rival business in order to damage consumer trust, is actually commonplace. Tencent and Alibaba, two of the world's largest companies, were each found to be using the technique against the other in 2014, culminating in a large and alarming public spat. 'Noticeably, neither of the companies bothered to deny the smear campaigns, testimony to how widespread – and acceptable – the practice of "black PR" has become' said the *South China Morning Post*.[5]

A similar approach appears to be emerging in the USA. California-based flight comparison service CheapAir reported in August 2018 that it had been contacted by a group called STD Company. The group had threatened it with a 'review bombing' campaign – coordinating high volumes of negative reviews and negative social media posts, unless it paid a ransom.

CheapAir shared e-mails it had received with tech website Motherboard: 'We are experts in destroying personal or company reputation online,' threatened STD Company in an e-mail sent in August 2018.[6] STD Company even showed CheapAir a tweet that been posted that read: 'CheapAir is a total fraud! I have lost $1,440 and they ignore my e-mails. People stay away from @cheapair.'

This is precisely the sort of feedback for which an inexperienced and anxious social media executive would reflexively apologize. And we don't need to look beyond aviation, one of the most low-friction industries, to find examples of this.

In the week commencing 15 November 2018, American Airlines apologized on social media more than 700 times; many of those were in response to off-the-cuff complaints and trivial gripes. But a significant portion were cultural criticisms and at least 11 of those contained serious accusations about racism.

This is where criticism becomes culture shaming of the sort that can permanently damage a brand's reputation and make its competitors appear more desirable by comparison: 'Dante at LAX is the WORST and most RACIST customer service rep we have ever dealt with @AmericanAir. Never flying American Airlines again!'[7]

American responded to six of the racism accusations, each time referencing their own anti-racism policies. It took just eight minutes for American Airlines to reply to the above tweet, with this response: 'Creating an inclusive environment for everyone is not just a goal; it's a big part of our culture. Please send your record locator via DM.'[8]

American Airlines are focused on defending their culture. They know the damage the perceptions of a toxic culture can do to their bottom line and won't let criticisms of it pass without acknowledgement. Imagine the effort and cost of reacting to every single criticism online like this. If a rival airline wanted to, they could tie American Airlines up in knots by firing off automated cultural criticisms.

CheapAir CEO Jeff Klee appeared prepared to stand firm against the threat to his brand's reputation: 'We're definitely not going to pay these cyber thugs, but we still have to devote a lot of time and resources to combating it.'[9]

They did the smart thing getting ahead of this problem. It would have been harder to control the damage if they hadn't first outed the threat. The other approach would have been to apologize first, ask questions later. But once the apology is on record, an organization is as good as guilty.

Should any of these 'black PR' companies decide to pivot from review bombing for ransom to on-demand public shaming, there exists an eager market ready to pay a lot of money. The infrastructure and marketplace already exists for this to happen. Online influencers already get paid to promote brands online and as of 2018, 75 per cent of members of the Association of National Advertisers say they work with influencers.[10] What's to stop a black PR firm hiring an influencer to go after a client's rival, demanding apologies it can then hold against them? After all, the chances of an inexperienced (or crisis-fatigued) social media executive or indeed, a frontline employee like the Starbucks cashier, simply accepting what their critics say and agreeing, is alarmingly high.

In fact, it's probably happening right now. A number of prominent social media influencers in the beauty industry claim they've already been approached and offered sums in the region of $85,000 to talk negatively about brands.[11] Make-up artist and social media influencer Kevin James Bennett, who has more than 40,000 Instagram followers (as of December 2018), claimed to know of other influencers who would take money from brands to 'trash' their rivals online too.[12, 13]

Another prominent beauty influencer, James Charles, who has more than 10 million Instagram followers (as of December 2018) said: 'I personally have never been offered a slandering campaign but I'm sure it does happen.'[14]

Influencers don't even need to be real people. There exists a fashion whistleblower Instagram account, 'Diet Prada', with 970,000 followers (as of December 2018) whose sole remit is criticizing fashion brands for an assortment of transgressions, from ripping off designs to cultural appropriation.

Although the identities of the people running the account are now known, they were anonymous from their launch in December 2014 until going public in October 2017, by which point they'd built a substantial following and fearsome reputation for publicly humiliating well-known brands.

Diet Prada has already extracted 'clarifications' from some of the world's most powerful fashion brands, including Gucci and Kim Kardashian. Their attention even pressured US luxury department chain Nordstrom into removing items from one of its collections over allegations of copying jewellery designs.

Nordstrom said in a statement:

> We take situations like this seriously and partnered with Lulu DK and Danielle Bernstein to remove each of the pieces in question. We're excited to offer our customers the chance to shop the rest of the collection on May 9.[15]

And when Dolce & Gabbana suffered possibly its biggest cultural crisis – it's had a few, admittedly – Diet Prada was the catalyst. D&G put out an advert that was undeniably offensive to Chinese people. Diet Prada was among the first to call it out.

Diet Prada then shared what are believed to be private messages between Stefano Gabbana and the journalist Michaela Phuong, in which Gabbana defends the advert, before making insulting remarks about China and Chinese people.

The subsequent outcry saw D&G's products removed from Chinese websites, calls for a Chinese boycott and humiliatingly, D&G forced to cancel a show in Shanghai. Diet Prada was the primary influence behind the fashion giant's public humiliation. Vice Media's 'Garage' outlet said Diet Prada 'chronicled the scandal with an almost perverse delight'.[16]

The influencer economy is huge, in terms of reach and power, as well as revenue.

The influencer economy is huge, in terms of reach and power, as well as revenue. In 2016, brands spent $81 billion paying influencers to say the right things.[17] There's no suggestion that Diet Prada is paid by anyone to criticize fashion brands online. But there's clearly a marketplace for this sort of activity.

Influencers have the proven ability to destroy a brand's reputation overnight and some brand owners are terrified of the influence an influencer could have on them. Even fake influencers have the capacity to scare brands into submission. The owner of a well-known sunglasses brand told culture magazine *The Atlantic* that he'd initially been confused when social media accounts he'd never heard of or worked with had started behaving as if they were in a commercial partnership with his brand, going as far as thanking his brand in Instagram posts and publicly stating they were working with him.

These users, it transpired, were attempting to pass themselves off as 'genuine' influencers by adopting the behaviours of well-known accounts; namely declaring a partnership, thanking their sponsors and promoting their products. The owner of the sunglasses brand was too scared to ask them to stop, despite the potential for reputational risk the fake brand ambassadors represented.

'These people are looking for the most amount of attention, so if they want to make it seem like they've been wronged in any way by a brand, they will.'[18] For this brand owner, the fear of upsetting an obscure Instagram account outweighed the fear of being lied about in public.

A shadow influencer economy could – and probably will – grow rapidly just as soon as the market conditions are right. Considering what we know about black PR, influencer marketing and the opportunities presented when a rival is publicly forced to apologize, a world where agencies have rosters of 'activist' accounts that will go after their clients' rivals isn't too hard to imagine. If you think this is far-fetched, consider what happened when Google changed its algorithm to eliminate spam from its search results.

Interflora and the unintended consequences of fighting Internet spam

For a short time in February 2013, the flower delivery website Interflora disappeared from Google's search results.[19] A site that had previously appeared in the results for highly profitable search terms like 'send flowers' and 'flower delivery' had completely vanished. It wouldn't even show up if you searched for 'interflora'. The disappearance happened between Valentine's Day and Mother's Day, Interflora's busiest time of year.

Rival flower delivery companies would have been delighted to see the market leader in online flower delivery effectively wiped out from the market. Without spending an extra marketing penny, they were cleaning up, just like that. So what happened?

Prior to 2012, it was easy to improve a website's performance in Google's search results through buying 'spam' links. This practice formed an element of what is called search engine optimization or 'SEO'. These links, bought in bulk from low-quality websites, could fool Google's algorithm into perceiving a website as being more popular and useful than it actually was.

The more popular and useful Google perceived a website, the higher it would appear in the search results for relevant search terms. If a website could rank well for certain key phrases, for example, 'mortgages for bad credit' or 'injury compensation lawyer', the owner of the website could get very rich very quickly. So for a time it was highly profitable to quickly increase the number of visitors to a website by purchasing those spam links.

In 2012, Google sought to stop this. It introduced an algorithm update that could identify whether a website was in receipt of paid-for links. The update was designed to lower the prominence in Google's search engine of spammy sites that had previously exploited the backdoor method of ranking.

If Google suspected a website of continuing this practice after the update, someone in their anti-spam team could manually remove the website from its index – a catastrophic outcome, given Google's almost monopolistic grasp on the search engine sector.

Interflora was the canary in the coalmine for companies manipulating Google's results. Once word got around that Interflora was on Google's naughty step, a cottage industry offering 'negative SEO' services emerged almost instantly. For a price, you could do to your rivals what Google had done to Interflora. The mafia would have been proud.

The ruse caught on. Businesses diverted marketing budget away from promoting their own websites and into damaging their competitor's websites. Rival companies were executing hit jobs all over the Internet.[20]

The practice became so widespread that companies began developing software to detect 'negative search engine optimization' being directed at their website. Google introduced its own tool so website owners could 'disavow' any spammy links pointing to their own website, effectively offering amnesty to all of the businesses involved.

It was alarmingly easy for organizations to damage their rivals using nothing more than a PayPal account. Victims of negative SEO had to divert funds to monitoring the spam links pointing at their site and if they were hit, they had to spend further resource disavowing them so Google didn't punish them. Lots of people got very rich by either harming their rivals, selling negative SEO and selling the tools to fix it.

Apply this thinking to crisis management. Within the framework of outrage capitalism, the incentives for manufactured cultural criticisms are obvious. And it will predominantly be cultural, not operational, criticism that gets weaponized; the former being far harder to disprove than the latter. For a business to see their competitors grovel and incur the costs of apologizing for unfounded but hard-to-disprove cultural crisis is to see an opportunity for growth. The online infrastructure exists and the media appetite for organizational humiliation is strong. The only thing standing between an organization and the potentially massive dividends of negative influencer marketing and a confected 'culture problem' is a robust crisis communications plan that includes guidance on dealing with cultural criticism.

Businesses diverted marketing budget into damaging their competitor's websites.

A lot of organizations simply aren't ready to deal with this threat though, and maybe they never will be. The risk of being tainted by a culture problem, even through an unfounded accusation, can be too high to contemplate. Ryan Holiday, an American PR consultant, former director of marketing at American Apparel and author of *Trust Me, I'm Lying: Confessions of a media manipulator* sees little point in fighting accusations when they're cultural.[21] Speaking of a hypothetical client accused of racism or sexism. Holidays says: 'I would tell him to bend over and take it. And then I'd apologize. I'd tell him the whole system is broken and evil, and I'm sorry it's attacking him. But there's nothing that can be done.'[22]

CHAPTER NINETEEN

Apology laundering

How a supermarket and an MP
were defrauded of 'sorry'

We're not dictating who should eat this sandwich.
WAITROSE, OCTOBER 2018

Apologies aren't free and giving them isn't cheap. Public atonement is subject to layers of complexity with which private person-to-person apologies aren't encumbered. There's more riding on an apology when you have an audience. It can affect shareholder wealth and influence the outcome of lawsuits, not to mention the entire reputation of an organization.

There's hay to be made in the sunshine of public humiliation. We've explored how that worked for Lyft and Uber, Burger King and KFC and how on-demand criticism could be the next iteration of influencer marketing. The media has skin in the game too. It stands to profit from the humiliation of a public organization as much as its rivals do.

When an apology sufficiently abases its giver, the media coverage often takes on a tenor of faux concern that makes clicking to read hard to resist. It's tough to say no to a headline that promises us humiliation, especially if it's someone we don't like. Humiliation offers two value streams to the media: the obvious revenue gleaned from page views, and of course, the chance to indulge in some partisan revelry. Tribalism demands that every side join in and members of the mainstream media appear happy to revel in the humiliation of their industry rivals.

It's tough to say no to a headline that promises us humiliation.

'*Guardian* is forced into a humiliating apology for its Corbyn train film report written by a hardline supporter' said the *Daily Mail* in October 2016.[1] Their turn for humiliation would come. 'The *Daily Mail* forced to issue humiliating apology for misleading Paris article', said lifestyle magazine *Shortlist* in February 2019.[2]

Humiliating apologies are a great way for media outlets to pursue the political opponents of their readers too. 'Nicola Sturgeon issues humiliating apology after Alex Salmond wins legal case over sexual harassment enquiry' says the *Telegraph* in January 2019 while the *Daily Mirror* reported in March 2017, 'America issues humiliating apology to Britain over claims MI6 helped Barack Obama spy on Donald Trump.'[3,4]

Then there's the viral news media. They don't go unrewarded when an organization issues a degrading apology. The profit model of outrage capitalism demands they report as many organizational apologies as possible, dragging reader attention away from other things and inviting us all to get angry about a pair of socks or a badly worded advert.

Pay-per-view apologies

In 1998, Japan finally apologized to British prisoners of war held in Japan during World War II. It had been a long time coming. The apology was well put, Japanese Prime Minister Ryutaro Hashimoto expressed genuine remorse, adding: 'This will not bring back the dead. But I hope the British people will see it in the spirit in which it is intended.'[5]

This apology wasn't notable only for its historical significance, but for how it was delivered. Hashimoto didn't go on TV or write a letter, he published his apology in *The Sun* newspaper. Shortly after publication, the BBC claimed that Downing Street had encouraged Ryutaro to apologize exclusively in *The Sun* and that they 'may have liaised with *The Sun*, which supported Labour in last year's election, to furnish them with the scoop'.[6] In what the *Independent*'s Joan Smith called 'the age of the privatized apology' the victims of Japan's conduct during World War II and intended recipients of Hashimoto's apology would actually have to pay to read it.[7]

The media has long facilitated the value exchange system that underpins the distribution and acquisition of public apologies. In accepting the reality of this pseudo-economic system, so must we accept the reality that apologies are – clearly and depressingly – transactional. And where transactions are made, fraud can flourish. People to whom an apology does not belong will often find themselves in possession of one nonetheless.

The comedian and *Guardian* columnist David Mitchell calls this 'the extortion racket in public life':

> Once you've demanded an apology, you can logically continue to demand it until you receive it. Often those called upon to apologize will do so just to silence the clamour – they can't match the complainants for bloody-mindedness.[8]

For the initiators of the most high-profile public humiliation – the advocacy groups, the Twitter influencers and the various self-appointed custodians of public conduct who make a hobby (or a career) from triggering product withdrawals, apologies and scrapped marketing campaigns – the gains in public influence can be impressive.

Gillian Duffy, recipient of an apology from Prime Minister Gordon Brown in 2010 (see Chapter 9), extracted an impressive amount of value from his mea culpa; her views on politics were still being sought by the mainstream media as late as 2016.[9] And in 2009, the formerly unknown Carl Larson was lauded as a hero when he pressured airline JetBlue into dropping their baggage charge for folding bikes. He received plenty of media coverage too. CNN hailed him as a pushy blogger who changed the airline industry.[10] Is there anyone who doesn't benefit when a corporate giant falls on its sword?

Even on the rare occasions that those called upon to say sorry refuse to do it, an apology can nonetheless make its way onto the public record. Understanding the perverse incentives of outrage capitalism, it would be naive to assume that the media's interest in apologies ends at simply reporting on them. They are a heavily invested participant in the outrage economy.

Apology laundering – how the media manipulated a row about relish

Only one employee at the UK-based Elsenham Quality Foods, makers of Gentleman's Relish, knows the recipe. It's a closely guarded trade secret adding mystique to the product's no doubt countless other charms. And because Gentleman's Relish is trade-marked, retailers need to be careful about what they call their products containing similarly configured anchovy pastes. Waitrose, faced with the challenge of simultaneously marketing the sand-wich and keeping the presumably watchful lawyers at Elsenham Quality Foods happy, had to come up with a name conspicuous enough to entice lovers of the delicious salty spread, without infringing Elsenham's rights. Hence the name 'Gentleman's Smoked Chicken Caesar Roll'.

When TV presenter, comic and prominent social media personality Amy Lamé spotted this particular chicken sandwich out in the wild, the packaging seemed to present her with a problem. The Gentleman's Smoked Chicken Caesar Roll she saw in a branch of Waitrose in October 2018 gave her cause to take issue with the apparent gendering of food products.

Lamé sent a friendly if somewhat sarcastic tweet to the official Waitrose account, tagging in the campaign group 'Everyday Sexism' with a picture of the offending product: 'I never knew sandwiches were gender specific. I'm female but thankfully @waitrose let me purchase this anyway.'[11]

Yes, it's a weird name for a sandwich. But the truth is, Waitrose was never marketing their sandwich at men. They were marketing it at fans of Gentleman's Relish. It's not clear whether Lamé genuinely believed Waitrose had intended to alienate her with this sandwich, or if she was simply drawing attention to the gendering of product names more generally. Nor was it actually important. For right or wrong, the call-out was on. Waitrose had a potential culture crisis on their hands.

Within 48 hours of her tweet, the *Telegraph*, the *Independent*, the *Express*, Fox News, *Daily Mail*, MSN, *The Sun*, and a range of local outlets had all reported on the so-called 'sexist sandwich' and the inevitable apology from Waitrose.[12–18]

As social media call-outs go, this one was pretty mild. By the end of 2018, the original tweet had been 'liked' just 186 times, retweeted 47 times and attracted 1,672 comments. It was hardly a viral sensation, but there was sufficient drama to pique the interest of viral news journalists.

The Sun reported that Waitrose was 'quick to apologize';[19] the *Independent* reported that Waitrose had apologized to 'anyone offended';[20] and dozens of smaller outlets ran similar lines, describing the humiliating climbdown for the retailer.

Waitrose's journey from Twitter opprobrium to humiliating apology may by now seem an ancient crisis management path. But in this particular episode, something was different. Waitrose never actually said sorry. Nor did they 'apologize', express 'regret' or even admit they'd 'got things wrong'. They didn't even distribute a statement. The only people who got a response on the matter were two journalists who rang the press office and asked for one. Both got the same response:

> It's never our intention to cause offence – we're not dictating who should eat this sandwich – we hope anyone who tries it will love the distinctive flavours. However, we are planning to change the name of the sandwich soon.[21]

That's not an apology. Yet pretty much all of the UK mainstream and much of the viral news media reported that one of the UK's best-known retail brands had said sorry for its sexist sandwich. How did this happen? The answer lies in this instance with the *Telegraph*. They were among the first to report on the situation and were first to get a statement from the Waitrose press office.

Admittedly, the statement does bear some of the characteristics of a modern corporate apology. It's meek, it contains a degree of moral licensing and it proposes a remedy. But it's categorically not an apology. Nor should it be. Waitrose didn't owe anyone an apology here. But that doesn't matter.

Once the *Telegraph* had reported that Waitrose had apologized, the retailer was cast as a humiliated victim of consumer power, shamed and forced to examine its obvious latent sexism. Waitrose had failed to live up to an arbitrary standard to which it never actually consented.

The media wasn't just reporting on an apology here; they'd actually created one from nothing.

Once the statement had been processed by the viral news media clearing house and stamped as 'sorry', it gained value as a media asset. It conferred social capital onto anyone offended by the sandwich. And it gave the media some outrage to write about. Waitrose became just another organization with a culture problem who said sorry.

The *Telegraph* reporter who first claimed that Waitrose had apologized, said he interpreted the words 'it's never our intention to cause offence' as Waitrose saying sorry. Laundering Waitrose's explanation into an apology in this way isn't some harmless act of poetic licence. That would be to assume that apologies don't come at a cost to the organization giving them. The statement Waitrose gave was deliberately and explicitly not an apology. At a time when organizations are reflexively apologetic, it's notable, but far less newsworthy, when one declines to say sorry.

The media wasn't just reporting on an apology here; they'd actually created one from nothing. It may seem like semantic quibbling. 'It's never our intention to cause offence' is apologetic in its tone, but – and this is worth repeating – it's not an apology. Given what we know about the impact on organizations of issuing a public apology, particularly as it relates to liability and the negative impact to shareholders of being seen to apologize when no apology is due, the media was the villain here. Not Waitrose.

The media has assumed the role of judge as well as jury. Organizations aren't sorry until the media tell us they're sorry, and even if they're not, that same media might decide that actually, they are. They do this while scrutinizing the sincerity and validity of the other corporate apologies they demanded on our behalf. But here they also fulfil a curious secondary function, laundering a bland corporate boilerplate so it comes out smelling like 'sorry' and creating a story where there never was one.

If this habit becomes a media norm, organizations will be faced with a challenge. Already anxious of accidentally admitting liability, they may be forced to issue categorical refusals of apology in case their clarifications are misinterpreted.

What was in it for the *Telegraph* to write this up as an apology when there are so many other actual apologies to write about? The viral news media has very specific tastes when it comes to outrage. It doesn't matter that consumers were well catered for already. Certain flavours of outrage become popular. The more we click on the headlines, the more of those same headlines we get.

Gentleman's Smoked Chicken Caesar Sandwichgate is inescapably trivial – a social media squabble over a sandwich that Waitrose wanted no part of. But the means by which their words were laundered to become a public apology are not trivial. It set them on a path to humiliation.

The more we click on the headlines, the more of those same headlines we get.

When, just over six months later, they put out an 'Ugly Duckling' themed Easter chocolate trio, they found themselves faced with yet more eccentrically trivial criticisms. This time people were accusing Waitrose of being racist, because the dark chocolate duckling was the 'ugly' duckling (the white chocolate duck was 'fluffy' and the milk chocolate duck was 'crispy'). Perhaps suffering from a bout of crisis fatigue, Waitrose decided people were right to be offended by their 140-gram dark chocolate ducklings. This time the apology was explicit. They appeared to wave the white flag almost immediately.

A spokesperson for Waitrose said: 'We are very sorry for any upset caused by the name of this product, it was absolutely not our intention to cause any offence. We removed the product from sale several weeks ago while we changed the labelling and our ducklings are now back on sale.'[22]

False confessions and the weaponization of vague language

Journalists on the hunt for a compliant headline aren't the only ones willing to magic up an apology from nowhere. Politicians do it too and UK Labour MP Dame Margaret Hodge understands only too well the damage that can be caused by a fabricated apology.

In July 2018 the Labour Party launched a controversial disciplinary investigation against the MP after she'd accused the party leader Jeremy Corbyn of being a racist and anti-semite. The Labour Party had offered to drop the investigation if Hodge issued an apology. A transactional offer that put a high value on Hodge saying sorry.

Hodge publicly refused to apologize, but the investigation was eventually dropped anyway. However, in a letter from Labour's general secretary Jennie Formby to Dame Margaret Hodge advising her that the investigation had been dropped, Formby referred to a conversation between Hodge and Labour chief whip Nick Brown in which Hodge had apparently 'expressed regret' for the way she'd spoken to Corbyn.

Hodge maintained that this did not happen. A letter from Hodge's lawyer to Jennie Formby, which Hodge made public, stated:

> While your decision is welcomed, the basis on which you seek to explain your belated volte-face is entirely disingenuous. You refer to an apparent discussion which took place between our client and the opposition chief whip in which she 'expressed regret'.
>
> Our client discussed this matter with the opposition chief whip over two weeks ago, and has had no further discussions. She did not express regret. As you are aware, our client will not apologize for her conduct or words, as she did nothing wrong.

One of the key problems in this exchange is the inherent pliability of the term 'expressed regret'. It is vague to the point of meaningless and offers the accuser the cover of plausible deniability. If left unchallenged, the expression of regret colours the events unfairly. If challenged, it's easy enough for the accuser to claim that they interpreted regret in good faith. Hodge had no choice but to issue a robust rebuttal of Formby's claim.

Reflecting on the apology falsely attributed to her, Hodge commented in an e-mail to the authors:

> In this time of intense political turmoil it is particularly important that apologies and expressions of regret are not misconstrued or more dangerously used for an individual's advantage.

I was angered by Jennie Formby's false claim that I had 'expressed regret' – when no such comment had been made – as these claims can often show events in a completely new light. I was fortunate in that I had my position as a Member of Parliament and legal representation so that I could counter these false claims, however, many others do not which can have worrying consequences.

If I had been unable to set the record straight on this issue it could have quickly created the impression that my deep frustration with Jeremy Corbyn was not sincere or genuine. The reality is that my misgivings then, and now, are deeply felt and I do not express any regret.

Apologies are important. Not giving an apology when one is due can be hugely injurious to the victim. And giving unnecessary apologies can be damaging to the apologizer, robbing them of credibility and in some cases, market value. The 2018 study 'The Value of Apology: How do corporate apologies moderate the stock market reaction to non-financial corporate crises?' found that organizations facing undue criticism perform better financially when 'refraining from apologizing when the firm is not directly responsible' and that they suffer financially when they give unnecessary apologies.[23]

Giving unnecessary apologies can be damaging to the apologizer.

So it seems quite a mean trick to pin an apology on an organization or individual when they categorically did not apologize. Dame Margaret Hodge had to go the expense and effort of having her lawyers refute the allegation that she'd said sorry. Waitrose took a different approach. After their statement was misconstrued as an apology, they kept their heads down and waited for it to blow over, which it eventually did.

Their restraint counts for nothing though when the thing most people remember is the reports of their 'apology'. Nobody gained from this episode but the viral news media; Waitrose were humiliated, a delicious-sounding sandwich appears to have been discontinued and consumers are no better off for any of the fuss that was made. The sad thing is, if the media were that desperate to pin something nasty on Waitrose, they'd only have had to wait 15 days. On 31 October, the editor of *Waitrose Food* magazine William Sitwell resigned after it was revealed he'd joked about killing vegans in an e-mail to a freelance writer.[24]

CHAPTER TWENTY

Apologizing on behalf of others

Lessons from car makers, presidents and freelance apologizers

Father, forgive them; for they know not what they do.

LUKE 23:34

Hidden away in the countryside of Japan's Shizuoka Prefecture, there's a derelict shack. The shack was remarkable to Tokyo-based journalist Taryn Siegel who visited in 2018 only for the fact it is located at least 40 minutes' walk from the nearest bus stop.[1] Inside are two couches, a small table and a desk. Nothing else. The shack is the unofficial headquarters of Nihon Shazai Daikokao – one of Japan's many 'apology agencies' – small to medium-sized organizations that apologize on behalf of others.

The translated version of its website invites visitors to 'please leave me bad things!' The menu of available apologies is exhaustive, covering every possible configuration of shame, guilt and embarrassment. Hire an apology agent to say sorry to your spouse (apologies for infidelity no problem), grovel to your boss, make amends with a neighbour or simply say sorry for lying to a friend.

In a country with some of the most densely packed urban centres on earth and a culture of honour, it's probably no surprise that there's a market for apologies-by-proxy. People are busy, or as is the case for some clients of Nihon Shazai Daikokao, they're being avoided by the people they want to say sorry to, so why not outsource your sorrow?

It's probably no surprise that there's a market for apologies-by-proxy.

A lucrative trade it might be for the conduits of your atonement – Nihon Shazai Daikokao charges around £24 per hour for the basic apology service – but does outsourcing rob an apology of its sincerity? And how does that work for public apologies?

There are two main reasons to give a public apology on behalf of others and none of them are to do with the business model of Japan's apology agencies. But both are controversial.

Passive–aggressive proxy apologies

When Geordie Greig took over as editor of the London *Evening Standard* newspaper in 2009, he announced his tenure with an apology campaign. Posters on the Tube and buses listed the ways in which the paper was sorry. One read 'sorry for being predictable', another 'sorry for being negative'. Greig had commissioned research to discover what Londoners really thought of their city's daily newspaper. The apologies were direct reflections of that research.

The three-week campaign was seen by some as Greig heralding a fresh new start for the *Standard*, but others couldn't help but see it as a waspish swipe at his predecessor Veronica Wadley.

Writing about the campaign at the time, the *Guardian*'s Roy Greenslade – a former newspaper editor himself and a professor of journalism – asserted that Wadley would see the apologies as an 'attack on her editorial approach'.[2] By apologizing on her behalf, Greig had possibly issued Wadley a very public, very humiliating insult. It's one way of saying 'under new management' though.

Uber found itself under new management after founder Travis Kalanick quit. His stewardship had seen Uber bounce from one crisis to the next. New CEO Dara Khosrowshahi took over in August 2017 and spent months overseeing Uber's 'Moving Forward' campaign. It wasn't an apology as such but the messaging was very much 'sorry about the last guy'. Every pledge Khosrowshahi made, from improving Uber's culture to bolstering workers' rights, were answers to the criticisms Kalanick had faced.

Apologizing on behalf of others, or on behalf of an organization, can be tricky. Not everyone inside the organization will agree that an apology is due, regardless of what it looks like from the outside. These apologies can alienate stakeholders and draw fierce, often unfounded criticism. In February 2019 UK Labour MP Chris Williamson was filmed at a meeting complaining to fellow party members that Labour had been 'too apologetic' in its handling of their much publicized anti-semitism crisis. Williamson apparently resented apologies being made on his behalf. His criticism of Labour's apologies inevitably drew criticism back towards him. Yet his obvious disdain for Labour's apparent habit for atonement eventually forced him to issue – you guessed it – his own apology.

Williamson's statement ran to more than 300 words, but it wasn't until the end of the third paragraph that he found the words he hated so much. 'I deeply regret, and apologize for, my recent choice of words.' He wasn't sorry for what he said, but how he said it and the deliberately evasive and, as Tom Watson Labour's deputy leader put it, 'heavily caveated' mea culpa, was hidden in the middle. He spent the first two paragraphs equivocating and reminding us of his spotless record as an 'anti-racist'. He spent the final two paragraphs telling us why the Labour Party needs people like him. Labour didn't necessarily see it that way and they suspended him pending an investigation.

There's definitely an element of performativity to apologies on behalf of others.

There's definitely an element of performativity to apologies on behalf of others. These apologies are almost exclusively given in front of audiences, often televised and sometimes promoted in advance. So the people giving them had better be confident those for whom they say sorry aren't going to object. One way of lowering this risk is to wait a few years, or even a couple of centuries, before saying sorry.

Historical apologies

By far the most notable reason for apologizing on behalf of others is the offer of redress for a significant historical grievance. This is predominantly within the purview of nation states, churches and mega-corporations. History has judged that an apology is due and those deemed to owe it are no longer around to give it. It's a function of both international diplomacy and domestic policy as well as an increasingly popular corporate PR exercise.

Towards the end of the Cold War era, international diplomacy was characterized by leaders saying sorry on behalf of their predecessors: Ronald Reagan said sorry in 1988 for the internment of Japanese citizens during World War II; Boris Yeltsin in 1992 for the Katyn Massacre of Polish military; Jacques Chirac in 1995 for the Vichy Government's treatment of Jews during World War II; FW de Klerk in 1996 for South African apartheid; King Harald V of Norway in 1997 for its historic treatment of the Sami people;

and Ryutaro Hashimoto in 1998 for Japan's treatment of prisoners of war – just some of the most notable national mea culpas.

Germany, for obvious reasons, has long been the model nation for historical apologies. Contrition is embroidered into German post-war culture. South Africa's post-Apartheid politicians would go on to adopt the German standard for national contrition. Jan-Werner Mueller of the Princeton University Center for Human Values credits the German model for South Africa's post-Apartheid Truth and Reconciliation process. 'Human rights activists and politicians in South Africa, for instance, closely studied German trials, public commemoration and schoolbooks.'[3] He says China, unhappy with Japan's handling of World War II, recommended they also follow the 'German model'.

This style of apologetic diplomacy often reflected a nation's prevailing cultural and economic preoccupations. The United States said it with dollars in 1988, paying each interned Japanese citizen $20,000 in compensation.[4] That was at the tail-end of an economic boom. But when Congress came to issue a formal apology for slavery and Jim Crow era discrimination 30 years later in 2008 they were staring down the barrel of a financial crisis. They did this apology on the cheap. Congress actually added a legal disclaimer to the Senate resolution that read: 'Nothing in this resolution authorizes or supports any claim against the United States; or serves as a settlement of any claim against the United States.'[5]

Stephen Harper's Canadian government had done the opposite in 2007, offering money but no apology. Canada had promised a formal apology as part of a $1.9 billion compensation package for Native Canadian children forced to attend residential schools, but reneged and made the settlement without saying sorry.[6] A spokesperson for the Union of British Columbian Indian Chiefs said: 'We are extremely disappointed that the current government does not understand the significant role an apology would have in the healing and reconciliation process for our people.'[7] Harper's government eventually issued the apology in 2008.[8]

It was around the same time that Australian Prime Minister Kevin Rudd formally apologized to the 'Stolen Generation' – Indigenous Australians who'd suffered at the hands of their government for hundreds of years. Since 1938, Australia had held a national Day of Mourning to commemorate the land loss and suffering of Indigenous Australians, but no government had ever said sorry. Rudd's predecessor John Howard had resisted the findings of a 1997 report recommending he apologize, saying he didn't 'subscribe to the black armband view of history'.[9]

He'd moved a 'motion of regret', but it didn't include an apology. Opposition leader at the time Kim Beazley had encouraged Howard to make the apology. In 1999, in response to his resistance, Australia's Day of Mourning became 'National Sorry Day', but the formal apology remained elusive. Nine years later, Kevin Rudd's first act as prime minister was to say sorry. It had been a feature of his election campaign and when he delivered on his promise he became the first Australian leader to formally apologize to Australia's indigenous people.

Other national leaders have issued less anticipated but nonetheless welcome historical apologies: David Cameron, the British Prime Minister in 2010 for the Bloody Sunday killings in Northern Ireland in January 1972, and Recep Tayyip Erdoğan in 2011 for the 1930 killing of 13,000 ethnic Kurds by the Turkish military.

Saying sorry for the sins of your predecessors can be a low-risk, high-reward public relations endeavour.

Not all of these nation state apologies were universally popular. Early on in his administration, President Obama's bridge-building style of diplomacy saw him embark on what his critics called an 'apology tour'. In 2010, Mitt Romney's response was to write a book called *No Apology: The case for American greatness*. National apologies were becoming divisive. Then Justin Trudeau arrived on the scene as prime minister of Canada to take national atonement to entirely new levels.

When Trudeau took office in 2015, national apologies stopped being notable for their scarcity. Trudeau, famous for his strong commitment to social justice, began issuing formal national apologies at a rapid rate, officially saying sorry four times in his first three years as prime minister, the first coming inside six months. Even the BBC, noting the contrast of his prolific output compared with international and even domestic norms, had to ask whether he apologized too much. They had a point. After issuing a formal apology for the 1914 Komagata Maru incident in which Sikh, Muslim and Hindu passengers were denied entry to Canada and sent back to India, there was – for some reason – an event to celebrate his apology. At the event, Trudeau took the opportunity to apologize for a third time to a member of Parliament he'd accidentally nudged in the crowded chamber days earlier.[10]

By 2018 Trudeau had issued six formal apologies on behalf of his country, one of which, to members of the Tsilhqot'in community in British Columbia, addressed an incident that had happened 156 years prior. Trudeau's appetite for contrition prompted Canadian author Linda Besner to remark: 'Canada's sorriest prime minister is getting on people's nerves.'[11]

That's a remarkable amount of apologizing, especially for the son of Pierre Trudeau, prime minister of Canada between 1980 and 1984. Trudeau senior was more conservative with his contrition, saying in 1984: 'I do not see how I can apologize for some historic event to which we or these people in this House were not a party.'[12]

A 2010 study into perceptions of apologies in the banking industry noted that:

Public apologies are now the norm for senior politicians who routinely express contrition for historical events such as slavery, apartheid and genocide. However, these events, by their very nature, are not attributable to the apologizer(s) and nor are the apologizees directly affected by them.[13]

In other words, saying sorry for the sins of your predecessors can be a low-risk, high-reward public relations endeavour.

The challenge posed by what academic and author Pramod K Nayar calls 'trans-generational guilt' is deciding when to stop. How far back into its own history can a nation or organization go before the apologies start ringing hollow? Timing is massively influential on whether the apology hits or misses. Perhaps that's why, in March 2019, when Mexico's president Andrés Manuel López Obrador wrote to King Felipe VI of Spain and to Pope Francis to see if either of them fancied saying sorry for the 1521 Spanish conquest of the Aztecs, his response was met with bemusement. Spain's foreign minister said it was 'weird to receive now this request for an apology for events that occurred 500 years ago'.[14]

This habit for national atonement started with German Chancellor Willy Brandt. On visiting the monument to the Warsaw ghetto uprising in 1970, Brandt fell to his knees. He didn't apologize. He didn't actually say anything, later writing in his memoirs: 'I did what people do when words fail them.' That same year, *Time* magazine made Brandt their Man of the Year. Maybe that's why the habit caught on.

National apologies have long conferred on the giver the power to foster reconciliation abroad and at home. Less recognized is the power they have to breed domestic shame and resentment. High-profile apologies, combined with a declining willingness for citizens to carry the shame of their ancestors, can be grist to the mill for those seeking to capitalize.

National apologies have long conferred on the giver the power to foster reconciliation abroad and at home.

Germany's 'memory culture', the once revered national tendency for self-examination and contrition, is wearing thin for some of its citizens.[15] In 2017 far right politician Björn Höcke called on his country to stop apologizing for the past.[16,17] This backlash might have been a long time coming. Even at the time of Willy Brandt's famous gesture, not all Germans believed it was necessary. A poll for *Der Spiegel* conducted at the time of the 'Kniefall' found that 48 per cent of West Germans thought it was excessive, 11 per cent had no opinion while 41 per cent thought it was appropriate.

Other unintended consequences

Do the deeds for which a nation apologizes have to be in living memory for the apology to resonate properly? When Japanese Prime Minister Ryutaro Hashimoto apologized via the pages of *The Sun* newspaper to British prisoners of war in 1998, many of those held by Japan during World War II were still alive, but they were old. One former prisoner noted the timing and didn't consider Hashimoto's column to be a genuine apology because of it.

Arthur Titherington, secretary of the Japanese Labour Camp Survivors Association told the BBC: 'This is very far from what we wanted and my members will without doubt reject these offers. The Japanese government is basically waiting for us all to die out and they think they can get away without apologizing or offering compensation.'[18]

For all the diplomatic and campaigning value national historical atonement has, it doesn't always fulfil the core function of an apology. Nayar sees them as providing: 'A minimal return to a certain form of civic engagement between former perpetrators and victims, or descendants of both. It opens up a space where the speech act works as a bridge between the two.'[19] This creates new problems. By apologizing so broadly, the apology confers onto its recipients collective responsibility to either accept or reject. It is never that simple.

Historical corporate apologies

The Mitsubishi company was one of the beneficiaries of prisoner labour during World War II. When the company made the decision to apologize on behalf of its predecessors to the prisoners it had used in its mines, they first contacted Kinue Tokudome, a Japanese-born author living in California. Tokudome is the founder and executive director of an organization called the US–Japan Dialogue on POWs. Mitsubishi wanted to ask her if she thought the prisoners of war would accept their apology.

Tokudome explained to Mitsubishi that she knew a prisoner of war called Jim Murphy. He was one of the few surviving Japanese prisoners of war well enough to travel to receive the apology. In an interview with National Public Radio she explained how Jim Murphy had wanted an apology for years, but his reasons for wanting one had recently changed.[20] At first, Tokudome explained, Murphy had wanted to hear an apology so he could move on with his life. The older he got, the less that mattered. But when the offer of an apology came, from Mitsubishi via Tokudome, Murphy was conflicted. He still wanted an apology, but knew many of his dead comrades would never have accepted one had they been alive to hear it. So how he could he accept it on their behalves?

Murphy's internal conflict is just one of the many unintended consequences of organizations and governments issuing historical apologies. These apologies can be good for healing historical wounds, but they're also great PR for the person issuing the apology since that person is invariably not guilty of the thing they are apologizing for.

Five years after his 2011 apology for the killing of ethnic Kurds, Turkey's president Recep Tayyip Erdoğan reportedly found himself apologizing to Russia for a controversy attributed to his own presidency.[21] Russia accepted his apology for downing one of their warplanes and diplomatic ties were resumed. Does it matter to the recipients of his first apology that he went on to apologize for shooting down a plane? Or that in the same year as that apology he faced an attempted coup d'état by sections of his own army who accused him of disregarding human rights?[22]

If you're going to apologize on behalf of others, you're going to need a spotless record of your own. Even the compulsively apologetic Justin Trudeau is learning this. In March 2019 he was accused of apologizing for the wrong things when trying to handle his own corruption scandal.[23,24] Instead of apologizing for the actions of our ancestors perhaps today's leaders might be better off focusing on ensuring future generations don't have to apologize for theirs.

CHAPTER TWENTY-ONE

£1 million in sales in four days

Discover the unexpected benefits of not saying sorry

We won't apologize to the irrational extremists who
are causing criminal damage to our adverts. 😤😳💪
PROTEIN WORLD TWITTER ACCOUNT, 27 APRIL 2015

Protein World was, until quite recently, a relatively obscure fitness supplement brand. Most of their early marketing activity involved reality TV stars plugging their low-fat protein shakes in glossy lifestyle magazines. Then in April 2015, the company invested £250,000 in a limited-run billboard campaign.

The billboard advert featured fitness model Renee Somerfield in a yellow bikini, accompanied by the strapline 'Are you beach body ready?' At first glance, the campaign had that distinct whiff of being a little out of touch; it looked like an apparently male-focused brand reviving old-fashioned female beauty tropes. It wasn't in-your-face offensive, but it was certainly out of place in 2015's 'embrace your imperfections' culture of body positivity leveraged by the likes of Dove and Pantene.

The advert encapsulated everything the growing movement of body positivity stood against; the model, toned and confident, rib bones visible, drew the eye to the slogan. The campaign felt like a creative misjudgement. Dove would later launch a parody of it with three curvy models and the strapline 'Yes. We are beach body ready'.[1]

Dated it may have been, but there was nothing specifically offensive about the advert. The Committee of Advertising Practice (CAP), the body that writes the advertising codes enforced by the Advertising Standards Authority, had already seen the creative and 'advised that it was unlikely to cause serious or widespread offence'.[2]

What the regulators think about an advert isn't always a reliable predictor of how consumers react. A year earlier, Victoria's Secret and Topshop had both faced widespread accusations of body-shaming women.[3,4] Both avoided regulator attention but were forced to make costly campaign alterations, the former being the subject of a 32,000 signature petition demanding they apologize.[5] Anyone fluent in the language of social media activism could see this campaign had everything required to become a major cultural moment. It was a matter of when, not if, Protein World would feel the backlash.

What the regulators think about an advert isn't always a reliable predictor of how consumers react.

It didn't take long either. Within a few days of the posters appearing on the London Underground, commuters started defacing them, adding their own messages of body positivity and criticizing Protein World on Twitter. There were two trending hashtags and a Change.org petition demanding the adverts be removed. More than 40,000 people signed it, and 378 people complained to the Advertising Standards Authority.[6] There was even a protest planned to take place in London's Hyde Park. This was looking bad for Protein World.

The machinery to extract a humiliating public apology was in motion. The viral news media, having extensively reported on the growing controversy, were waiting for Protein World to apologize and deliver to them their hard-earned editorial pay-off. Other brands were ready to cash in with parodies and activists were standing by to criticize and reject the apology when it eventually came. All that was missing from the equation was Protein World's cooperation. That cooperation, crucial in the viral news apology ecosystem, was conspicuous by its absence.

The missing piece of the jigsaw

For an authentic corporate humiliation narrative, the viral news media requires three elements: a moment of controversy, be that a misjudged remark or unpopular advert; a social media reaction, even a handful of tweets from obscure accounts will do; and an apology. The first two elements were in place, but Protein World were holding out on the third. Without their apology, the only accurate headlines were of the 'people are upset' variety. The media wanted to say 'Protein World apologize for "vile" and "sexist" advert after social media backlash'.

Almost three days had passed since the first articles reporting the 'sexist' and 'body-shaming' adverts went live and not a peep from Protein World. By now, a brand under this much intense scrutiny would be expected to have crumbled. We should have already been in the think piece – 'Why Protein World need to do more than apologize' – stage of the outrage cycle.

On 24 April, nine days after the *Guardian* had first written[7] about the adverts, Protein World gave a statement to BBC's Newsbeat. It wasn't the statement people were expecting. 'It is a shame that in 2015 there are still a minority who aren't focusing on celebrating those who aspire to be healthier, fitter and stronger.'[8]

Ouch. 'Celebrating', 'aspire', 'healthier' – Protein World were talking back, using the language of the body positivity movement to shame their critics. Not only were they doubling down; they were doing it with a smirk. Where were the hollow promises to do better, the faux introspection and corporate soul-searching? Brands weren't supposed to stick up for themselves, were they?

They seemed to be enjoying it too. This wasn't in the script and their critics were confused. They told Protein World what a PR disaster they were having and Protein World couldn't have seemed happier. CEO Arjun Seth even bragged on social media that his PR team would be receiving bonuses.[9] This wasn't going to plan for anyone except Protein World.

Marketing director Richard Staveley said the furore around the campaign had produced nothing but impressive gains for the company, citing 20,000 new customers, £1 million revenue in four days, 20,000 new social media followers and 133 individual pieces of media coverage reaching an audience of 113 million at an estimated advert equivalency value of £320,663.[10,11]

Although the viral news media continued to report this as a PR fail for Protein World, with the Indy 100 claiming 'everyone is still really angry'.[12] Protein World had fostered a powerful 'us vs them' mentality between their critics and their advocates. Twitter users were now urging Protein World to 'stay strong' and thanking them for being 'inspirational'.[13]

When it comes to high volumes of social media feedback, strategic communications specialist Chris Lewis, founder of strategic communications agency LEWIS, urges pragmatism:

> It's easier to exercise judgement when social media is monitored correctly. Where some people are upset, a judgement call is needed firstly on whether to respond at all. Sometimes, responding can just draw attention and create a martyr.

Martyr is the right word and Protein World refused to create a single one.[14] They did acquire a growing band of brand advocates though.

One social media user even wrote: 'I'm a chubby girl and I am not offended by Protein World's ad, I am inspired by it. Fantastic advertising guys, haters do make you famous.'[15]

Alienation marketing

It's hard to imagine that Protein World didn't expect at least some of this. Whether or not they knew 'beach body ready' would create this level of attention, they obviously had a plan for dealing with it. They also had an ace in their back pocket. They didn't care about the criticism. As it related to their crisis response strategy, their nonchalance was a feature, not a bug.

Protein World aren't the only brand to turn not apologizing into a marketing strategy.

And Protein World aren't the only brand to turn *not* apologizing into a marketing strategy. A handful of creative communicators have long been alive to the possibilities that this kind of constructive insolence can bring. Craft brewery BrewDog won new fans with a particularly petulant #sorrynotsorry response to regulator sanctions.[16] The founder of London's Brick Lane Coffee, famous on social media for its outrage-inducing chalkboard messages, simply said: 'Don't explain, don't complain' when challenged by the London *Evening Standard* over some of their riskier creative signage that went viral.[17]

Discount retailer Poundland demonstrated similar plucky resilience in the face of public criticism. Their 2017 'naughty elf' campaign was branded misogynistic and sexist, before being banned by the Advertising Standards Authority.[18] A spokesperson for the retailer not only refused to apologize, they called it a 'storm in a teacup', adding 'we're just pleased the number of people who didn't get the joke is so small'.[19]

Tellingly, each of these brands would go on to repeat the very behaviour that first got them in trouble. Protein World took their 'Beach Body Ready' campaign to the United States in July 2015, receiving a warmer welcome than they did in London, Brick Lane Coffee continued with ever edgier chalkboard messages, and Poundland brought the naughty elf back for Christmas 2018, proclaiming in advance that it would be the 'advertising regulator's worst nightmare'.[20]

The media were showing signs too that they understood the value of organizations resisting the temptation to say sorry. 'It appears Poundland knew its customers because there was plenty of praise for the cut-price Christmas campaign', said *Metro*'s Katie Buck,[21] before listing a selection of comments from social media from people who saw the funny side of a toy elf simulating a sex act on a Barbie doll.

For some brands, it's that simple. Accepting criticism can be easy, especially if a brand hasn't built its public persona on being inherently 'good' or 'nice'. These brands expect criticism and are prepared for it. They stand to gain more from their loyal customers and potential customers than they could ever lose from their critics and the media.

The people in charge of protecting and enhancing the reputations of these brands understood one important thing that their reflexively apologetic counterparts at other organizations did not.

They knew instinctively that their customers didn't want them to apologize. Protein World, for example, sell a product aimed at gym goers. The product is designed to aid weight loss. Only people interested in spending money on body transformation products are of commercial value to Protein World. By robustly defending their advert, Protein World was robustly defending the values of its existing and potential customers.

For all the studies and experts urging brands to speak to a higher social purpose, Protein World showed us another way: a robust communications plan that accepts criticism as an inevitability can be a profitable path to growth. Alex Smith, marketing measurement and evaluation specialist at London agency Sense called it integrity.

Writing in *Campaign*, he said: 'What Protein World has done is become one of the first high-profile brands ever to show genuine integrity, and it is reaping the rewards', concluding that, 'However obtuse it may sound, Protein World has become more meaningful to its audience than all the Innocents, Patagonias, Ben & Jerry's and Body Shops rolled together.'[22]

These brands were quite prepared to alienate non-customers and in doing so they reinforced the values that their actual customers cared about: fun, political incorrectness and irreverence. When brands understand the distinction between *customers* and *audience,* they can put together a more authentic response. The more they know their own customers, the less they need to say sorry.

After the initial outrage died down, the Protein World ad was eventually banned by the ASA, but not for any of the reasons above. The ASA disputed some of the weight loss claims made in the small print. Regulators may have won the battle, but Protein World won the war.

The 'feel-bad factor'

Brands chiefly use their understanding of consumers to make those customers feel good, or at least they try to; think Dove's Campaign For Real Beauty or Budweiser's Stand By You campaign. The 2019 Super Bowl, one of the world's biggest advertising events, was a never-ending parade of self-esteem boosters and feel-good spots from the likes of Bud, Toyota and Airbnb.

Adweek's Erik Oster summarized the spectacle as, 'A beer brand touting its disaster relief efforts. A car brand supporting gender equality. A vacation rental company pushing for diversity', adding that, 'Recent years have seen a rise in the number of brands aligning themselves with causes, a trend that has found its way into advertising's biggest night – the Super Bowl.'[23]

Smart brands are learning how to amplify criticism, outrage and hurt feelings and turn them into marketing wins.

Using the same logic, but inverting the 'make customers feel good' approach so it becomes a 'make non-customers feel bad' approach allows marketers to reinforce their values by emphasizing what they are *not*. Smart brands are learning how to amplify criticism, outrage and hurt feelings and turn them into marketing wins. The only trick is to not say sorry.

The power of tribalism

It's useful to think of consumers and audience groups as cultural 'tribes', each of which contain multiple smaller, overlapping groups: tribes-within-tribes. Social media, now the default communications channel for brands, tends to silo people into two main tribal identities: progressive and traditional. This is the crucial intersection of alienation marketing, where the feel-bad factor is felt most intensely.

Brands too, fall into these two main tribal silos. Starbucks, Ben & Jerry's, Patagonia clearly and deliberately align with progressive values. On the other side of the house, Chick-fil-A (a company so toxic to the progressive tribe that in June 2018 Twitter CEO Jack Dorsey apologized simply for eating at one of their restaurants), UK pub chain Wetherspoons and US craft supply store Hobby Lobby wear their traditionalism loud and proud.[24]

By hitching their wagon to a specific divisive issue, brands can communicate powerfully with one tribe by alienating another.

Of course, brands are acutely sensitive to the culture's ever-evolving social contours and can be impressively nimble when commercial expediency demands it. Within just a few years Procter & Gamble, the world's biggest advertiser, pivoted from telling us through their own ads that they were a 'proud sponsor of moms' – the logic being that of course it's mothers who buy nappies, detergent and groceries – to then telling us, through their controversial 'We Believe in the Best in Men' campaign for Gillette, that gender stereotypes are harmful.

Brands can communicate powerfully with one tribe by alienating another.

Levi's have 'crossed the floor' too. In 2018, the denim brand once synonymous with gun-slinging cowboys announced a partnership with gun control group Everytown for Gun Safety. 'While taking a stand can be unpopular with some, doing nothing is no longer an option' said Chip Bergh, Levi's chief executive.[25] What he didn't say was, unpopular with whom.

Pew Research Centre data suggests gun ownership is most common among older, rural, non-college-educated people and least popular among younger, urban, college-educated people.[26] This is the exact demographic that New Yorker and former Procter & Gamble executive Bergh calls the 'lost generation' of Levi's customers and one he is keen to win back from the likes of Diesel.[27] Bergh knows young people haven't thought Levis were cool since the 90s. Gun owners are a demographic he's willing to alienate to put that right.

The National Rifle Association were quick to spot this too, accusing Levi's directly of alienating their members for profit. 'We can only assume that Levi's accountants have determined that resulting skinny jeans sales will be enough to offset the permanent damage to their once-cherished brand.'[28]

The reason brands are so keen to be on the right side of a cultural moment is because, as the theory goes anyway, it works. A study of 1,000 US consumers by marketing company Sprout

Social found that around two-thirds of consumers want the brands they consume to 'take a stand' politically.[29] It all comes back to the idea that consumption is a 'self-expressive' activity.[30] When Uber inadvertently undermined protests against President Trump's travel ban, rival Lyft differentiated itself, promising to 'stand firmly against these actions, and will not be silent on issues that threaten the values of our community'.[31]

When Nike announced an endorsement deal with the NFL's Colin Kaepernick, the iconic player behind the #takeaknee national anthem protest against police racism, furious patriots filmed themselves destroying Nike merchandise in anger. The performative outrage was off the charts. This wasn't about how much outrage Nike was attracting, but from whom they were attracting it.

President Trump said the advert sent a 'terrible message';[32] country singer John Rich, who performed at Trump's inauguration gala, filmed his sound engineer cutting the Nike Swoosh from his socks;[33] Andrew H Scott, mayor of Coal Run, Kentucky said he was 'officially done' with Nike.[34]

A cynical observer might ask just how on earth a youth-orientated urban sportswear brand like Nike would survive the ire of President Trump, the mayor of a 1,500-population town in Kentucky and a country and western singer. Then again, maybe it's obvious.

The campaign's strapline was 'Believe in something, even if it means sacrificing everything'. Nike knew exactly what they were sacrificing: Trump supporters, country and western singers and people who get upset about fellow Americans not respecting the national anthem. Sales of Nike products jumped 31 per cent in the week after the launch of the campaign. *Time* magazine said: 'Despite outrage, Nike sales increased 31 per cent after Kaepernick ad.' But it wasn't despite the outrage, it was because of it.

The opportunity for brands is clear. Pick a side and never apologize to the opposition. By alienating one tribe, and refusing to say sorry about it, brands can send what seems like a costly signal to their own tribe – 'hey, we share your values, now watch us alienate the "enemy"'. This signal isn't as costly as it seems though. There is little risk in alienating a tribe that has neither the means nor the ability to buy your product in greater numbers than the tribe to which you're signalling. As Patagonia founder Yvon Chouinard, a man who understands brand purpose better than most, famously said: 'If you're not pissing off 50 per cent of people, you're not trying hard enough.'[35]

And it's not always necessary to alienate an entire tribe in order to delight your own.

Like all tribes, cultural demographics have tribal elders. These influential figureheads become proxies for the virtues and aspirations of the tribe. Or, in some cases, aspirant cultural figureheads attach themselves to tribes.

Broadcaster Piers Morgan is an example. As a supporter of the traditional values, 'anti-PC gone mad' tribe, he frequently lambasts the so-called 'snowflake' generation for their perceived oversensitivity and willingness to take offence.

It must have been a source of delight then, for UK bakery chain Greggs, when in January 2019 Morgan commented on their vegan sausage roll, branding them 'PC-ravaged clowns' on Twitter, amplifying the product launch in the process. Greggs' response was simple: 'Oh hello Piers, we've been expecting you.'

And, of course, they may well have been. Piers Morgan and Greggs have shared the same PR firm in the past.[36, 37] The pithy response received more than 20,000 retweets and more than 145,000 'likes'. Multiple Greggs branches sold out of vegan sausage rolls shortly after. Taylor Herring, the PR agency that has represented both parties, denied that the stunt was orchestrated, but somebody, somewhere clearly understood the value of leveraging people's distaste for a public figure like Morgan. He later tweeted to Greggs that they owed him a 'large cheque'.

Two weeks later, Morgan helped amplify another brand's marketing message. This time it was Gillette, who launched their controversial 'We Believe in the Best in Men' campaign.

Once again, Morgan had an opinion, referring to the creative as 'virtue-signalling PC guff' and vowed to reconsider his position as a lifelong Gillette customer.

Morgan's Twitter conniptions aside, the advert attracted a lot of criticism. Less than two months after its launch it had 29 million YouTube views and 1.2 million downvotes.[38] Alienating this many people, the vast majority of them men, doesn't seem like the smartest commercial decision for Gillette. But then, almost half of the people who buy Gillette men's razors are women. According to research from management consultancy Kantar:

> the gender split of buyers for 'male' razors is 50.5 per cent male and 49.5 per cent female… and that's not just women buying for their sons and husbands; 1 in 5 women (18 per cent in the UK, 22 per cent in the US) choose a male-branded razor.[39]

Campaign magazine's trends editor Nicola Kemp spotted the upside for Gillette immediately, noting that 'pissing off Morgan is a valid marketing strategy'.[40] She's entirely correct too. As brands discover the goodwill and brand affinity that can be generated by alienation, we should expect an increase in them courting performative outrage.

CHAPTER TWENTY-TWO

Don't mistake kindness for weakness

Why the UK's 'nicest' brand refused to say sorry

*The motif on the aloe vera toilet tissue, which we have been selling
for over five years, is categorically of an aloe vera leaf.*

MARKS & SPENCER, JANUARY 2019

I n 2018, public opinion experts YouGov ranked Marks &
Spencer as the fourth best-perceived high street fashion brand
in the UK. In the year prior, they ranked it as the brand best
perceived by women.[1] To most who live in the UK, M&S is *the*
quintessentially nice brand. It's where you'd buy your grand-
mother's Christmas present, or pick up some bits for a picnic.
People like M&S for their ethically-sourced food hall favourites
and their little cans of mojito. Even critics concede that whatever
else it may be, M&S is 'a reliable litmus test for a certain kind of
bourgeois gentility'.[2]

That said, we should never confuse their inherent niceness for weakness. Marks & Spencer have got a hidden tough streak. You'll see it in their approach to addressing criticism. They take a refreshingly no-nonsense, meat-and-potatoes approach.

In November 2018, when the brand found itself at the centre of a social media mini-scandal, they gave what should be considered a masterclass in reputation management.

A shopper in Nottingham had spotted a window display they didn't like. It featured images of models wearing a range of clothes, from women in frilly knickers to men in suits. The shopper, focusing on the contrast between the men in suits and women in knickers, said the display was 'vomit inducing' and told social media that they were specifically annoyed by 'normalization of damaging gender stereotypes'.[3]

The viral news media eagerly picked up on the story and repeated the shopper's most eye-catching claims in scare quotes. They smelled an easy win. The situation bore all of the hallmarks of a reflexive apology-waiting-to-happen. Even a feminism charity got involved, demanding to know who signed the campaign off. Surely M&S would apologize for the offence and alter the display? That's what firms do nowadays.

Before exploring what Marks & Spencer did right, we should consider what they could have done wrong. Thankfully, 2018 was rich with examples of brands nervously apologizing to their social media critics.

A few weeks before the M&S window display 'nontroversy', a luxury hotel in Brisbane had found itself facing remarkably similar criticisms for an advert showing a man and woman enjoying breakfast in bed. Sofitel Brisbane's problem, if you could call it that, was that the man was reading the financial pages while the woman was reading a fashion magazine. The advert, even by 2018's hypersensitive standards, was pretty innocuous. Yet it seemed to sufficiently irritate a property reporter at *The Australian*. The journalist wrote on Twitter: 'Hi @sofitelbrisbane, your breakfast looks delicious…

just wanted to let you know I'm a woman and I also read the *Financial Review* every day.'[4]

Her tweet, honestly, didn't attract much interaction. As of January 2019, it had 128 retweets, 903 likes and around 400 comments, some shared her irritation but most took issue with her criticism, not the content of the advert. It didn't matter though. The hotel, like M&S, had been shamed, by a blue-tick-verified journalist no less.

That fact alone made this a news story, albeit not a big one. The *Northern Star*, serving the town of Lismore in New South Wales, was the only outlet to pick it up to start with. Their headline 'Hotel Ad Angers Women' suggested that deep down they knew this wasn't much of a scoop.

This episode should have been nothing but a minor scuffle confined to social media and one local news outlet. Then Sofitel did what many anxious organizations do when criticized – they apologized, tweeting from their now-deleted account: 'We appreciate you voicing your concerns. There was no intention of portraying a stereotype, but we recognize it and apologize for any offence it has caused.'

Not only did they say sorry, they cancelled the advert and effectively invited their critics to keep their criticism up, adding that: 'The creative has been pulled from any future activity. Feel free to send us a DM if you'd like to discuss further.'[5]

Can you guess what happened next? It wasn't, as Sofitel would have hoped, that the problem went away. Their apology drew worldwide coverage. Yahoo. com, News Corporation Australia, Fox News, the *Daily Mail*, the *Daily Mirror* – all of them lapped it up. With one tweet of contrition from the hotel, an absolute non-story became a major social media talking point.[6–10]

It can't be stressed enough that this story was going precisely nowhere until the apology. With all due respect to the *Northern Star* and the various verified Twitter accounts criticizing the advert, this wasn't a situation Sofitel should have been worrying about, let alone apologizing for. But not apologizing is far easier said than done. Only those unlucky social media managers who've been there understand the intensity of stress that unexpected media scrutiny and social media criticism generates.

A crucial detail worth noting here is that the hotel, owned by French multinational AccorHotels, made the apology from its local Twitter account. There were no responses from either Sofitel head office or its parent group. Until the criticism about the advert, the Sofitel Brisbane account had posted local promotions and pictures from its restaurant. It was by no means a corporate Twitter account and this response looked like the work of an anxious social media executive with little capacity or training for handling any level of media scrutiny. Issuing a panic apology and hoping the criticism goes away is not a crisis management strategy.

This story was going precisely nowhere until the apology.

The extraction of this apology was presented in most reports as the story of plucky Twitter users taking on a corporate giant. In hindsight though, it appears more like a handful of local journalists demanding an apology from a junior staff member, or worse, an untrained hotel employee who had no involvement in the advert. The Sofitel Brisbane Twitter account was deleted on 10 October, one day after the apology made headlines around the world.

How to defend your organization against accusations of sexism and selling blasphemous toilet tissue

So if that's how not to handle petty online criticisms, how do you deal with them? Fast forward a few weeks to the M&S episode and those observing might have expected a similar outcome. M&S didn't fall into the apology trap though. In response to the many criticisms they were facing, a spokesperson did what a lot of under-fire spokespeople dare not to do. They put facts before feelings:

> M&S sells more underwear, in more shapes, sizes and styles, than any other retailer, especially at Christmas. We've highlighted one combination in our windows, which are part of a wider campaign that features a large variety of must-have Christmas moments, from David Gandy washing up in an M&S suit through to families snuggling up in our matching PJs.[11]

Despite the volume of criticism and media attention, they simply refused to say sorry. And in doing so they denied the media the missing word they were waiting for so eagerly. Without a 'sorry' around which to anchor the story, outlets resorted to vague claims about the display sparking a debate, or causing a 'sexism row'.[12]

In taking this approach, M&S relieved themselves immediately of the costly burden of saying sorry. They didn't need to make any promises to do better, to reflect or make things right. Their communications team and frontline staff didn't need to absorb the additional scrutiny that comes with saying sorry. It was simply business as usual.

As consumers, we've been trained to expect a very specific response to this kind of situation. Brands are supposed to say sorry, aren't they? That's the transaction. Someone criticizes you, the media stirs the pot a little bit, you say sorry and the attention you didn't ask for goes away. Sofitel's social media person obliged, M&S didn't.

M&S defended their display robustly and sent out a clear message that there was little point for their critics or the media in pursuing it. Had there been a hint of anxiety in their statement, a concession to the feelings of those criticizing them, or an 'it's never our intention to offend' preamble, it wouldn't have worked.

Former news journalist and now editor at the communications training provider Media First, Adam Fisher painted a vivid picture of how it might have played out, that consumers might have expected M&S to:

> apologize profusely for the transgression, state that it takes the issues seriously and claim that it had learned its lesson. Maybe we might have been told that a window designer had lost their employment as a result of the fallout.[13]

When the expected response doesn't come, there's just not that much people can do about it. There's an important lesson here, so it bears repeating. There's not much anyone can do to you if you don't say sorry. Even threatening a boycott is futile when the organization you're targeting isn't prepared to back down. M&S had created a template for handling trivial criticism and they didn't have to wait long to try it out again.

When the expected response doesn't come, there's just not that much people can do about it.

In January 2019, just over eight weeks after the window display criticism, they were in the firing line again. This time because somebody with access to a social media account believed they could see the Arabic word for 'Allah' imprinted on Marks & Spencer's three-ply aloe vera toilet paper.[14]

Cast your mind back to H&M's socks crisis for a second. Causing offence to a specific religion, even in this post-deferential age, is high risk. Regardless of the facts, the optics are unforgiving. Even people of other religions or no religion at all seem to find it distasteful. We mustn't forget how quick Tesco was to apologize to Christians for a 2017 Good Friday beer promotion. Small brands too, understand the potential damage of religious offence. The Cheshire Brewhouse, a microbrewery near Macclesfield, changed its packaging and apologized to Hindu Council UK for using an Om symbol on one of their cans.[15]

M&S had it worse than all these brands though. They were accused of the ultimate religious disrespect, by putting an image on toilet paper. A Change.org petition demanding the product's immediate removal hit almost 5,000 signatures in its first six days.[16] There was a #boycottmarksandspencer campaign on social media. Coverage of the criticism was global and M&S, just like H&M, had just finished dealing with high-profile criticism of their advertising choices. Yet they managed to resist the temptation either to apologize or withdraw the products.

In a statement on Twitter, M&S said: 'The motif on the aloe vera toilet tissue, which we have been selling for over five years, is categorically of an aloe vera leaf and we have investigated and confirmed this with our suppliers.'[17]

Take a moment to breathe in the intoxicating bluntness of that statement. It's deliberately and assertively bland, so dull and categorical that you can almost feel the press officer's irritation at having to write it. There is no concession to hurt feelings, no 'we're sorry if you find this offensive', no claims to 'care deeply about…'. Just the facts. 'It is an aloe vera leaf, now go away.'

And they didn't just post this message once. They posted it in response to at least seven different Twitter accounts criticizing them, without changing a word. That's important too. A common habit among social media managers is to 'mix up' the wording from an approved statement to disguise the fact that it's a prepared template. Take a look at the United Airlines Twitter feed to see how this works. M&S didn't even bother doing that though.

And of course, why would they bother? The aloe vera truthers making all the noise were not worth taking seriously. They may have earnestly believed that Marks & Spencer had

People believe lots of things. It doesn't mean they deserve an apology when reality conflicts with their beliefs.

deliberately made blasphemous toilet roll, but so what? People believe lots of things. It doesn't mean they deserve an apology when reality conflicts with their beliefs. The media knew M&S weren't deliberately selling this toilet roll to wind people up.

M&S knew that the media knew this. Yet in their hunger to get people clicking on their stories, the viral news media gave undue prominence to a cranky conspiracy theory. It was just something for them to write about.

Redefining the 'communications crisis'

Marks & Spencer proved two things here: media coverage and social media criticisms do not necessarily represent a reputational crisis; and responding to criticism does not necessarily mean saying sorry. Handled properly, frivolous criticism has limited potential to damage a reputation, even when it involves touchy subjects like religion.

Communications teams that understand the difference between their social media audience and their real-life customers have a distinct advantage over those that don't. Social media isn't real life. It confers unearned credibility and authority onto people who would otherwise have no influence over a brand's reputation. These social media nobodies, literal nobodies sometimes – studies have shown that bots and automated accounts can amplify inflammatory content and outrage rapidly and easily – are causing organizations to humiliate themselves with impulsive apologies they didn't need to give.[18] The very platforms upon which brands stake their reputation are designed specifically to reward outrage and yet it's vanishingly rare for brands to do what M&S did. It's an enduring myth that social media criticism is always a big deal.

The other myth is that negative media attention requires a crisis response. Negative media attention is not ideal of course, but it's also not the disaster many brands believe it is. Take Protein World. The media went for them in a big way over the 'Beach Body Ready' campaign, yet they *gained* customers. Trust in the mass media, although improving, is low. Gallup estimate that less than half of Americans trust the media either 'a fair amount' or 'a great deal'.[19]

The key thing to remember here is that the viral news media will report on pretty much any situation in which a brand may be expected to deliver a humiliating apology. It's a key driver of the outrage economy. Organizations should recognize their own power to make supply-side interventions. They can simply not say sorry when they've done nothing wrong.

Marks & Spencer have a standard of conduct and they will apologize when they fall short. Their apologies for tangible shortcomings prove this. But they also have a sense of proportion and of what does not warrant an apology. That changes how they respond to criticism. Criticism for trivial issues only becomes a crisis if an organization can't handle criticism.

By any meaningful metric, Marks & Spencer has not suffered from not apologizing, either for their toilet paper or their window display. Social media sentiment about the brand is positive; their share price didn't suffer after either episode, in fact it went up both times, although this probably has more to do with Christmas than whether the markets care about what people on social media are saying.[20] Customers are still shopping at Marks & Spencer.

Criticism for trivial issues only becomes a crisis if an organization can't handle criticism.

It is a criminally under-observed fact that refusing to apologize is often the quickest and most effective way to stop a reputational crisis before it happens. Saying sorry has a cost. Organizations are obliged to avoid unnecessary costs. Failing to do so costs jobs.

And jobs, or more specifically the people doing them, are frequently the overlooked collateral damage of approval-seeking apologies. Starbucks taught us this. And other brands can afford to heed the lesson. Saying sorry means – in theory – accepting blame. Accepting blame means someone, somewhere in the organization, takes responsibility. Nervous, ill-prepared organizations are often only too happy to let their people pay the cost of their apology.

One member of counter staff at the St Paul, Minnesota branch of fast-food chain Chipotle learned this to her cost.[21] The staff member and colleagues were filmed refusing to serve customers they believed had previously left without paying in a common scam known as 'dine and dash'. One of the first things Chipotle management did when the video was published online was to apologize, and then they fired one of the servers in question. When it emerged shortly after that the staff's suspicions were correct, and the customers in question had actually bragged on social media about their scam, Chipotle management rehired her, and issued a second apology, to the member of staff they'd thrown under the bus because social media demanded it.

What can we learn from M&S?

M&S has a very distinctive way of communicating. They avoid waffle and get straight to facts, leaving no room for wilful misinterpretations. In both examples above, they have calmly rebuffed the criticism without wandering into generalities, a common unforced error of many corporate apologies. It's rare that organizations are able to set the terms on which they handle criticism. Lots of people were telling M&S they were having a PR nightmare, but the organization knew differently. They were not prepared to hit the panic button.

This is because Marks & Spencer are cut from similar cloth to Ben & Jerry's and Patagonia. They're not perfect, but they do have the kind of social purpose credentials – sustainability initiatives, supply chain ethics and a historically acclaimed pay and benefits culture – that eliminate the requirement for approval-seeking public conduct.

Organizations that have 'reversed into' social purpose as a marketing tactic, as Alex Weller of Patagonia put it, don't have the benefit of the same sure-footedness. These purpose-as-marketing brands appear needy and want to be loved, so they apologize a lot and will happily burden their staff with the cost of doing so. Because M&S are sure of their ground and know what they do and do not stand for, they don't feel forced to court goodwill when criticized. In short, they are capable and prepared to handle criticism.

CHAPTER TWENTY-THREE

Conclusion

*How to manage the apology impulse
and deliver meaningful responses*

The act of apologizing is in crisis. Organizations are confused and gripped by a range of anxieties: the fear of humiliation discourages them from addressing failure, the (unfounded) fear of inviting litigation prevents them from giving apologies when they're most needed, and the fear of social media criticism compels them to apologize when they really don't need to. This collective anxiety is driving down the value of 'sorry' and driving up the cost of crisis communications.

It's a myth that social media has ushered in a new age of brand authenticity. Social media is facilitating consumer and media habits we're yet to fully understand, making it harder for organizations to communicate with sincerity, especially during times of crisis, when sincerity and authenticity are what everyone needs most.

This book has shown, with particular thanks to the many organizations who got it wrong (and the few who got it right), how *not* to communicate during a crisis. But identifying failure is only half the job. What can any industry learn from these failures to deliver meaningful apologies that provide genuine value to our customers? How can organizations apologize in a way that fosters accountability, respect and delivers restitution, without humiliating the giver? Here's what we've learned from writing this book.

Collective anxiety is driving down the value of 'sorry' and driving up the cost of crisis communications.

Don't make promises you can't keep

An organization's stated corporate, social and cultural values – and whether or not they align with their day-to-day operations – have proven to be a strong indicator of how often and how earnestly they will apologize. These stated values, whether explicit – like Google's 'don't be evil' code of conduct mantra – or otherwise implied through advertising, marketing or advocacy campaigns, often set unrealistic expectations of operational conduct.

It's a wholly unnecessary burden. Organizations, especially consumer brands, are setting themselves up to apologize more than necessary by publicly aiming for a standard of conduct that they have no hope of achieving. Claiming to project 'global messages of unity' (Pepsi), or to be 'raising women's self-esteem and helping them reach their full potential' (Dove) or simply saying 'don't be evil' in their code of conduct (Google) almost dares consumers to focus on shortcomings. As we've explored, corporate social responsibility is a good thing, but not if it's just a marketing gimmick. It needs to be backed by a tangible and unassailable commitment to the chosen cause.

Patagonia, Ben & Jerry's and Marks & Spencer are three brands for whom social purpose is part of the business model. They are also notable for how few public apologies they give and their ability to tolerate and response to criticism rationally. They're confident in their ability to do the right thing and they don't overcompensate by saying sorry for trivialities.

Tacking on a lofty purpose or mission as a marketing exercise means that when brands behave like a normal large organization or business – doing things like advertising in popular (or unpopular) newspapers, marketing products to specific demographics or outsourcing to developing countries – it looks bad in comparison. Proportionality is key for organizations in helping consumers manage their expectations and to lessen the disappointment when they inevitably indulge in 'business' behaviour. This doesn't mean dispensing with creativity or rubbing people's faces in the quest for profit. It just means not over-committing to standards of moral purity in the quest for consumer palatability and being seen as 'good'.

A better approach is to be honest, realistic and embedding social purpose (or whatever you want to call it) into day-to-day operations – while obviously not trying to be evil – and to set realistic expectations as a result.

What's wrong with 'offering straightforward financial products' or 'restoring value and style in clothing and fashion' like Marks and Spencer? Consumers completely understand that a business needs to make sales and generate profit. Acknowledging this apparently inconvenient fact, or at least not hiding from it, is the first step on the way to managing expectations.

Have a plan

According to a 2014 study by Unmetric, American Airlines is, or at least was, the most apologetic airline in the world. Between

January and April 2014, they issued 23,353 public apologies via social media. They were sorry approximately 200 times a day. Their official spokesperson explained at the time that neither American, nor US Airways with whom they merged in 2012, had 'an established protocol for deciding when to say sorry'. Adding that 'the brands do treat customers' tweets as though they were inbound calls'.[1] Not having a plan for handling criticism means saying sorry is your only option. Even if you say it with your fingers crossed behind your back.

Most organizations have a crisis communications plan for when predictable things go badly wrong. But what about a plan for dealing with high, or even moderate, volumes of criticism when things haven't necessarily gone badly wrong, but you've still managed to upset people? Criticism isn't a crisis. But when all you have is a crisis response, even small things start to feel like one. With a few notable exceptions, no organization expects to be constantly deluged with negative feedback or find itself in a reputational mess it can't contain. Not having a plan leads to hasty, short-term thinking. Organizations clamour to stem the tide of criticism without considering *why* they are being criticized and if it's valid.

When Paperchase were criticized on social media for running a promotion with the *Daily Mail*, they effectively outsourced their crisis response to social media in the absence of a plan. The *Daily Mail* claimed that the criticism amounted to no more than 150 direct tweets and 250 Facebook comments and that Paperchase had been 'bullied' into backing out of future partnerships.[2] Perhaps Paperchase had succumbed to the cognitive bias known as the 'spotlight effect', where perceptions of the amount of attention received are significantly overestimated. Or maybe they just panicked. United Airlines had to deal with

Not having a plan for handling criticism means saying sorry is your only option.

1.2 million Twitter mentions and 135,000 Facebook comments during the 're-accommodation' affair. That's a genuine crisis. But when, as Paperchase did, you ask the inhabitants of Twitter if you owe them an apology, you'll probably end up giving one.

The apology response plan doesn't need to be complex. In fact, you only need to ask yourself three questions to get started: Are we at fault? If so, *how* sorry do we need to be? How do we put it right?

Step 1 – Decide if you are you sorry

Answering this question isn't hard if you *are* obviously at fault. Most organizations know when they've messed up. It's when the failure isn't necessarily obvious that the question demands a period of honest self-reflection. That self-reflection must account for internal policy and address whether or not the conduct in question accords with or contradicts the organization's stated aims. It may be that the criticism is valid. What was OK 20 years ago isn't OK any more. Maybe the organization being criticized needs to hear the criticism. Expected standards of conduct necessarily vary between organizations and industries, and that matters. Maybe your industry has moved on from outdated communications norms, or maybe it hasn't. Protein World can get away with using toned and tanned swimwear models in their marketing, Innocent Smoothies probably can't.

If you have nothing to be sorry for, you have a number of options. None of them involve saying sorry. This isn't just a matter of wording. You must not say sorry. Remember the 2018 study that proved saying sorry when you did nothing wrong damages the financial fortunes of your organization?[3]

How to not say sorry

So what can you do instead? You can clarify your position and discourage further criticism, as Marks & Spencer did when accused of selling blasphemous toilet paper. The UK charity Comic Relief can also provide a lesson in handling criticism without saying sorry. In March 2019 David Lammy MP criticized the charity for portraying a distorted vision of African countries. It was a fair criticism, but that doesn't mean Comic Relief owed him or anyone an apology. They saw things differently, responding that they 'make no apologies' for producing documentaries about African countries in pursuit of their charitable goals.

The lesson here is, if you are going to clarify, be unequivocal. Avoid alluding to contrition. Don't clarify that you did nothing wrong but then apologize if anyone was offended (that you did nothing wrong). You can be generous, in the style of Ben & Jerry's, while simultaneously not being sorry. 'Thanks for your feedback, we'll take your points on board, but we stand by our decision/advert/pricing policy…'. Or you can do nothing. There's a lot to be said for saying nothing.

And saying nothing is definitely preferable to trying to appease your critic, especially if you have no plans to change anything about how you do business. When organizations aren't at fault, but behave like they are, we see the most costly and humiliating failures of crisis communications. H&M said it best about the apparently blasphemous socks: 'Because our customers have complained, we have chosen to recall the items.' Product recalls aren't cheap either.

It doesn't have to be like this. JetBlue provided us with the model apology in 2007. Ten years later, they provided us with the model response to the question 'are we at fault?' In July 2017 the airline made headlines for refusing to apologize to a family of five that they had removed from a flight for belligerent and threatening behaviour towards crew and passengers.[1] It would have been tempting for JetBlue to do what many other airlines have done and simply apologize the problem away, but they showed integrity by backing the actions of their staff. A JetBlue spokesperson told the *Daily Mail* they were thinking of banning the family altogether. 'We are investigating whether the customers' behaviour warrants restrictions on JetBlue travel and we thank our crew members for their professional handling of this unfortunate incident.'[5]

This was brave. The family's mother had filmed the flight crew escorting them from the cabin and the video ended up on social media. As Seth Kaplan of aviation trade publication *Airline Weekly* noted to CBS News at the time: 'Social media has changed the way people interact with companies. It seemed like airlines were, you know, falling all over themselves to apologize for absolutely anything.'[6] JetBlue proved to be the exception. Kaplan added: 'You know what? The customer's not always right.'

Step 2 – Decide how sorry you are

Once you've decided that your organization is at fault, it's time to decide just how sorry you need to be. And that's not as easy as it sounds. Contrition is a spectrum. Airbnb proved, with their eccentric and over-the-top claims of being 'paralysed' by the 'tragedy' of a vandalized holiday rental, that over-egging the atonement can rob future apologies of much needed credibility. They had nowhere to go linguistically when they had to address far more serious matters. A sense of proportion and a commitment to plain language is invaluable here; no hyperbole, no euphemisms and no passive voice.

The third question, 'how do we put this right?', is crucial. It's the first step in establishing a path to recovery.

Step 3 – Decide what you are going to do about it

The first and most obvious thing you need to do is say sorry. Don't *apologize* or *express regret*; say **sorry**. Hopefully there are enough examples in this book of how *not* to do that. But how do you actually give a good one? Common to the best and most meaningful apologies we've looked at are *brevity, clarity* and *plain language*.

Keep it as short as possible. Make it clear what you are apologizing for and to whom. Centre the victims and speak to their experience. Own the failure and acknowledge the impact. Don't obfuscate or deflect, don't use the passive voice and do resist the temptation to speak to your own virtues or mitigating factors that will water down your atonement. As Benjamin Franklin apparently put it: 'Never ruin an apology with an excuse.' And keep it simple. Plain language is essential; short sentences, no fancy grammatical construction and absolutely no ifs, buts or maybes.

The degree to which you've failed should inform your choice of words. Don't say you're 'extremely sorry' if you're not. Save it for when you are. And, because you're clearly acknowledging how you failed and what impact it had, you don't need to throw in superlatives for extra impact. People will understand what you mean.

Consider your delivery method. Some apologies need to be public, some can be private. Some need to be far-reaching, some don't. Try not to smile too much. Studies have shown that smiling damages perceptions of the person giving the apology and can cause investors to lose trust in that organization.[7]

Consumers can tell how sorry you are by what you do to fix things.

The most important part of the apology comes next. Consumers can tell how sorry you are by what you do to fix things. General Motors, under the stewardship of CEO Mary Barra, embarked on a corporate culture shift after the 2014 ignition switch scandal, meaning their customers at least knew, if nothing else, that the company was trying to improve. The same goes for Johnson &

Johnson. Their example remains the definitive case study in 'putting things right'.

If you've ever grappled for longer than you'd prefer with the foil seal on a paracetamol bottle, you can thank James Burke and the Johnson & Johnson company (and their commitment to putting things right) for your short moment of frustration.[8] That type of packaging, annoying as it is, has probably saved lives. In 1982, seven people in Chicago died after consuming cyanide-laced extra-strength Tylenol capsules. The Tylenol murders, as they came to be known, led to the United States' first major non-automotive product recall. Johnson & Johnson's response, coordinated by then CEO James Burke, became the blueprint for modern crisis management. It's hard to overstate the cultural or business impact of that crisis. It caused widespread panic across the USA and led to copycat tampering incidents for years after. In 2018, *Chicago* magazine speculated that the incident might have been the United States' first incident of domestic terrorism.[9]

One of the first things James Burke did after he heard that investigators had linked the first of the deaths to Tylenol was to arrange a nationwide recall of all 31 million potentially affected bottles currently on sale.[10] At the time, there was no evidence that tainted capsules had been found anywhere outside of the greater Chicago area, but Burke wasn't taking any chances. The second thing he did was speak to the heads of news at the major US networks alone, to the horror of Johnson & Johnson's lawyers.[11]

He went in front of live TV audiences to answer questions and, despite not knowing where his firm stood legally, told the country to throw away their Tylenol capsules. Burke offered free replacements of Tylenol pills to anyone who could produce a Tylenol capsule packet. The pill form of the drug was impossible to tamper with in the same way as the capsules. No receipt was required for the exchange.

While the FBI investigated the poisonings, Johnson & Johnson were busy coming up with a robust plan to prevent their products being tampered with in future. Tamper-proof packaging was an innovation of necessity and it took Johnson & Johnson just under two months to come up with it. Burke went on TV to demonstrate it. He didn't oversell it, calling the new tamper-proof packaging 'the best protection we could reasonably devise'.[12] In a televised demonstration, Burke showed how the new packaging offered three barriers to entry. When he popped the outer plastic seal and unscrewed the lid to reveal the secure foil seal, the audience began clapping. Investigators eventually confirmed that the capsules had been tampered with after leaving Johnson & Johnson's facilities, effectively clearing them of any liability.

James Burke credits a document written in 1887 for his steady stewardship during the Tylenol crisis.[13] On its formation, the Johnson & Johnson company authored its corporate credo. Without realizing it, they'd created the blueprint of the modern crisis communications plan. Burke recalled in an interview for the book *Lasting Leadership: What you can learn from the top 25 business people of our times* how that credo outlined the firm's obligations and their order of priority: customers, employees, community, stockholders – in that order.[14] Burke believed that without this credo, he would have been unable to convince Johnson & Johnson to spend the necessary $100 million to recall the 31 million bottles of Tylenol.

Burke never actually said the words 'I am sorry' either. He didn't need to. His decisive action, both in protecting and compensating customers meant that no apology was due. The poisonings were a criminal enterprise and Tylenol was used as a weapon. In 2003 Burke was awarded the Presidential Medal of Freedom for his commitment to 'ethics-driven' business.[15] Speaking in a documentary Burke said: 'I get a lot of credit, but the fact is my job was made incredibly simple. There was nothing else I could have done.'[16]

Remember to take your time

A large part of the success behind the JetBlue 2007 model apology and the Tylenol crisis response is that they took their time to consider the right course of action and then they got on with delivering it. Time is also why modern organizations have been unable to emulate that success. Social media and viral news live or die by their ability to capture the moment and this demands an immediate response. Outrage capitalism abhors an apology vacuum, so organizations rush to do something – anything – to be seen to be addressing criticism. This inevitably means saying sorry.

JetBlue had a plan for restoring consumer trust and took care to implement it properly. Their now-famous YouTube apology came five days after the start of their operational crisis. Tylenol took months to fully respond. That's a lifetime in today's economy of on-demand contrition. JetBlue didn't rush into a reflexive apology because they didn't have to. Tylenol didn't rush their response because lives depended on them *not* rushing.

As counterintuitive as it will feel for today's highly connected organizations to *not* respond in real time, they should resist the temptation at all costs. This isn't a recommendation for organizations to ignore criticism or to drag their feet, but to take the appropriate time to reflect, plan and implement an appropriate response. Reactive and impulsive apologies are insincere. And letting consumer distaste inform internal policies and standards is not a crisis communications strategy. Consumers will absolutely hold organizations to their hastily made, panic-induced promises to do better. And if you need further convincing of the benefits of 'slow crisis management', consider the outcome of a 2005 study called 'Better Late Than Early: The influence of timing on apology effectiveness'.[17]

The study, published in the *Journal of Experimental Social Psychology,* found that the passage of time actually enhanced the impact of an apology and recipients of apologies that came later rather than sooner were more likely to be satisfied with the outcome. 'Knee-jerk' apologies are more likely to fall flat. The study also found that there might actually be a sweet spot. Apologies where the giver has clearly engaged in a period of reflection but hasn't left it so long that people don't feel forgotten about are most likely to work best.

To get our heads around the value of not apologizing reflexively and giving it some time, consider for a second what it would feel like if a high-profile person, perhaps someone with a lack of tact and diplomacy known for their refusal to say sorry, one day decided to break the habit of a lifetime.

Take the appropriate time to reflect, plan and implement an appropriate response.

Many, many (many) people believe President Donald Trump owes them an apology. Imagine that at his next press conference or during his next interview he said: 'Actually, I've been thinking about what I said about Hillary Clinton and I believe I owe her an apology. I was wrong to say what I said and I'm committing to being more thoughtful about my choice of words in future.' People's heads would explode. We'd question his motives. We'd want to know who'd kidnapped the real Donald Trump and of course we may find that, as the 2010 study into apology 'forecasting errors' revealed, the *idea* of him apologizing is actually far more satisfying than the reality. But we'd definitely sit up and take notice.

A note on demanding apologies

For all of the criticism we've levelled at communications professionals in this book, and for all the failures we've celebrated, it's hard not find a degree of sympathy for them. We've examined the various bad habits of outbound brand and organizational communications, but there's another side to it too. Communications professionals are more often than not the whipping boys and girls for the most visceral inbound consumer anger.

In April 2019, Twitter users started noticing some odd activity on the official Carlsberg Twitter account. The brand was paying to promote derogatory and unflattering tweets about its own product. Consumers assumed it was a mistake and many speculated that it was either the work of an incompetent or disgruntled staff member. It wasn't at all. It was part of a marketing campaign. Carlsberg announced a couple of weeks later that it was changing the recipe for its lager. The launch campaign featured Carlsberg employees reading mean tweets directed at the brand and the unflattering and sometimes frankly horrible tweets they'd promoted was the warm-up. It was funny, but also quite poignant in an odd way. Since when did brands and organizations sign up for the sort of flack consumers routinely throw at them?

Anger directed at organizational social media accounts doesn't just disappear into a vacuum. Somebody has to read it. In many cases, 'social listening' and sentiment analysis tools will capture it and report back to management teams how their organization is being perceived. It's someone's day job to collate this anger, outrage and disgust and the more of it there is, the more questions there are to answer.

Behind every corporate or organizational social media account is a person. A real person. With hobbies, friends, worries, career ambitions, anxieties and a whole host of other things they share in common with the people shouting at them. The corporate logo and the blue checkmark of verification aren't much of a shield when it's part of your job to be yelled at.

When the CFO of Domino's Pizza made some mildly anti-Brexit remarks on his personal Twitter account in March 2019, angry consumers rushed to the official Domino's account to vent their rage. It was a coordinated response. The poor executive staffing the social media accounts that day had to copy and paste the same reply more than 20 times in the space of a few hours, explaining that Domino's staff have their own opinions and they do not necessarily represent those of the company.

Did these angry Twitter users believe, in their incandescent 'fetch me the manager' Twitter rage that they were actually speaking to someone in a position to discipline the chief financial officer of the UK arm of the world's largest pizza seller? Or were they just so performatively outraged that they had to let off some steam? Either way, it wasn't the CFO taking the heat from his remarks. It was quite possibly someone he had never even met.

This book was written for communications professionals, but we're all consumers too. And like all of the other, albeit angrier and shoutier, consumers who made this book worth writing, it pays to remember that the people at the blunt end of that consumer anger are often the ones who least deserve to be there. The person responding to customer complaints, apologizing for the hundredth time that day or struggling to work through a backlog of angry comments is rarely the same person who wrote the policy, signed off the advert or designed the products those complaints are concerned with.

A lot of the worst apologies in this book wouldn't have even happened without consumer anger and the tools for those consumers to amplify and laser-focus it at a specific target. So before indulging in performatively outraged consumer pose-striking, it'd be nice if everyone – all of us, consumers, viral news media, social media companies and the communications industry – remembered that behind every organizational apology is a person, or a team of people, trying to do their job.

Notes

Chapter 1

1 Office for National Statistics (2019) Let's get married. OK – when?, www.ons.gov.uk/visualisations/marriages/marriages/index.html (archived at https://perma.cc/LL3J-X93D)
2 Office for National Statistics (2019) Let's get married. OK – when?, www.ons.gov.uk/visualisations/marriages/marriages/index.html (archived at https://perma.cc/LL3J-X93D)
3 Marketwatch (2019) Moss Bros. Group plc, www.marketwatch.com/investing/stock/mosb/financials (archived at https://perma.cc/C2ZQ-PNM3)
4 Grabmeier, J (2016) The 6 elements of an effective apology, according to science, Ohio State University, 12 April, news.osu.edu/the-6-elements-of-an-effective-apology-according-to-science/ (archived at https://perma.cc/DTA3-E9BT) [last accessed 26/11/2018]
5 Martin, B (2018) How psychologically entitled shoppers respond to service recovery apologies, *Emerald Insight*, www.emeraldinsight.com/doi/abs/10.1108/EJM-02-2017-0165 (archived at https://perma.cc/B7HV-EZA4)

Chapter 2

1 Kollewe, J (2018) Qatar Airways CEO apologises for suggesting a woman could not do his job, *Guardian*, www.theguardian.com/business/2018/jun/06/qatar-airways-ceo-apologises-for-suggesting-a-woman-could-not-do-his-job (archived at https://perma.cc/498V-MZVF)
2 Groden, C (2015) Volkswagen CEO issues video apology for emissions cheating scandal, *Fortune,* http://fortune.com/2015/09/22/volkswagen-apology-emissions-cheating/ (archived at https://perma.cc/JG8L-QN45)

3 Suleman, K (2015) Top of the month: Alton Towers delivers sensitive response to roller-coaster crash, *PR Week*, 13 July, www.prweek.com/ article/1355671/top-month-alton-towers-delivers-sensitive-response-roller-coaster-crash (archived at https://perma.cc/Z79Y-9L9G) [last accessed 29/03/2019]

4 Levin, S (2018) Google gender pay gap: women advance suit that could affect 8,300 workers, *Guardian,* www.theguardian.com/ technology/2018/oct/26/google-gender-pay-gap-women-class-action-lawsuit (archived at https://perma.cc/RHG6-CJB3)

5 Conger, K, Wakabayashi, D and Benner, K (2018) Google faces internal backlash over handling of sexual harassment, *New York Times,* www.nytimes.com/2018/10/31/technology/google-sexual-harassment-walkout.html (archived at https://perma.cc/FM4U-5GJE)

6 Bergen, M and Carr, A (2018) Where in the world is Larry Page?, Bloomberg News, www.bloomberg.com/news/features/2018-09-13/ larry-page-is-a-no-show-with-google-under-a-harsh-spotlight (archived at https://perma.cc/AV6C-GTH9)

7 Rosoff, M (2018) Larry Page's silence speaks volumes as Alphabet faces one ethical crisis after another, CNBC, 21 May, www.cnbc. com/2018/05/21/alphabet-leadership-vacuum-where-is-larry-page.html (archived at https://perma.cc/N5QF-CVV5) [last accessed 29/03/2019]

8 Kessler, A (2018) Where in the world is Larry Page? *Wall Street Journal*, 31 December, www.wsj.com/articles/where-in-the-world-is-larry-page-11546199677 (archived at https://perma.cc/3DY9-HUNW) [last accessed 29/03/2019]

9 US Senate (2018) Select Committee on Intelligence Hearing [video], www.intelligence.senate.gov/hearings/open-hearing-foreign-influence-operations%E2%80%99-use-social-media-platforms-company-witnesses (archived at https://perma.cc/6XGG-VD7R)

10 Bergen, M and Carr, A (2018) Where in the world is Larry Page?, Bloomberg News, www.bloomberg.com/news/features/2018-09-13/ larry-page-is-a-no-show-with-google-under-a-harsh-spotlight (archived at https://perma.cc/AV6C-GTH9)

11 Wei, H and Ran, Y (2017) Male versus female: How the gender of apologizers influences consumer forgiveness, *Journal of Business Ethics*, 21 January, /link.springer.com/article/10.1007/s10551-017-3440-7 [last accessed 01/05/2019]

12 Meyersohn, N (2018) Facebook's stock drops after Zuckerberg apologizes, CNN, 22 March, money.cnn.com/2018/03/22/news/companies/facebook-stock/index.html (archived at https://perma.cc/B4MY-4MBK) [last accessed 09/02/2019]

13 Miller, R (2018) An aquarium apologized for calling its sea otter 'thicc', *USA Today,* https://eu.usatoday.com/story/news/nation/2018/12/20/abby-thicc-sea-otter-monterey-bay-aquarium-apology/2376653002/ (archived at https://perma.cc/FGE5-2JPC)

14 Siegel, ST (2019) New York reporter gets fake news shirt removed from Bloomingdale's mannequin, *Adweek,* www.adweek.com/tvspy/new-york-reporter-gets-fake-news-shirt-removed-from-bloomingdales-mannequin/212409 (archived at https://perma.cc/2TBZ-375W)

15 Chung, F (2017) America's 'most hated start-up' apologises for trying to put corner stores out of business, News.com.au, www.news.com.au/finance/small-business/americas-most-hated-startup-apologises-for-trying-to-put-corner-stores-out-of-business/news-story/d17089b043853c2ce0d6b5fe9819d8df (archived at https://perma.cc/6YYT-K7JL)

16 Google search results (2019) 'Bodega startup most hated', www.google.com/search?ei=fdWlXKexMdHDxgP1saj4CA&q=bodega+startup+%22most-hated%22&oq=bodega+startup+%22most-hated%22&gs_l=psy-ab.3..33i29913.28301.30326..30884...0.0..0.100.188.1j1......0....1..gws-wiz.......0i71.HQBH4_d_Dro (archived at https://perma.cc/T7VG-HN42)

17 McDonald, P (2017) So, about our name..., Bodega [blog], 13 September, blog.bodega.ai/so-about-our-name-aa5bff63a92d (archived at https://perma.cc/V63A-UWT9) [last accessed 29/03/2019]

18 O'Connor, C (2014) Chick-fil-A CEO Cathy: gay marriage still wrong but I'll shut up about it and sell chicken, *Forbes,* www.forbes.com/sites/clareoconnor/2014/03/19/chick-fil-a-ceo-cathy-gay-marriage-still-wrong-but-ill-shut-up-about-it-and-sell-chicken/#3c78637e2fcb (archived at https://perma.cc/7WDH-3Y3B)

19 De Silva, M (2019) Five things Tesla CEO Elon Musk can still safely tweet about, Quartz, https://qz.com/1606410/five-things-tesla-ceo-elon-musk-can-still-safely-tweet-about/ (archived at https://perma.cc/DS3V-LCYE)

20 Peterson, H (2015) Whole Foods CEOs admit to overcharging customers, Business Insider, www.businessinsider.com/whole-foods-ceos-admit-to-overcharging-customers-2015-7?r=US&IR=T (archived at https://perma.cc/A755-Y33M)

21 Shane, D (2019) Volkswagen CEO apologizes after appearing to reference Nazi slogan, CNN, 15 March, edition.cnn.com/2019/03/15/business/herbert-diess-volkswagen-ceo-nazi-slogan/index.html (archived at https://perma.cc/45SP-YJ73) [last accessed 29/03/2019]

22 Shane, D (2019) Volkswagen CEO apologizes after appearing to reference Nazi slogan, CNN, 15 March, edition.cnn.com/2019/03/15/business/herbert-diess-volkswagen-ceo-nazi-slogan/index.html (archived at https://perma.cc/45SP-YJ73) [last accessed 29/03/2019]

23 McCann, E (2017) United's apologies: A timeline, *New York Times,* www.nytimes.com/2017/04/14/business/united-airlines-passenger-doctor.html (archived at https://perma.cc/N47E-XT53)

24 Ostrower, J (2013) United say flight 3411 wasn't overbooked. It just had no open seats left, CNN Business, https://money.cnn.com/2017/04/13/news/companies/united-3411-overbooked/index.html (archived at https://perma.cc/6JCX-AJ5Y)

Chapter 3

1 Winch, G (2013) The five ingredients of an effective apology, *Psychology Today*, 21 November, www.psychologytoday.com/us/blog/the-squeaky-wheel/201311/the-five-ingredients-effective-apology (archived at https://perma.cc/7GLG-BS9U) [last accessed 29/01/2019]

2 Goodwin, C and Ross, I (1992) Consumer responses to service failures: Influence of procedural and interactional fairness perceptions, *The Journal of Business Research*, September, www.researchgate.net/publication/222277919 (archived at https://perma.cc/76UV-9E65) [last accessed 29/01/2019]

3 Shakespeare, Stephan (2018) Topshop's brand perception metrics fall following Green accusations, YouGov, 31 October, yougov.co.uk/topics/consumer/articles-reports/2018/10/31/topshops-brand-perception-metrics-fall-following-g (archived at https://perma.cc/5643-GAG4) [last accessed 29/01/2019]

4 Shakespeare, Stephan (2018) Topshop's brand perception metrics fall following Green accusations, YouGov, 31 October, yougov.co.uk/topics/consumer/articles-reports/2018/10/31/topshops-brand-perception-metrics-fall-following-g (archived at https://perma.cc/5643-GAG4) [last accessed 29/01/2019]

5 Shakespeare, Stephan (2018) Topshop's brand perception metrics fall following Green accusations, YouGov, 31 October, yougov.co.uk/topics/consumer/articles-reports/2018/10/31/topshops-brand-perception-metrics-fall-following-g (archived at https://perma.cc/5643-GAG4) [last accessed 29/01/2019]

6 Burgess, S (2018) Topshop apologises and donates £25,000 to charity after removing feminist stall, Sky News, https://news.sky.com/story/topshop-apologies-and-donates-25-000-to-charity-after-removing-feminist-stall-11518592 (archived at https://perma.cc/HH3Z-UQ54)

7 Cardy, P (2015) Alton Towers Smiler operator who theme park blamed for crash horror is sacked, www.mirror.co.uk/news/uk-news/alton-towers-smiler-operator-who-6920989 (archived at https://perma.cc/LHY6-Y95Z)

8 Cockburn, H (2018) Police urge people to stop calling them about KFC chicken shortage, Independent, www.independent.co.uk/news/uk/home-news/police-urge-stop-calling-kfc-chicken-shortage-dhl-tower-hamlets-a8220321.html (archived at https://perma.cc/N96U-PKAV)

9 Kiefer, B (2018) Colonel Sanders makes a bold comeback in KFC's first campaign after chicken crisis, Campaign, www.campaignlive.co.uk/article/colonel-sanders-makes-bold-comeback-kfcs-first-campaign-chicken-crisis/1465900 (archived at https://perma.cc/VB45-Y7C3)

10 Associated Press (1997) Hugo Boss acknowledges link to Nazi regime, New York Times, archive, www.nytimes.com/1997/08/15/business/hugo-boss-acknowledges-link-to-nazi-regime.html (archived at https://perma.cc/PBQ3-FDW4)

11 United States Holocaust Memorial Museum (nd) Holocaust Encyclopedia, The 'People's Car' and the Nazi State, https://encyclopedia.ushmm.org/content/en/article/volkswagen-1 (archived at https://perma.cc/N2H6-9RLJ)

12 Tesco (2019) Twitter, 1 February, https://twitter.com/Tesco/status/1091294129034801153 (archived at https://perma.cc/U482-MFUS) [last accessed 01/02/2019]

13 Halperin, B, Ho, B, List, JA and Muir, I (2018) Toward an understanding of the economics of apologies: evidence from a large-scale natural field experiment, September, s3.amazonaws.com/fieldexperiments-papers2/papers/00644.pdf (archived at https://perma.cc/G5MN-JDEN) [last accessed 28/11/2018]

14 Singh, J (2018) Frontline problem-solving effectiveness: A dynamic analysis of verbal and nonverbal cues, *Journal of Marketing Research*, April, https://journals.sagepub.com/doi/10.1509/jmr.15.0243 (archived at https://perma.cc/YV9N-XGSM) [last accessed 01/02/2019]

15 Wei, H and Ran, Y (2017) Male versus female: How the gender of apologizers influences consumer forgiveness, *Journal of Business Ethics*, 21 January, /link.springer.com/article/10.1007/s10551-017-3440-7 [last accessed 01/05/2019]

16 *Harvard Business Review* (2018) 'Sorry' is not enough, January, https://hbr.org/2018/01/sorry-is-not-enough (archived at https://perma.cc/9G46-YVA8) [last accessed 01/02/2019]

17 Care, A (2019) The truth about Build-a-Bear 'pay your age' event rumours, *Nottingham Post,* www.nottinghampost.com/whats-on/shopping/truth-build-bear-pay-your-2700366 (archived at https://perma.cc/FCG8-FM4U)

18 Google Finance (nd) Build-a-Bear Workshop Inc, www.google.com/search?tbm=fin&q=NYSE:+BBW&stick=H4sIAAAAAAAAAONgecRoyi3w8sc9YSmdSWtOXmNU4-IKzsgvd80rySypFJLgYoOy-KR4uLj0c_UNzKuyCyoKeRaxcvpFBrtaKTg5hQMAy7mteEYAAAA&biw=1440&bih=717#scso=_Y8ioXMnRCbWq1fAP2NCKsA42:0 (archived at https://perma.cc/CPT6-ANS9)

19 Nix, E (2017) Tuskegee Experiment: The infamous syphilis study, A&E Television Networks, www.history.com/news/the-infamous-40-year-tuskegee-study (archived at https://perma.cc/W2B3-YQNX)

20 Katz, RV, Kegeles, SS, Kressin, NR, Green, BL, James, SA, Wang, MQ, Russell, SL and Claudio, C (2008) Awareness of the Tuskegee syphilis study and the US presidential apology and their influence on minority participation in biomedical research, *American Journal of Public Health*, www.ncbi.nlm.nih.gov/pmc/articles/PMC2377291/ (archived at https://perma.cc/R9G5-FWPT)

21 Harvey, T (2018) Too little, too late? The effects of historical intergroup apologies, University of New England, https://blog.une.edu.au/socialpsychology/2018/01/11/too-little-too-late-the-effects-of-historical-intergroup-apologies/ (archived at https://perma.cc/SAW6-EXXC)

22 Corkery, M (2016) Wells Fargo fined $185 million for fraudulently opening accounts, *New York Times*, www.nytimes.com/2016/09/09/business/dealbook/wells-fargo-fined-for-years-of-harm-to-customers.html (archived at https://perma.cc/P5LP-BQVQ)

23 Byrne, C (2002) Mirror says sorry to Bing, *Guardian*, www.theguardian.com/media/2002/oct/22/pressandpublishing.privacy (archived at https://perma.cc/2BLM-D99G)

24 BBC News (2002) Bing proclaims victory over Mirror, 22 October, news.bbc.co.uk/1/hi/entertainment/2353203.stm (archived at https://perma.cc/7PPG-MGQY) [last accessed 01/05/2019]

25 Isidore, C (2015) Death toll for GM ignition switch: 124, CNN Business, https://money.cnn.com/2015/12/10/news/companies/gm-recall-ignition-switch-death-toll/index.html (archived at https://perma.cc/D2ZH-CG22)

26 McClean, P (2016) Merlin fined £5m for Alton Towers rollercoaster crash, *Financial Times*, 27 September, www.ft.com/content/967773ce-84a2-11e6-a29c-6e7d9515ad15 (archived at https://perma.cc/HS3G-63VX) [last accessed 10/08/2018]

27 ten Brinke and Adams, GS (2015) Saving face? When emotion displays during public apologies mitigate damage to organizational performance, *Organizational Behavior and Human Decision Processes*, 1 June, citeseerx.ist.psu.edu/viewdoc/download?doi=10.1.1.706.2307&rep=rep1&type=pdf (archived at https://perma.cc/9LY5-GL9M) [last accessed 29/03/2019]

28 Statista (nd) Attendance at Alton Towers theme park in the United Kingdom (UK) from 2009 to 2017* (in millions), www.statista.com/statistics/641549/attendance-at-alton-towers-uk-theme-park/ (archived at https://perma.cc/EF86-F82Y)

29 Statista (nd) Alton Towers rollercoaster crash: influence on theme park visitors in the UK 2017, www.statista.com/statistics/688605/alton-towers-rollercoaster-crash-influence-in-the-united-kingdom-uk/ (archived at https://perma.cc/7UAR-PRPL)

30 Pugh, G (2015) Sack Kay Burley after awful interviewing of Alton Towers CEO Nick Varney, Change.org, www.change.org/p/sky-news-sack-kay-burley-after-awful-interviewing-of-alton-towers-ceo-nick-varney (archived at https://perma.cc/93CU-AKW9) [last accessed 10/08/2018]

31 Ho, B and Liu, E (2010) Does sorry work? The impact of apology laws on medical malpractice, Johnson School Research Paper Series No. 04-2011, https://papers.ssrn.com/sol3/papers.cfm?abstract_id=1744225 (archived at https://perma.cc/FGK3-X6C9)

32 UK Government (2006) Compensation Act 2006, UK Parliament, www.legislation.gov.uk/ukpga/2006/29/section/2?view=plain (archived at https://perma.cc/6J5D-MPJM) [last accessed 27/04/2019]

33 Burne James, S (2017) PRs launch 'Apology Clause' campaign to tell businesses they can apologise without legal liability worry, *PR Week,* www.prweek.com/article/1449915/prs-launch-apology-clause-campaign-tell-businesses-apologise-without-legal-liability-worry (archived at https://perma.cc/AD9H-RGNR)

34 Balsomini, P and Pileri, G (2018) Autostrade vows to rebuild bridge; stops short of apology, Reuters, https://uk.reuters.com/article/uk-italy-motorway-collapse/autostrade-vows-to-rebuild-bridge-stops-short-of-apology-idUKKBN1L3071?il=0 (archived at https://perma.cc/4THA-2KQX)

Chapter 4

1 McDermott, J (2014) Should brands apologize so much in social media?, Digiday UK, 16 April, digiday.com/marketing/brands-apology-social-media/ (archived at https://perma.cc/4QY5-YQDZ) [last accessed 29/03/2019]

2 Taylor, J (2011) UK banks fund deadly cluster bomb industry, *Independent,* www.independent.co.uk/news/uk/home-news/uk-banks-fund-deadly-cluster-bomb-industry-2338168.html (archived at https://perma.cc/T2VK-EYLV)

3 BBC News (2008) Current account debate in numbers, http://news.bbc.co.uk/1/hi/business/7509375.stm (archived at https://perma.cc/EP2F-R3NP)

4 Burns, J (2017) Uber apologizes in email to ex-riders: former staffer calls it 'all optics', *Forbes*, www.forbes.com/sites/ janetwburns/2017/06/17/uber-apologizes-in-email-to-ex-riders-former-staffer-calls-it-all-optics/#649c989c6265 (archived at https://perma. cc/56YJ-8GWP)

5 Isaac, M (2017) *New York Times*, www.nytimes.com/2017/02/19/ business/uber-sexual-harassment-investigation.html (archived at https://perma.cc/6KHV-K5QK)

6 Quackenbush, C (2018) Uber is under federal investigation for gender discrimination, reports say, *Time*, http://time.com/5340575/uber-federal-investigation-gender-discrimination/ (archived at https://perma. cc/5A9E-JQBN)

7 Isaac, M (2017) Uber founder Travis Kalanick resigns as CEO, *New York Times*, www.nytimes.com/2017/06/21/technology/uber-ceo-travis-kalanick.html (archived at https://perma.cc/X7RQ-C66L)

Chapter 5

1 Heid, J (2009) Herb Kelleher made JetBlue's founder cry, *D Magazine*, www.dmagazine.com/frontburner/2009/09/herb-kelleher-made-jetblues-founder-cry/ (archived at https://perma.cc/98S8-FFXJ)

2 Rifkin, G (2019) Herb Kelleher, whose Southwest Airlines reshaped the industry, dies at 87, *New York Times*, 3 January, www.nytimes. com/2019/01/03/obituaries/herb-kelleher-whose-southwest-airlines-reshaped-the-industry-dies-at-87.html (archived at https://perma. cc/3D9T-CGEA) [last accessed 01/03/2019]

3 Rifkin, G (2019) Herb Kelleher, whose Southwest Airlines reshaped the industry, dies at 87, *New York Times*, 3 January, www.nytimes. com/2019/01/03/obituaries/herb-kelleher-whose-southwest-airlines-reshaped-the-industry-dies-at-87.html (archived at https://perma. cc/3D9T-CGEA) [last accessed 01/03/2019]

4 Carville, P and Begala, J (2002) *Buck Up, Suck Up... and Come Back When You Foul Up: 12 winning secrets from the war room*, Simon & Schuster, New York

5 McDermott, J (2014) Should brands apologize so much in social media, Digiday UK, https://digiday.com/marketing/brands-apology-social-media/ (archived at https://perma.cc/7GAQ-EH2E)

6 Eblin Group (2009) Jet Blue Founder's advice for leaders: Have your cry and keep going [blog], https://eblingroup.com/blog/jet-blue-founders-advice-for-leaders-have-your-cry-and-keep-going/ (archived at https://perma.cc/9XDS-TRBC)

7 Oldest.org (2005) First backflip on YouTube [video], www.oldest.org/entertainment/videos-on-youtube/ (archived at https://perma.cc/62VZ-2QZS)

8 Gianatasio, D (2013) JetBlue knows how to communicate with customers in social, and when to shut up, *Adweek*, 9 September, www.adweek.com/brand-marketing/jetblue-knows-how-communicate-customers-social-and-when-shut-152246/ (archived at https://perma.cc/W73W-WTEN) [last accessed 01/03/2019]

9 Weiss, T (2007) JetBlue's Survival School, *Forbes*, 20 February, forbes.com/2007/02/20/neeleman-jet-blue-lead-cx_tw_0220jetblueceo.html#11388bcf6195[last accessed 27/02/2019]

10 Gianatasio, D (2013) JetBlue knows how to communicate with customers in social, and when to shut up, *Adweek*, 9 September, www.adweek.com/brand-marketing/jetblue-knows-how-communicate-customers-social-and-when-shut-152246/ (archived at https://perma.cc/W73W-WTEN) [last accessed 01/03/2019]

11 Gianatasio, D (2013) JetBlue knows how to communicate with customers in social, and when to shut up, *Adweek*, 9 September, www.adweek.com/brand-marketing/jetblue-knows-how-communicate-customers-social-and-when-shut-152246/ (archived at https://perma.cc/W73W-WTEN) [last accessed 01/03/2019]

Chapter 6

1 Geddes, L (2016) Why do the British say sorry so much?, BBC, 24 February, www.bbc.com/future/story/20160223-why-do-the-british-say-sorry-so-much (archived at https://perma.cc/8GA8-CNQZ) [last accessed 15/08/2018]

2 Google (2018) Google Books Ngram Viewer [online tool], books. google.com/ngrams (archived at https://perma.cc/LBR8-7RAN) [last accessed 15/08/2018]

3 Mental Health Today (2017) People were happier in 1957 than today, according to research, www.mentalhealthtoday.co.uk/people-were-happier-in-1957-than-today-according-to-research (archived at https://perma.cc/5BHS-6B69)

4 Faull, J (2016) Tesco claims customer trust at a four year high as resurgence continues, The Drum 05 October, www.thedrum.com/news/2016/10/05/tesco-claims-customer-trust-four-year-high-resurgence-continues (archived at https://perma.cc/MU8Z-VXBY) [last accessed 31.7.2018]

5 Kokalitcheva, K (2016) Twitter encourages more businesses to interact with upset customers, *Fortune,* http://fortune.com/2016/10/05/twitter-customer-service-study/ (archived at https://perma.cc/GL2N-HQV2)

6 Carr, D (2014) Risks abound as reporters play in traffic, *New York Times*, 23 March, www.nytimes.com/2014/03/24/business/media/risks-abound-as-reporters-play-in-traffic.html (archived at https://perma.cc/SC7P-W3WW) [last accessed 27/8/2018]

7 Sanders, S (2017) Upworthy was one of the hottest sites ever. You won't believe what happened next, National Public Radio, 20 June, www.npr.org/sections/alltechconsidered/2017/06/20/533529538/upworthy-was-one-of-the-hottest-sites-ever-you-wont-believe-what-happened-next?t=1535384358722 (archived at https://perma.cc/7NCK-DT8C)

8 Barakat, C (2014) Viral content on social media: Headline tips by Upworthy, *Adweek*, 14 January, www.adweek.com/digital/viral-content-social-media-headline-tips-upworthy/ (archived at https://perma.cc/475T-YEG5) [last accessed 24/08/2018]

9 Abad-Santos, A (2015) 2015: A year of fake outrage and backlash that made us feel better, Vox.com, 23 December, www.vox.com/2015/12/23/10659910/2015-outrage (archived at https://perma.cc/3W2H-BQYB) [last accessed 27/8/2018]

10 Barakat, C (2014) Viral content on social media: Headline tips by Upworthy, *Adweek*, 14 January, www.adweek.com/digital/viral-content-social-media-headline-tips-upworthy/ (archived at https://perma.cc/475T-YEG5) [last accessed 24/08/2018]

11 Upworthy, (2018) Why advertise with Upworthy? www.upworthy. com/advertise (archived at https://perma.cc/UF9U-X6PQ) [last accessed 27/08/2018]

12 Upworthy, (2018) Why advertise with Upworthy? www.upworthy. com/advertise (archived at https://perma.cc/UF9U-X6PQ) [last accessed 27/08/2018]

13 Anonymous (2017) I write viral news for a living. What it's like will shock you, Wired, www.wired.co.uk/article/viral-news-psychology-human-nature (archived at https://perma.cc/XA5E-VTUW)

14 Anonymous (2017) I write viral news for a living. What it's like will shock you, Wired, www.wired.co.uk/article/viral-news-psychology-human-nature (archived at https://perma.cc/XA5E-VTUW)

15 Oxford Living Dictionaries (2018) www.lexico.com/en/definition/call_someone_out (archived at https://perma.cc/55JB-6X72) [last accessed 27/08/2018]

16 Spary, S, (2018) This Mum has called out Clarks over the difference in its shoes for girls and boys, Buzzfeed, 9 August, www.buzzfeed.com/saraspary (archived at https://perma.cc/V68V-F9LZ) [last accessed 24/08/2018]

17 Watts, S (2017) I'm the woman who called out United and I'm sick of sexism, Time, 27 March, http://time.com/4714476/united-leggings-ban-shannon-watts-why-it-was-sexist/ (archived at https://perma.cc/DXV3-BG6W) [last accessed 24/08/2018]

18 Kannenberg, L (2018) How to restore brand credibility after having screwed up publicly, The Next Web, 4 March, thenextweb.com/contributors/2018/03/04/restoring-brand-credibility-in-the-face-of-call-out-culture/ (archived at https://perma.cc/ZNM2-FVWT) [last accessed 24/08/2018]

19 Kannenberg, L (2018) How to restore brand credibility after having screwed up publicly, The Next Web, 4 March, thenextweb.com/contributors/2018/03/04/restoring-brand-credibility-in-the-face-of-call-out-culture/ (archived at https://perma.cc/ZNM2-FVWT) [last accessed 24/08/2018]

20 Friedersdorf, C (2017) The destructiveness of call-out culture on campus, The Atlantic, 8 May, www.theatlantic.com/politics/archive/2017/05/call-out-culture-is-stressing-out-college-students/524679/ (archived at https://perma.cc/UX9X-RBUQ) [last accessed 24/08/2018]

21 Benjamin, K (2019) Lush ditches UK social media accounts, *Campaign*, 10 April, www.campaignlive.co.uk/article/lush-ditches-uk-social-media-accounts/1581564 (archived at https://perma.cc/64R5-Q7KS) [last accessed 10/04/2019]

22 BBC News (2018) Weatherspoon pub chain shuts its social media accounts, www.bbc.co.uk/news/business-43781281 (archived at https://perma.cc/C2GG-VB2R)

23 Shaer, M (2014) What emotion goes viral the fastest? *The Smithsonian,* www.smithsonianmag.com/science-nature/what-emotion-goes-viral-fastest-180950182/ (archived at https://perma.cc/5LAW-FNRE)

24 Stadd, A (2014) Anger spreads faster than any other emotion on Twitter, *Adweek,* www.adweek.com/digital/anger-twitter/ (archived at https://perma.cc/EB5B-TNX4)

25 Kannenberg, L (2018) How to restore brand credibility after having screwed up publicly, The Next Web, 4 March, thenextweb.com/contributors/2018/03/04/restoring-brand-credibility-in-the-face-of-call-out-culture/ (archived at https://perma.cc/ZNM2-FVWT) [last accessed 24/08/2018]

26 Panahi, R (2018) Why companies shouldn't be spooked by online bullies, *The Herald Sun*, 16 September, www.heraldsun.com.au/news/opinion/rita-panahi/why-companies-shouldnt-be-spooked-by-online-bullies/news-story/df8bafa4e1cea22916d79cc785355ba3 (archived at https://perma.cc/8L5J-JXML) [last accessed 19/9/2018]

Chapter 7

1 Reuters, (2018) Plane skids off Turkish runway and plunges towards sea, Reuters, 4 January, www.reuters.com/article/us-turkey-airplane/plane-skids-off-turkish-runway-and-plunges-towards-sea-idUSKBN1F30C1 (archived at https://perma.cc/N2P8-4VDU) [last accessed 10/08/2018]

2 Czarnecki, S (2017) Timeline of a crisis: How Equifax botched its breach, *PR Week*, 27 November, www.prweek.com/article/1450723/timeline-crisis-equifax-botched-its-breach (archived at https://perma.cc/964F-ND4Y) [last accessed 27/8/2018]

3 Equifax (2017) Equifax announces cybersecurity incident involving consumer information, Cision PR Newswire, www.prnewswire.com/news-releases/equifax-announces-cybersecurity-incident-involving-consumer-information-300515960.html (archived at https://perma.cc/4TQ4-X75G)

4 Equifax (2017) Equifax announces cybersecurity incident involving consumer information, 7 September, https://investor.equifax.com/news-and-events/news/2017/09-07-2017-213000628 (archived at https://perma.cc/2QRD-T7Y6) [last accessed 27/8/2018]

5 Equifax (2017) Equifax announces cybersecurity incident involving consumer information, 7 September, https://investor.equifax.com/news-and-events/news/2017/09-07-2017-213000628 (archived at https://perma.cc/2QRD-T7Y6) [last accessed 27/8/2018]

6 Merriam-Webster (2018) Re-accommodate, www.merriam-webster.com/dictionary/reaccommodate (archived at https://perma.cc/NT97-2GSY) [last accessed 15/08/2018]

7 Thomas, L (2017) United CEO says airline had to 're-accommodate' passenger, and the reaction was wild, CNBC News, www.cnbc.com/2017/04/10/united-ceo-says-airline-had-to-re-accommodate-passenger-and-twitter-is-having-a-riot.html (archived at https://perma.cc/KAN4-36FP)

8 Thomas, L (2017) Video surfaces of man being dragged from overbooked United flight', CNBC News, 10 April, www.cnbc.com/2017/04/10/video-surfaces-of-man-being-dragged-from-overbooked-united-flight.html (archived at https://perma.cc/NVA7-BSVR) [last accessed 15/08/2018]

9 Macias, M (2017) It may be time for United to 're-accommodate' CEO Oscar Munoz, CNBC Business News, 11 April, www.cnbc.com/2017/04/11/it-may-be-time-for-united-to-re-accommodate-ceo-oscar-munoz-commentary.html (archived at https://perma.cc/8B9A-B3Z2) [last accessed 15/08/2018]

10 Urban Dictionary (2017) Re-accommodate, www.urbandictionary.com/define.php?term=re-accommodate (archived at https://perma.cc/3T43-YC7H)

11 Thune, J, Nelson, W, Blunt, R and Cantwell, M (2017), United States Senate Committee on Commerce, Science and Transportation, letter to Chicago Department of Aviation, 7 April, www.commerce.senate.gov/

public/_cache/files/04f5c270-f404-4351-95cb-fb17b3277d25/4A395B
3AA6B66FCC0CD081434C4D9312.cst-to-united-and-o-hare.pdf
(archived at https://perma.cc/VTH9-C8WT) [last accessed 15/08/2018]

12 Wikipedia (2017) United Express Flight 3411 incident, en.wikipedia.
org/wiki/United_Express_Flight_3411_incident (archived at
https://perma.cc/G9SS-3DM8) [last accessed 15/08/2018]

13 Blakinger, K (2017) #arkema spox says: 'It's misleading to say it was
an explosion. It was an overpressurizatiom that was followed by a
fire', Twitter, 31 August, https://twitter.com/keribla/status/9032417912
64215040?lang=en (archived at https://perma.cc/PU5F-Z8D8) [last
accessed 15/08/2018]

14 Platoff, E (2018) As lawsuits over Texas chemical disaster add up,
advocates blame Arkema and rules regulating it, *Texas Tribune*, 30
March, www.texastribune.org/2018/03/30/arkema-disaster-harvey-
regulations-texas-crosby/ (archived at https://perma.cc/TF46-ZL2R)
[last accessed 15/08/2018]

15 Taggart, J (2017) The Energy 202: Trump wants more infrastructure.
So Interior aims to speed up environmental reviews, *Washington Post*,
8 September, www.washingtonpost.com/news/powerpost (archived at
https://perma.cc/GJ8U-RWGS) [last accessed 15/08/2018]

16 Taggart, J (2017) The Energy 202: Trump wants more infrastructure.
So Interior aims to speed up environmental reviews, *Washington Post*,
8 September, www.washingtonpost.com/news/powerpost (archived at
https://perma.cc/GJ8U-RWGS) [last accessed 15/08/2018]

Chapter 8

1 Mendleson, R (2014) Hair drug tests: A mother's anguish over losing
her girls, *The Star*, 8 December, www.thestar.com/news/
gta/2014/12/08/hair_drug_tests_a_mothers_anguish_over_losing_her_
girls.html (archived at https://perma.cc/E5D9-P3ZC) [last accessed
14/08/2018]

2 Mendleson, R (2017) Lawyers spar over whether class-action into
Motherisk drug-testing scandal should go ahead, *The Star*, 12 October,
www.thestar.com/news/gta/2017/10/12/lawyers-spar-over-whether-
class-action-into-motherisk-drug-testing-scandal-should-go-ahead.html
(archived at https://perma.cc/8UE3-NX92) [last accessed 14/08/2018]

3 Lorrigio, P (2018) Discredited Motherisk hair-testing program harmed vulnerable families: report, *The Canadian Press*, 26 February, www.theglobeandmail.com/news/national/discredited-motherisk-hair-testing-program-harmed-vulnerable-families-report/article38111582/ (archived at https://perma.cc/Y22Q-GZMV) [last accessed 14/08/2018]

4 Butler, S (2018) Co-op to be investigated over its treatment of suppliers, *Guardian,* 8 March, www.theguardian.com/business/2018/mar/08/co-op-investigated-treatment-suppliers-groceries-code-adjudicator (archived at https://perma.cc/RCQ9-4GFA) [last accessed 27/08/2018]

5 Shank, M and Bedat, M (2016) How Beyoncé's 'Ivy Park' label should solve sweatshop scandal: switch suppliers, Huffington Post, 26 May, www.huffingtonpost.com/michael-shank/how-beyonces-ivy-park-lab_b_10143234.html/ (archived at https://perma.cc/JG4K-YQA4) [last accessed 27/8/2018]

6 Shank, M and Bedat, M (2016) How Beyoncé's 'Ivy Park' label should solve sweatshop scandal: switch suppliers, Huffington Post, 26 May, www.huffingtonpost.com/ (archived at https://perma.cc/HG43-ELLD) [last accessed 27/8/2018]

7 Equifax (2017) Equifax announces cybersecurity incident involving consumer information, 7 September, https://investor.equifax.com/news-and-events/news/2017/09-07-2017-213000628 (archived at https://perma.cc/2QRD-T7Y6) [last accessed 27/8/2018]

8 McCrank, J and Finkle, J (2018) Equifax breach could be most costly in corporate history, Reuters, 2 March, www.reuters.com/article/us-equifax-cyber/equifax-breach-could-be-most-costly-in-corporate-history-idUSKCN1GE257 (archived at https://perma.cc/YJY3-HB6B) [last accessed 27/8/2018]

9 Statt, N (2016) Samsung runs full-page apology ads over Galaxy Note 7 recall, The Verge, 7 November, www.theverge.com/2016/11/7/13558442/samsung-galaxy-note-7-recall-apology-ad (archived at https://perma.cc/Q9FZ-XDJQ) [last accessed 27/8/2018]

10 Tyler, J (2016) KFC in Birmingham found to be covered in mice droppings, dirt, grime and grease, *Birmingham Mail*, 4 August, www.birminghammail.co.uk/news/midlands-news/kfc-birmingham-found-covered-mice-11706232 (archived at https://perma.cc/NBH3-6AEK) [last accessed 27/8/2018]

11 Gilbert, J (2018) Firefighters tackle blaze after double decker bus bursts into flames near quiet Scottish village, *Mirror*, 21 August, www.mirror.co.uk/news/uk-news/firefighters-tackle-blaze-after-double-13113610 (archived at https://perma.cc/X2DC-AGC5) [last accessed 27/8/2018]

12 Tiwari, P (2018) 'We are committed to protecting women's health... we are deeply sorry' – CervicalCheck issue apology, *Irish Independent*, 6 May, www.independent.ie/irish-news/health/we-are-committed-to-protecting-womens-health-we-are-deeply-sorry-cervicalcheck-issue-apology-36878635.html (archived at https://perma.cc/Q7LC-CERX) [last accessed 27/8/2018]

13 Orwell, G (1946) *Politics and the English Language*, www.orwell.ru/library/essays/politics/english/e_polit (archived at https://perma.cc/BZE4-4FTE)

14 *The Economist* (2011) Johnson [blog], Hating on hating on the passive voice, *The Economist*, 23 February, www.economist.com/johnson/2011/02/23/hating-on-hating-on-the-passive-voice (archived at https://perma.cc/Y3XH-UHZZ) [last accessed 27/8/2018]

15 Zimmer, B (2018) The passives of PricewaterhouseCoopers, Language Log, 27 February, http://languagelog.ldc.upenn.edu (archived at https://perma.cc/QD9A-9W5Q) [last accessed 27/08/2018]

16 Doyle, G (2017) The award for best use of passive voice in an apology goes to..., Twitter, 26 February, https://twitter.com/mgerrydoyle/status/836140212174508033 (archived at https://perma.cc/X9JS-CNV6) [last accessed 2708/2018]

17 Rosman, K (2017) Have never seen a greater painstaken use of the passive voice in an apology, Twitter, 27 February, https://twitter.com/katierosman/status/836186458457313280 (archived at https://perma.cc/48X3-24JZ) [last accessed 2708/2018]

18 Broder, J (2007) Familiar fallback for officials: 'Mistakes were made', *New York Times*, 14 March, www.nytimes.com/2007/03/14/washington/14mistakes.html (archived at https://perma.cc/WBU4-6JMY) [last accessed 29/03/2019]

19 Johnston Publishing (2018) Portsmouth couple outraged after train lighting grille falls on them – and company offers them a fiver in compensation, *The News*, 9 April, www.portsmouth.co.uk/news/

traffic-and-travel/portsmouth-couple-outraged-after-train-lighting-grille-falls-on-them-and-company-offers-them-a-fiver-in-compensation-1-8596150 (archived at https://perma.cc/KB6W-7B4B) [last accessed 11/06/2019]

20 Newsquest (2018) Mum claims children were treated like 'second class citizens' as one has arm trapped in bus door and other denied disability access, *The Mail*, 20 August, www.nwemail.co.uk/news/barrow/16587604.mum-claims-children-were-treated-like-second-class-citizens-as-one-has-arm-trapped-in-bus-door-and-other-denied-disability-access/ (archived at https://perma.cc/5NX8-GHEP) [last accessed 11/06/2019]

Chapter 9

1 Ronson, J (2015) *So You've Been Publicly Shamed*, Picador, London

2 Ronson, J (2015) *So You've Been Publicly Shamed*, Picador, London

3 Zahavi, A and Zahavi, A (1999) *The Handicap Principle: A missing piece of Darwin's puzzle*, Oxford University Press, Oxford

4 Wills, E (2018) H&M pulls range of socks over pattern that resembles Arabic word for Allah, *Evening Standard,* www.standard.co.uk/news/world/hm-pulls-range-of-socks-over-pattern-that-resembles-arabic-word-for-allah-a3753386.html (archived at https://perma.cc/CCJ7-F52X)

5 *Guardian* (2018) Gap sorry for selling T-shirt with 'incorrect' map of China, 15 May, www.theguardian.com/world/2018/may/15/gap-sorry-t-shirt-map-china (archived at https://perma.cc/FA55-SP4J)

6 Murphy, C (2018) Topman explains why controversial '96' T-shirt was released and 'apologise unreservedly', *Liverpool Echo,* www.liverpoolecho.co.uk/news/liverpool-news/topman-explains-controversial-96-shirt-14419024 (archived at https://perma.cc/WS9S-PGL5)

7 Woolcock, N (2018) Racism row over all white shortlist in Next mothers' contest, *The Times,* www.thetimes.co.uk/article/racism-row-over-all-white-shortlist-in-next-mothers-contest-vn2v0kgb5 (archived at https://perma.cc/7MEQ-5ANH)

8 Petter, O (2018) Boohoo accused of sexism after offering women discounts for feeling 'second best' during world cup, *Independent,* www.independent.co.uk/life-style/fashion/boohoo-world-cup-sexism-women-discount-offers-online-fashion-shopping-a8422481.html (archived at https://perma.cc/NYC5-JPDJ)

9 Kerr, C (2018) H&M pulls socks from stores in row over 'Allah pattern', *Express,* www.express.co.uk/news/ uk/911494/h-and-m-socks-allah-pulled-shelves-controversy-squiggle-stopped-recalled (archived at https://perma.cc/4ZGS-4CJ5)

10 Abdulrazaq, T (2018) Twitter, 3 February, https://twitter.com/ thewarjournal/status/959926885240201216 (archived at https:// perma.cc/NW32-2EM8) [last accessed 8/8/2018]

11 Arrington, M (2011) Airbnb offers unconditional apology, and $50,000 insurance guarantee, TechCrunch, 1 August, https://techcrunch.com/2011/08/01/airbnb-offers-unconditional-apology-and-50000-insurance-guarantee/ (archived at https://perma.cc/ WSQ5-N9XJ) [last accessed 27/8/2018]

12 Hannam, K (2017) Airbnb hosts in Australia charged with raping and murdering their guest, *Fortune,* 30 October, https://fortune. com/2017/10/30/airbnb-murder-melbourne/ (archived at https://perma. cc/BC6J-7NKB) [last accessed 27/8/2018]

13 Moore, C (2018) General Election 2010: Gordon Brown was undone by the media, not Gillian Duffy, *Telegraph,* 3 May, telegraph.co.uk/ news/election-2010/7671436/General-Election-2010-Gordon-Brown-was-undone-by-the-media-not-Gillian-Duffy.html (archived at https://perma.cc/2RR8-9LQF) [last accessed 11/06/2019]

14 O'Reilly, G (2010) PR professionals criticise Gordon Brown's apology following 'bigot' slur, *PR Week,* 28 April, www.prweek.com/ article/999931/pr-professionals-criticise-gordon-browns-apology-following-bigot-slur (archived at https://perma.cc/FP67-CTQG) [last accessed 17/08/2018]

15 Zatat, N (2018) Canadian prime minister Justin Trudeau called out a woman for being racist – and this is why he's not apologising, Indy100, 21 August, www.indy100.com/article/justin-trudeau-racist-woman-canada-illegal-immigrant-comment-8501546 (archived at https://perma.cc/M29K-MRNP) [last accessed 22/02/2019]

16 Wright, M (2018) Boris Johnson and the awful art of the empty political apology, *The New European,* 13 August, www.theneweuropean.co.uk/top-stories/boris-johnson-apology-burka-1-5649321 (archived at https://perma.cc/BX5X-7JBA) [last accessed 14/08/2018]

17 Jones, N (2006) Brownites v Blairites – the full story, BBC, 7 September, https://news.bbc.co.uk/1/hi/uk_politics/5323960.stm (archived at https://perma.cc/S9ZJ-6XMG) [last accessed 12/06/2019]

Chapter 10

1 Ibrahim, Y (1998) British Petroleum is buying Amoco in $48.2 billion deal, *New York Times,* www.nytimes.com/1998/08/12/business/british-petroleum-is-buying-amoco-in-48.2-billion-deal.html (archived at https://perma.cc/2KHP-WBF2)

2 Reuters (2010) BP CEO apologizes for 'thoughtless' oil spill comment, www.reuters.com/article/us-oil-spill-bp-apology/bp-ceo-apologizes-for-thoughtless-oil-spill-comment-idUSTRE6515NQ20100602 (archived at https://perma.cc/TDN3-LTGF)

3 *Telegraph* (2011) Ten largest oil spills in history, www.telegraph.co.uk/news/worldnews/australiaandthepacific/newzealand/8812598/10-largest-oil-spills-in-history.html (archived at https://perma.cc/SL42-4M95)

4 Beam, C (2010) Oil Slick: how BP is handling is PR disaster, Slate, https://slate.com/news-and-politics/2010/05/what-p-r-experts-think-of-bp-s-response-to-the-oil-spill.html?via=gdpr-consent (archived at https://perma.cc/HJ7D-TE7X)

5 Seitz-Wald, A (2010) Trying to shirk responsibility for spill, BP CEO predicts 'lots of illegitimate' lawsuits because 'this is America', Think Progress, https://thinkprogress.org/trying-to-shirk-responsibility-for-spill-bp-ceo-predicts-lots-of-illegitimate-lawsuits-because-this-cb78e8a39f71/ (archived at https://perma.cc/FR55-VZGF)

6 Lyons, LE (2011) 'I'd like my life back': Corporate personhood and the BP oil disaster, University of Hawaii Press, www.jstor.org/stable/23541181?seq=1#page_scan_tab_contents (archived at https://perma.cc/RE65-52B8) [last accessed 22/02/2019]

7 Reuters (2010) BP CEO apologizes for 'thoughtless' oil spill comment, www.reuters.com/article/us-oil-spill-bp-apology/bp-ceo-apologizes-for-thoughtless-oil-spill-comment-idUSTRE6515NQ20100602 (archived at https://perma.cc/TDN3-LTGF)

8 BBC News (2010) BP boss Tony Hayward's gaffes, 20 June, www.bbc.com/news/10360084 (archived at https://perma.cc/5N3V-X7EY)

9 Chance, D, Cicon, J and Ferris, SP (2015) Honesty can keep companies' stock prices up during hard times, University of Missouri-Columbia, 26 May, www.sciencedaily.com/releases/2015/05/150526132359.htm (archived at https://perma.cc/D275-W4HW) [last accessed 09/02/2019]

10 Tiedens, LZ (2001) Anger and advancement versus sadness and subjugation: The effect of negative emotion expressions on social status conferral, *Journal of Personality and Social Psychology*, May, web.mit.edu/curhan/www/docs/Articles/15341_Readings/Affect/Tiedens.pdf (archived at https://perma.cc/XV6T-EMTQ) [last accessed 01/02/2019]

Chapter 11

1 De Cremer, D, Pillutla, MM and Folmer, CR (2010) How important is an apology to you?: Forecasting errors in evaluating the value of apologies, *Psychological Science*, 1 December, journals.sagepub.com/doi/abs/10.1177/0956797610391101 (archived at https://perma.cc/F3XD-DRZF) [last accessed 27/04/2019]

2 Zuckerberg, M (2018) Hard questions: update on Cambridge Analytica, Facebook, https://newsroom.fb.com/news/2018/03/hard-questions-cambridge-analytica/ (archived at https://perma.cc/822A-2ELR)

3 Zuckerberg, M (2010) From Facebook, answering privacy concerns with new settings, *Washington Post*, 24 May, www.washingtonpost.com/wp-dyn/content/article/2010/05/23/AR2010052303828.html (archived at https://perma.cc/S77N-K76G) [last accessed 22/02/2019]

4 Meyersohn, N (2018) Facebook's stock drops after Zuckerberg apologizes, CNN News, https://money.cnn.com/2018/03/22/news/companies/facebook-stock/index.html (archived at https://perma.cc/QWA6-6WU5)

5 McKenzie, S (2018) Facebook's Mark Zuckerberg says sorry in full-page newspaper ads, CNN World, https://edition.cnn.com/2018/03/25/europe/facebook-zuckerberg-cambridge-analytica-sorry-ads-newspapers-intl/index.html (archived at https://perma.cc/J7QP-Y5SB)

6 Meyersohn, N (2018) Facebook's stock drops after Zuckerberg apologizes, CNN News, https://money.cnn.com/2018/03/22/news/companies/facebook-stock/index.html (archived at https://perma.cc/QWA6-6WU5)

7 Meyersohn, N (2018) Facebook's stock drops after Zuckerberg apologizes, CNN News, https://money.cnn.com/2018/03/22/news/companies/facebook-stock/index.html (archived at https://perma.cc/QWA6-6WU5)

8 Volz, D and Ingram, D (2018) Facebook's Zuckerberg unscathed by congressional grilling, stock rises, Reuters, 11 April, www.reuters.com/article/us-facebook-privacy-zuckerberg/facebooks-zuckerberg-unscathed-by-congressional-grilling-stock-rises-idUSKBN1HI1CJ (archived at https://perma.cc/QK43-53HF) [last accessed 27/02/2019]

9 United (2017) United Airlines CEO Oscar Munoz named *PRWeek*'s 'Communicator of the Year' , United Airlines Newsroom Resources, 17 March, https://hub.united.com/united–ceo-communicator-of-year-2567373427.html (archived at https://perma.cc/HW99-UUEX) [last accessed 06/02/2019]

10 United (2017) United Airlines CEO Oscar Munoz named *PRWeek*'s 'Communicator of the Year', United Airlines Newsroom Resources, 17 March, https://hub.united.com/united–ceo-communicator-of-year-2567373427.html (archived at https://perma.cc/HW99-UUEX) [last accessed 06/02/2019]

11 *PR Week* (2017) United Airlines CEO Oscar Munoz named PRWeek US Communicator of the Year, *PRWeek*, 9 March, www.prweek.com/article/1426909/united-airlines-ceo-oscar-munoz-named-prweek-us-communicator-year (archived at https://perma.cc/C9AJ-L3FM) [last accessed 06/02/2019]

12 McCann, E (2017) United's apologies: A timeline, *New York Times*, www.nytimes.com/2017/04/14/business/united-airlines-passenger-doctor.html (archived at https://perma.cc/N47E-XT53)

13 Shen, L (2017) United Airlines stock drops $1.4 billion after passenger-removal controversy, *Fortune*, http://fortune.com/2017/04/11/united-airlines-stock-drop/ (archived at https://perma.cc/XN4Y-YJ8B)

14 Fickensher, L (2018) Papa John's founder admits to deal with woman accusing him of sexual harassment, *New York Post,* https://nypost. com/2018/10/01/papa-johns-founder-admits-to-deals-with-women-accusing-him-of-sexual-harassment/ (archived at https://perma.cc/ P78Z-Q9UW)

15 Wolfson, A (2013) 'Papa John' makes no apology for wealth, Obamacare remarks, *USA Today,* https://eu.usatoday.com/story/ money/business/2013/01/14/pizza-papa-john-schnatter/1566364/ (archived at https://perma.cc/PQM2-Y6K4)

16 Kirsch, N (2018) John Schnatter sues Papa John's, backtracks admission to use of racial slur, *Forbes,* www.forbes.com/sites/ noahkirsch/2018/07/26/john-schnatter-sues-papa-johns-calls-reports-over-his-use-of-n-word-false/#3adeb2471b74 (archived at https:// perma.cc/W55X-HE2X)

17 Whitten, S and Handley, L (2018) Family of KFC's Colonel Sanders defends him amid Papa John's racial slur scandal, CNBC Marketing, www.cnbc.com/2018/07/19/family-of-kfc-colonel-defends-him-amid-papa-johns-racial-slur-scandal.html (archived at https://perma. cc/5TTY-TCHA)

18 Moye, David (2018) Papa John's CEO attempts damage control but not an apology, Huffington Post, 14 July, www.huffingtonpost.co.uk/entry/ papa-johns-damage-control_n_5b49237de4b0bc69a78749ea (archived at https://perma.cc/8YFA-WW53) [last accessed 01/02/2019]

Chapter 12

1 Lebow, RN (2018) My innocent joke about lingerie and an insidious culture of censorship: Leading academic says trouble caused by a one-liner he cracked in a lift left him reeling, *Daily Mail*, www. dailymail.co.uk/news/article-5738391/PROFESSOR-RICHARD-NED-LEBOW-innocent-joke-lingerie-insidious-culture-censorship.html (archived at https://perma.cc/R4RF-VM3E)

2 Sky News (2018) Academic refuses to apologise for 'lame' lingerie joke, https://news.sky.com/story/academic-refuses-to-apologise-for-lame-lingerie-joke-11368097 (archived at https://perma.cc/VF6J-PQAJ)

3 Marcus, R (2018) She called his elevator joke offensive. He called her complaint 'frivolous.' Who's right? *Washington Post*, www. washingtonpost.com/opinions/she-called-his-elevator-joke-offensive-he-called-her-complaint-frivolous-whos-right/2018/05/03/43ba4084-4ee1-11e8-af46-b1d6dc0d9bfe_story.html?utm_term=.a9a400b8232a (archived at https://perma.cc/H86L-RPVU)

4 Marcus, R (2018) She called his elevator joke offensive. He called her complaint 'frivolous'. Who's right? *Washington Post*, www. washingtonpost.com/opinions/she-called-his-elevator-joke-offensive-he-called-her-complaint-frivolous-whos-right/2018/05/03/43ba4084-4ee1-11e8-af46-b1d6dc0d9bfe_story.html?utm_term=.a9a400b8232a (archived at https://perma.cc/H86L-RPVU)

5 Friedersdorf, C (2018) Is 'ladies lingerie' a harmless joke or harassment? *The Atlantic*, www.theatlantic.com/politics/archive/2018/05/is-this-old-lingerie-joke-harmless-or-harassment/559760/ (archived at https://perma.cc/UWM9-DC24)

6 Parke, C (2018) Male professor faces sanction for elevator joke, calls it 'chilling example of political correctness', Fox News, www.foxnews.com/us/male-professor-faces-sanction-for-elevator-joke-calls-it-chilling-example-of-political-correctness (archived at https://perma.cc/BRM4-7PKP)

7 Mangan, K (2018) Dispute over 'lingerie' comment persists, as society rejects professor's appeal, *Chronicle of Higher Education*, www. chronicle.com/article/Dispute-Over-Lingerie-/245094 (archived at https://perma.cc/87F9-3BVS)

8 YouGov (2018) Should obesity be treated as a disease? Plus, family at weddings, and ladies lingerie joke results [survey results] https://yougov.co.uk/opi/surveys/results?utm_source=Twitter&utm_medium=daily_questions&utm_campaign=question_3#/survey/88d60672-5822-11e8-9add-95bf9f28ce1a/question/238c315d-5823-11e8-8c47-fb7f8d9b865b/age (archived at https://perma.cc/YAC5-R68D)

9 Smith, CE, Anderson, D and Strassberger, A (2018) Say you're sorry: Children distinguish between willingly given and coerced expressions of remorse, Wayne State University Press, April, www.jstor.org/stable/10.13110/merrpalmquar1982.64.2.0275?seq=1#page_scan_tab_contents (archived at https://perma.cc/L8UM-SLPJ) [last accessed 09/02/2019]

NOTES

10 Sky News (2018) Academic refuses to apologise for 'lame' lingerie joke, https://news.sky.com/story/academic-refuses-to-apologise-for-lame-lingerie-joke-11368097 (archived at https://perma.cc/VF6J-PQAJ)

11 Francescani, C (2019) A court-ordered apology to a 10-year-old leaves his family furious, ABC News, 19 January, abcnews.go.com/US/court-ordered-apology-10-year-leaves-family-furious/story?id=60483458 (archived at https://perma.cc/C8D3-T55R) [last accessed 19/02/2019]

12 Francescani, C (2019) A court-ordered apology to a 10-year-old leaves his family furious, ABC News, 19 January, abcnews.go.com/US/court-ordered-apology-10-year-leaves-family-furious/story?id=60483458 (archived at https://perma.cc/C8D3-T55R) [last accessed 19/02/2019]

13 Kuchler, H (2018) Facebook forced to apologise again over abuse posts, *Financial Times*, 18 July, www.ft.com/content/dd8b7daa-8a18-11e8-b18d-0181731a0340 (archived at https://perma.cc/2UVX-AMG2) [last accessed 19/02/2019]

14 Peterson, H (2018) Twitter CEO Jack Dorsey forced to apologise for eating Chick-fil-A during Pride Month, Business Insider, 12 June, www.businessinsider.com.au/twitter-ceo-apology-chick-fil-a-gay-pride-month-2018-6 (archived at https://perma.cc/S63K-S78S) [last accessed 19/02/2019]

15 Kids with Food Allergies (2018) Letter to the makers of the Peter Rabbit movie: Jokes about food allergies can put people in danger, https://community.kidswithfoodallergies.org/blog/letter-to-the-makers-of-the-peter-rabbit-movie-jokes-about-food-allergies-can-put-people-in-danger?fbclid=IwAR1V5S6sD725somBAJnFQlVEaeOBJa5MTpTz70R5yiaLN-Ap01xj5O-PB20 (archived at https://perma.cc/R2VQ-E46Q)

16 Kids with Food Allergies (2016) 15 easy ways to make a difference and raise food allergy awareness, 22 April, community.kidswithfoodallergies.org/blog/15-easy-ways-to-make-a-difference-and-raise-food-allergy-awareness (archived at https://perma.cc/U99C-4F27) [last accessed 19/02/2019]

17 Bieler, S (2016) Psoriasis on the silver screen: The one place where your spots disappear, National Psoriasis Foundation, www.psoriasis.org/blog/psoriasis-silver-screen (archived at https://perma.cc/J8QF-8ZY4)

18 Fortin, J (2018) Sony apologizes for Peter Rabbit movie allergy scene, *New York Times,* www.nytimes.com/2018/02/12/arts/peter-rabbit-food-allergy.html (archived at https://perma.cc/D7YG-AV3C)

19 Mendelson, S (2018) Sony should not have to apologize for the 'Peter Rabbit' controversy, *Forbes*, 12 February, www.forbes.com/sites/scottmendelson/2018/02/12/sony-should-not-have-to-apologize-for-the-peter-rabbit-controversy/ (archived at https://perma.cc/FD86-6GK7) [last accessed 19/02/2019]

20 Levine, DM (2012) Banking the least trusted industry in America: Report, Huffington Post, www.huffingtonpost.co.uk/2012/03/16/financial-industry-trust_n_1353564.html (archived at https://perma.cc/S4SJ-VSGG)

21 Thomas-Mason, L (2016) Furious Newcastle United fan throws season ticket at Steve McClaren, *Metro*, https://metro.co.uk/2016/03/05/furiousnewcastle-united-fan-throws-season-ticket-at-steve-mcclaren-5735384/ (archived at https://perma.cc/3LRP-H8ZD)

22 Office of National Statistics (2018) Median gross weekly earnings by place of work, Great Britain, April 2015, www.ons.gov.uk/visualisations/nesscontent/dvc126/ (archived at https://perma.cc/QU6X-G2DC)

23 Newcastle United FC (2015) Season tickets on general sale, www.nufc.co.uk/news/archive/season-tickets-on-general-sale (archived at https://perma.cc/2WUV-5UVY)

24 Conghaile, PO (2018) 'Someone else will take their seat' – Ryanair responds to backlash as free 10kg cabin bag era ends, *Irish Independent*, www.independent.ie/life/travel/someone-else-will-take-their-seat-ryanair-responds-to-backlash-as-free-10kg-cabin-bag-era-ends-37248759.html (archived at https://perma.cc/TL8S-A69R)

Chapter 13

1 Whipple, T (2017) Dogs take the lead when it comes to winning human empathy, *The Times,* www.thetimes.co.uk/article/dogs-take-the-lead-when-it-comes-to-winning-human-empathy-7598cmck2 (archived at https://perma.cc/7ATQ-J4M6)

2 Hirtzer, M (2018) United CEO acknowledges airline's mistake in puppy's death, Reuters, www.reuters.com/article/us-ual-dog-munoz/ united-ceo-acknowledges-airlines-mistake-in-puppys-death-idUSKBN1GX30L (archived at https://perma.cc/4UZL-R3MH)

3 Levin J, Arluke, A and Irvine, L (2017) Are people more disturbed by dog or human suffering? *Society and Animals*, 25 (1), https://brill.com/ abstract/journals/soan/25/1/article-p1_1.xml (archived at https:// perma.cc/AQQ6-CPBL)

4 Associated Press (2018) United CEO on puppy death: 'We got it wrong', AP News, 21 March, www.apnews.com/ a96ac49d20b24fe0922ec7f91e08f30f (archived at https://perma. cc/4F3E-FA2H)

5 Associated Press (2018) United CEO on puppy death: 'We got it wrong' [video], 21 March, www.youtube.com/watch?v=ZmreLErb-yY (archived at https://perma.cc/M34T-9UQE)

6 Zuckerberg, M (2010) From Facebook, answering privacy concerns with new settings, *Washington Post*, 24 May, www.washingtonpost.com/ wp-dyn/content/article/2010/05/23/AR2010052303828.html (archived at https://perma.cc/S77N-K76G) [last accessed 22/02/2019]

7 Zuckerberg, M (2010) From Facebook, answering privacy concerns with new settings, *Washington Post*, 24 May, www.washingtonpost.com/ wp-dyn/content/article/2010/05/23/AR2010052303828.html (archived at https://perma.cc/S77N-K76G) [last accessed 22/02/2019]

8 Tufecki, Z (2018) Why Zuckerberg's 14-year apology tour hasn't fixed Facebook, Wired, www.wired.com/story/why-zuckerberg-14-year-apology-tour-hasnt-fixed-facebook/

9 Glenza, J (2015) Bud Light sorry for 'removing no from your vocabulary for the night' label, *Guardian*, www.theguardian.com/ business/2015/apr/29/bud-light-slogan-no-means-no (archived at https://perma.cc/4C3E-93YW)

10 Wattles, J (2017) Dove apologizes for ad: We 'missed the mark' representing black women, CNN Business, https://money.cnn. com/2017/10/08/news/companies/dove-apology-racist-ad/index.html (archived at https://perma.cc/A2L9-7BAV)

11 Callahan, C (2019) Jameela Jamil called out Avon for body-shaming cellulite ads, *Today*, www.today.com/series/love-your-body/jameela-jamil-called-avon-out-their-cellulite-ads-t147276 (archived at https:// perma.cc/U9P6-B2V2)

12 Zatat, N (2018) Heineken admits it 'missed the mark' with 'terribly racist' advert, Indy100, 26 March, www.indy100.com/article/heineken-racist-advert-apology-light-beer-missed-mark-twitter-marketing-campaign-8273791 (archived at https://perma.cc/MY63-HMD8) [last accessed 22/02/2019]

13 Statista (nd) Revenue of Anheuser-Busch InBev (AB InBev) worldwide from 2005 to 2018 (in million U.S. dollars), www.statista.com/statistics/269112/revenue-of-anheuser-busch-inbev-worldwide/ (archived at https://perma.cc/PLZ9-3RCS)

14 Unilever (2018) Unilever full year 2017 results, www.unilever.com/Images/ir-q4-results-presentation_tcm244-515320_en.pdf (archived at https://perma.cc/YF82-UD58)

15 PepsiCo (2018) PepsiCo 2017 Annual Report, www.pepsico.com/docs/album/annual-reports/pepsico-inc-2017-annual-report.pdf (archived at https://perma.cc/5ML6-B4HF)

16 Hospitality Ireland (2018) Heineken posts 5% increase in revenue in 2017, www.hospitalityireland.com/heineken-posts-5-increase-revenue-2017/55745 (archived at https://perma.cc/CG5K-52M6) – (converted from Euro)

17 Cision PR Newswire (2018) Avon reports fourth-quarter and full-year 2017 results, PR Newswire, www.prnewswire.com/news-releases/avon-reports-fourth-quarter-and-full-year-2017-results-300599156.html (archived at https://perma.cc/66ZF-6XCP)

18 Statista (nd) Spending on marketing data in the United States from 2016 to 2018 (in million U.S. dollars), www.statista.com/statistics/818881/usa-marketing-data-spend/ (archived at https://perma.cc/F3F7-4SBC)

19 TripAdvisor (2015) Sometimes mistakes happen... will likely give it another try but... [guest review], www.tripadvisor.co.uk/ShowUserReviews-g1015443-d7894598-r274700617-Cerveceria_Los_Arbolitos-Olvera_Province_of_Cadiz_Andalucia.html (archived at https://perma.cc/5BTR-C82X)

20 Wright, R (2018) Saudi Arabia's investigation of Jamal Khashoggi's murder is a tragic farce, *The New Yorker,* www.newyorker.com/news/news-desk/saudi-arabias-investigation-of-jamal-khashoggis-murder-is-a-tragic-farce (archived at https://perma.cc/9NG3-2FDG)

21 Wright, R (2018) Saudi Arabia's investigation of Jamal Khashoggi's murder is a tragic farce, *The New Yorker*, www.newyorker.com/news/news-desk/saudi-arabias-investigation-of-jamal-khashoggis-murder-is-a-tragic-farce (archived at https://perma.cc/9NG3-2FDG) [last accessed 22/02/2019]

22 *Express* (2013) Bank's head in apology to US regulator, *Express*, www.express.co.uk/finance/city/386060/Bank-s-head-in-apology-to-US-regulator (archived at https://perma.cc/9UXW-2UP3)

Chapter 14

1 Schau, HJ and Gilly, MC (2003)We are what we post? Self-presentation in personal web space, Oxford University Press, 1 December, www.jstor.org/stable/10.1086/378616?seq=1#metadata_info_tab_contents (archived at https://perma.cc/7PJ7-RFKH) [last accessed 28/11/2018]

2 Sinek, S (2009) How great leaders inspire action,Ted.com [video], www.ted.com/talks/simon_sinek_how_great_leaders_inspire_action?language=en (archived at https://perma.cc/3A63-GJUR)

3 Sharp, B (2011) The flawed Stengel study of business growth, 30 December, byronsharp.wordpress.com/2011/12/30/flawed-stengel-study/ (archived at https://perma.cc/2Y7L-SEV9) [last accessed 20/05/2019]

4 McCarthy, J (2018) Richard Shotton on brand purpose: 'marketers have fallen out of love with marketing', The Drum, 22 November, www.thedrum.com/news/2018/11/22/richard-shotton-brand-purpose-marketers-have-fallen-out-love-with-marketing (archived at https://perma.cc/67WK-USEW) [last accessed 28/11/2018]

5 Craik, L (2017) How beauty giant Dove went from empowering to patronizing, *Guardian*, www.theguardian.com/fashion/2017/may/15/beauty-giant-dove-body-shaped-bottles-repair-damage (archived at https://perma.cc/NK5H-M5W9)

6 Brown, A (2017) I'm washing my hands of Dove's patronizing 'real beauty': give me back my old shower gel bottle, *Daily Record*, www.dailyrecord.co.uk/news/business-consumer/im-washing-hands-doves-patronising-10388911 (archived at https://perma.cc/9HQH-ZZ9F)

7 Kurtzleben, D (2015) How Dove went from moisturising to patronising, Vox.com, www.vox.com/2014/4/25/5652462/how-dove-went-from-a-soap-to-a-brand-feminists-love-to-hate (archived at https://perma.cc/EXP9-Y57Z)

8 Chumsky, S (2015) Why Dove's 'Choose Beautiful' campaign sparked a backlash, *Fortune*, http://fortune.com/2015/04/15/why-doves-choose-beautiful-campaign-sparked-a-backlash/ (archived at https://perma.cc/KX24-NPWC)

9 Phelvin, P and Wallop, H (2008) Innocent Smoothies accused over environmental marketing, *Telegraph*, 01 August, www.telegraph.co.uk/news/2484148/Innocent-Smoothies-accused-over-environmental-marketing.html (archived at https://perma.cc/FC4B-ETK3) [last accessed 28/11/2018]

10 Phelvin, P and Wallop, H (2008) Innocent Smoothies accused over environmental marketing, *Telegraph*, 01 August, www.telegraph.co.uk/news/2484148/Innocent-Smoothies-accused-over-environmental-marketing.html (archived at https://perma.cc/FC4B-ETK3) [last accessed 28/11/2018]

11 Rogers, C (2018) Patagonia on why brands 'can't reverse into purpose' through marketing, *Marketing Week*, 18 July, www.marketingweek.com/2018/07/18/patagonia-you-cant-reverse-into-values-through-marketing/ (archived at https://perma.cc/6PRF-9Y2W) [last accessed 28/11/2018]

12 Winer, S (2018) Ben & Jerry's anti-Trump flavor gives Israelis brain freeze, *The Times of Israel*, 1 December, www.timesofisrael.com/ben-jerrys-anti-trump-flavor-gives-israelis-brain-freeze/ (archived at https://perma.cc/UC8D-GTWE) [last accessed 28/11/2018]

13 Winer, S (2018) Ben & Jerry's anti-Trump flavor gives Israelis brain freeze, *The Times of Israel*, 1 December, www.timesofisrael.com/ben-jerrys-anti-trump-flavor-gives-israelis-brain-freeze/ (archived at https://perma.cc/UC8D-GTWE) [last accessed 28/11/2018]

14 Ben and Jerry's (2018) Twitter, @benandjerrys, 30 October, https://twitter.com/benandjerrys/status/1058207773278650369 (archived at https://perma.cc/TJW8-CTRG) [last accessed 28/11/2018]

15 Barnes, T (2017) UCL forced to apologise for 'dreaming of a white campus' tweet, 14 December, *Independent*, www.independent.co.uk/news/education/education-news/ucl-white-campus-tweet-christmas-apologise-snow-racism-lawn-university-college-london-a8110746.html (archived at https://perma.cc/ER5U-JMWA) [last accessed 12/06/2019]

16 Barnes, T (2017) UCL forced to apologise for 'dreaming of a white campus' tweet, 14 December, *Independent,* www.independent.co.uk/news/education/education-news/ucl-white-campus-tweet-christmas-apologise-snow-racism-lawn-university-college-london-a8110746.html (archived at https://perma.cc/ER5U-JMWA) [last accessed 12/06/2019]

17 Kemp, N (2018) Zoopla apologises for #Metoo ad blunder, *Campaign,* 1 February, campaignlive.co.uk (archived at https://perma.cc/BRS2-BKRJ) [last accessed 23/11/2018]

18 Advertising Standards Authority (2015) Advertising and religion: Avoiding offence, 13 March, www.asa.org.uk/news/advertising-and-religion-avoiding-offence.html (archived at https://perma.cc/D7HH-LK64) [last accessed 28/11/2018]

19 Kemp, N (2018) Zoopla apologises for #Metoo ad blunder, *Campaign,* 1 February, campaignlive.co.uk (archived at https://perma.cc/BRS2-BKRJ) [last accessed 23/11/2018]

20 Kemp, N (2018) Zoopla apologises for #Metoo ad blunder, *Campaign,* 1 February, campaignlive.co.uk (archived at https://perma.cc/BRS2-BKRJ) [last accessed 23/11/2018]

21 Greenfield, P (2017) Paperchase apologises for Daily Mail promotion after online backlash, 20 November, *Guardian,* www.independent.co.uk/news www.theguardian.com/media/2017/nov/20/paperchase-apologises-for-daily-mail-promotion-after-online-backlash [last accessed 18/11/2017]

22 Paperchase (2017) Twitter, 18 November, https://twitter.com/FromPaperchase/status/931885424909398016 (archived at https://perma.cc/3C7S-JR4F) [last accessed 23/11/2018]

23 Paperchase (2017) Twitter, 18 November, https://twitter.com/FromPaperchase/status/932541140657688577 (archived at https://perma.cc/4U9M-8JYF) [last accessed 23/11/2018]

24 Monllos, K (2017) Lessons Learned From the 5 Biggest Brand Fails of 2017: Uber, Pepsi, *Adweek,* www.adweek.com/brand-marketing/lessons-learned-from-the-5-biggest-brand-fails-of-2017-uber-pepsi-dove-and-more/ (archived at https://perma.cc/3C2W-GCWD) [last accessed 4/12/2018]

25 King, Bernice (2017) If only Daddy would have known about the power of #Pepsi, Twitter, 5 April, https://twitter.com/BerniceKing/status/849656699464056832 (archived at https://perma.cc/ATV8-9ULD) [last accessed 12/06/2019]

26 Franck, J (2017) 'Clearly we missed the mark': Pepsi just pulled this controversial ad, Business Insider, www.businessinsider.com/pepsi-pulled-controversial-ad-kendall-jenner-2017-4?r=US&IR=T (archived at https://perma.cc/85S7-XW8A)

Chapter 15

1 Rousseau, J-J (1903) *The Confessions of Jean Jacques Rousseau*, Aldus Society, London
2 Oliver, A (2019) Mother was no carousing floozie! *Mail on Sunday,* www.dailymail.co.uk/news/article-6712873/Princess-Margarets-son-write-biography-attacking-Crowns-portrayal-her.html (archived at https://perma.cc/9ALK-MV9X)
3 Scrivenor, P (2016) *Mad Toffs: The British Upper Classes at Their Best and Worst,* John Blake Publishing, London
4 Bensinger, K and Vartabedian, R (2009) Report reveals details on San Diego crach that led to recall, *Seattle Times,* www.seattletimes.com/nation-world/report-reveals-details-on-san-diego-crash-that-led-to-recall/ (archived at https://perma.cc/2HQA-DF8C)
5 Ross, B (2010) Toyota CEO apologizes to his customers: 'I Am Deeply Sorry', ABC News, https://abcnews.go.com/Blotter/toyota-ceo-apologizes-deeply/story?id=9700622 (archived at https://perma.cc/HZY2-VTBN)
6 Ross, B (2010) Toyota CEO apologizes to his customers: 'I Am Deeply Sorry', ABC News, https://abcnews.go.com/Blotter/toyota-ceo-apologizes-deeply/story?id=9700622 (archived at https://perma.cc/HZY2-VTBN)
7 BBC News (2010) MPs told to repay £1.1m expenses, http://news.bbc.co.uk/1/hi/uk_politics/8496729.stm (archived at https://perma.cc/G7XZ-SLG6)
8 *Guardian* (2009) 'Humiliated' Tory MP Peter Viggers quits over duck island expense claim, *Guardian,* www.theguardian.com/politics/2009/may/23/mps-expenses-conservatives (archived at https://perma.cc/CY4M-4PEQ)
9 Allen, N (2009) MPs' expenses: Sir Peter Viggers claimed for £1,600 floating duck island, *Telegraph,* www.telegraph.co.uk/news/newstopics/mps-expenses/5357568/MPs-expenses-Sir-Peter-Viggers-claimed-for-1600-floating-duck-island.html (archived at https://perma.cc/E8AH-HMHX)

10 Nikkhah, R (2009) MPs' expenses: Sir Peter Viggers' ducks rejected their floating island, *Telegraph*, www.telegraph.co.uk/news/newstopics/mps-expenses/5375613/MPs-expenses-Sir-Peter-Viggers-ducks-rejected-their-floating-island.html (archived at https://perma.cc/W34E-3WKC)

11 *The Star* (2011) 'Free Libya 'gets a lifeline', *Toronto Star*, 19 March, www.thestar.com/opinion/editorials/2011/03/19/free_libyagets_a_lifeline.html (archived at https://perma.cc/YQB6-SVUC) [last accessed 18/11/2018]

12 Maxwell, K (2011) Buzzword: Optics, The MacMillan Dictionary, 18 March, www.macmillandictionary.com/ (archived at https://perma.cc/4ACB-933G) [last accessed 18/11/2018]

13 Maxwell, K (2011) Buzzword: Optics, The MacMillan Dictionary, 18 March, www.macmillandictionary.com/us/buzzword/entries/optics.html (archived at https://perma.cc/C4EX-UY3P) [last accessed 18/11/2018]

14 Sky News (2011) Topman Withdraws 'Offensive' T-Shirts, https://news.sky.com/story/topman-withdraws-offensive-t-shirts-10485908 (archived at https://perma.cc/7V3L-Q44X)

15 Webb, S (2014) Topman forced to apologise after selling jacket with SS symbol on chest, *Daily Mail,* www.dailymail.co.uk/news/article-2603624/Topman-forced-apologise-selling-jacket-SS-symbol-chest.html (archived at https://perma.cc/UA3S-GDP8)

16 McGovern, A (2018) Hi @Topman. No idea what is behind this, but it is very unfortunate. Hope you can discontinue the tshirt asap please, Twitter, 15 March, https://twitter.com/Alison_McGovern/status/974398690000547840 (archived at https://perma.cc/TAW4-VHG7) [last accessed 19/02/2019]

17 Nsubuga, J (2018) Topman under fire after releasing 'insulting Hillsborough disaster t-shirt', *Metro*, https://metro.co.uk/2018/03/16/topman-fire-releasing-insulting-hillsborough-disaster-t-shirt-7391737/ (archived at https://perma.cc/B92A-29HP)?

18 Sharman, J (2018) Topman stops selling red '96' T-shirt after fury from Liverpool fans and Hillsborough survivors, *Independent,* www.independent.co.uk/news/uk/home-news/topman-liverpool-fc-fans-hillsborough-disaster-karma-tshirt-anger-a8258686.html (archived at https://perma.cc/LUK2-29SJ)

19 Powell, T (2018) Topman 96 shirt: red top which 'inadvertently mocks Hillsborough disaster' with 'what goes around comes around' slogan is slammed, *Evening Standard,* www.standard.co.uk/news/uk/liverpool-fans-slam-red-topman-shirt-which-inadvertently-mocks-hillsborough-disaster-a3791371.html (archived at https://perma.cc/M75F-DSEN)

20 Weaver, M (2018) Topman withdraws T-shirt from sale after Hillsborough row, *Guardian,* www.theguardian.com/uk-news/2018/mar/16/topman-withdraws-t-shirt-from-sale-after-hillsborough-row (archived at https://perma.cc/7969-95WP)

Chapter 16

1 Johnson, K (2018) Starbucks CEO: Reprehensible outcome in Philadelphia incident, Starbucks.com, https://stories.starbucks.com/press/2018/starbucks-ceo-reprehensible-outcome-in-philadelphia-incident/ (archived at https://perma.cc/CZD6-7NXX)

2 Fletcher, C and Patton, L (2018) Starbucks' training shutdown could cost it $16.7 million in lost sales, *AdAge*, 18 April, adage.com/article/cmo-strategy/starbucks-training-shutdown-cost-16-7-million/313191 (archived at https://perma.cc/7VQR-JZA8) [last accessed 28/11/2018]

3 Sharpe, B (2018) Hotep Jesus talks Starbucks prank on FOX News with Laura Ingraham [video], YouTube, www.youtube.com/watch?v=_uom5-aTvCY (archived at https://perma.cc/DXY7-EB29)

4 Hyken, S (2018) Starbucks gets an A in crisis management, *Forbes*, 10 May, www.forbes.com/sites/shephyken/2018/05/10/starbucks-gets-an-a-in-crisis-management/#13cdac457998 (archived at https://perma.cc/6CB6-5VZY) [last accessed 28/11/2018]

5 Doubek, J (2018) Starbucks: No purchase needed to use the restroom, NPR, www.npr.org/sections/thetwo-way/2018/05/11/610337214/starbucks-will-give-people-the-key-to-restroom-regardless-of-purchase-ceo-says (archived at https://perma.cc/MTG4-FQB8)

6 Sorkin, AR (2019) Howard Schultz draws fire from Trump and Bloomberg over 2020 plans, *New York Times,* www.nytimes.com/2019/01/27/us/politics/howard-schultz-president-2020.html (archived at https://perma.cc/74LK-6V8N)

Chapter 17

1 Smith, A (2010) BP's television ad blitz, CNN Money, https://money. cnn.com/2010/06/03/news/companies/bp_hayward_ad/index.htm (archived at https://perma.cc/4LNB-PHE6)

2 YouGov (2010) Omnibus poll, Huffington Post, https://big.assets. huffingtonpost.com/toplines_oilspill_0312132013.pdf (archived at https://perma.cc/TG79-JRMH)

3 YouGov (2010) Omnibus poll, Huffington Post, https://big.assets. huffingtonpost.com/toplines_oilspill_0312132013.pdf (archived at https://perma.cc/TG79-JRMH) [last accessed 06/02/2019]

4 Bourdon, W (2018) 4 lessons of what not to do when you mess up, learned from Uber's apology tour, *Adweek*, www.adweek.com/ creativity/4-lessons-of-what-not-to-do-when-you-mess-up-learned-from-ubers-apology-tour/ (archived at https://perma.cc/8LTU-UCYW)

5 Bourdon, W (2018) 4 lessons of what not to do when you mess up, learned from Uber's apology Tour, *Adweek*, www.adweek.com/ creativity/4-lessons-of-what-not-to-do-when-you-mess-up-learned-from-ubers-apology-tour/ (archived at https://perma.cc/8LTU-UCYW)

6 Alpha (2018) Do people find corporate apology advertisements to be effective?, Alpha, 21 June, platform.alphahq.com/report/19d29022e8c 624c5801283393a63d805 (archived at https://perma.cc/2CTV-T5AL) [last accessed 09/02/2019]

7 Shepherd, A (2018) Why Jack Dorsey's apology tour backfired, *The New Republic,* https://newrepublic.com/article/150798/jack-dorseys-apology-tour-backfired (archived at https://perma.cc/AP6U-9S96)

8 Katz, AJ (2018) Here's How Much It Costs to Advertise in This Year's NBA Finals, *Adweek,* www.adweek.com/tv-video/heres-how-much-it-costs-to-advertise-in-this-years-nba-finals/ (archived at https://perma. cc/4GT2-EZ3A)

9 Bennett College (2019) The Papa John's Foundation donates $500,000 to Bennett College, Bennett College website, 14 January, www.bennett. edu/news/the-papa-johns-foundation-donates-500000-to-bennett-college/ (archived at https://perma.cc/CS2S-2ZZS) [last accessed 06/02/2019]

10 Bennett College (2019) The Papa John's Foundation donates $500,000 to Bennett College, Bennett College website, 14 January, www.bennett. edu/news/the-papa-johns-foundation-donates-500000-to-bennett-college/ (archived at https://perma.cc/CS2S-2ZZS) [last accessed 06/02/2019]

11 Burges, S (2018) Topshop apologises and donates £25,000 to charity after removing feminist stall, Sky News, https://news.sky.com/story/topshop-apologies-and-donates-25-000-to-charity-after-removing-feminist-stall-11518592 (archived at https://perma.cc/HH3Z-UQ54)

12 MSN News (2018) Scarlett Curtis Explains The TopShop/'Feminist's Don't Wear Pink' Controversy, www.msn.com/en-us/lifestyle/lifestyle-buzz/scarlett-curtis-explains-the-topshop-feminists-dont-wear-pink-controversy/vi-BBO7eR0 (archived at https://perma.cc/V3KA-KVG3)

13 Heffer, G (2018) HMRC spends £10,000 on flowers to say 'sorry' for tax mistakes, Sky News, 31 November, news.sky.com/story/amp/hmrc-spends-10000-on-flowers-to-say-sorry-for-tax-mistakes-11540764) [last accessed 06/02/2019]

14 Kickstarter (2013) We were wrong [blog], www.kickstarter.com/blog/we-were-wrong (archived at https://perma.cc/9YYP-B7JC)

15 Wall, M (2018) Aer Lingus apologises to staff over 'stealing' claim, *The Irish Times,* www.irishtimes.com/news/ireland/irish-news/aer-lingus-apologises-to-staff-over-stealing-claim-1.3723656 (archived at https://perma.cc/JU92-WK4Q)

16 Kim, T (2018) Elon Musk makes the 'most valuable apology of all time' on Tesla's earnings call, CNBC, 2 August, www.cnbc.com/2018/08/02/wall-street-says-elon-musks-contrition-on-tesla-call-could-be-most-v.html (archived at https://perma.cc/G9QJ-UY64) [last accessed 2/8/2018]

17 Kim, T (2018) Elon Musk makes the 'most valuable apology of all time' on Tesla's earnings call, CNBC, 2 August, www.cnbc.com/2018/08/02/wall-street-says-elon-musks-contrition-on-tesla-call-could-be-most-v.html (archived at https://perma.cc/G9QJ-UY64) [last accessed 2/8/2018]

18 Lieberman, D (2011) Netflix CEO Reed Hastings' apology fails to stop stock slide, Deadline, https://deadline.com/2011/09/netflix-ceo-reed-hastings-apology-fails-to-stop-stock-slide-173487/ (archived at https://perma.cc/M2QM-AJXC)

19 Lieberman, D (2011) Netflix CEO Reed Hastings' apology fails to stop stock slide, Deadline, https://deadline.com/2011/09/netflix-ceo-reed-hastings-apology-fails-to-stop-stock-slide-173487/ (archived at https://perma.cc/M2QM-AJXC)

20 Meyersohn, N (2018) Facebook's stock drops after Zuckerberg apologizes, CNN, 22 March, https://money.cnn.com/2018/03/22/news/companies/facebook-stock/index.html (archived at https://perma.cc/QWA6-6WU5) [last accessed 09/02/2019]

21 Balakrishnan, A (2017) Scandals may have knocked $10 billion off Uber's value, a report says, CNBC, www.cnbc.com/2017/04/25/uber-stock-price-drops-amid-sexism-investigation-greyballing-and-apple-run-in-the-information.html (archived at https://perma.cc/RE32-HYG3)

22 Kotasova, I (2017) United loses $250 million of its market value, CNN Money, https://money.cnn.com/2017/04/11/investing/united-airlines-stock-passenger-flight-video/ (archived at https://perma.cc/UZ4B-N6XE)

23 Racine, MD, Wilson, C and Wynes, M (2018)The Value of Apology: How do corporate apologies moderate the stock market reaction to non-financial corporate crises? *Journal of Business Ethics*, October, www.researchgate.net/publication/328411361_The_Value_of_Apology_How_do_Corporate_Apologies_Moderate_the_Stock_Market_Reaction_to_Non-Financial_Corporate_Crises (archived at https://perma.cc/5PCR-Y68L) [last accessed 06/02/2019]

24 Reid, W (2018) Dissecting the anatomy of two corporate apologies, University of Virginia, https://news.virginia.edu/content/dissecting-anatomy-two-corporate-apologies (archived at https://perma.cc/22VW-LPRN)

25 Mulholland, R (2013) Croat group says it will drop suit against Bob Dylan if he apologises for 'race slur', *Telegraph*, 3 December, www.telegraph.co.uk/news/worldnews/europe/france/10491697/Croat-group-says-it-will-drop-suit-against-Bob-Dylan-if-he-apologises-for-race-slur.html (archived at https://perma.cc/W2CG-K3LK) [last accessed 06/02/2019]

26 McMichael, BJ, Van Horn, R and Viscusi, WK (2018) Sorry is never enough: How state apology laws fail to reduce medical malpractice liability risk, 6 February, Stanford Law Review, Forthcoming, https://ssrn.com/abstract=2883693 (archived at https://perma.cc/9S2J-RQBK)

27 Morton, H (2018) Medical Professional Apologies Statutes, National Conference of State Legislatures, www.ncsl.org/research/financial-services-and-commerce/medical-professional-apologies-statutes.aspx (archived at https://perma.cc/6F74-7TRD)

28 McMichael, BJ, Van Horn, R and Viscusi, WK (2018) Sorry is never enough: How state apology laws fail to reduce medical malpractice liability risk, 6 February, Stanford Law Review, Forthcoming, https://ssrn.com/abstract=2883693 (archived at https://perma.cc/9S2J-RQBK)

29 McMichael, BJ, Van Horn, R and Viscusi, WK (2018) Sorry is never enough: How state apology laws fail to reduce medical malpractice liability risk, 6 February, Stanford Law Review, Forthcoming, https://ssrn.com/abstract=2883693 (archived at https://perma.cc/9S2J-RQBK) [select Open in PDF browser and see page 1]

30 Duff-Brown, B (2018) In patient injury cases, revealing facts, offering apology does not lead to increase in lawsuits, Stanford Medicine News Centre, 2 October, med.stanford.edu/news/all-news/2017/10/in-patient-injury-cases-offering-apology-does-not-lead-to-lawsuit-increase.html (archived at https://perma.cc/4JD6-C45K) [last accessed 06/02/2019]

31 Duff-Brown, B (2018) In patient injury cases, revealing facts, offering apology does not lead to increase in lawsuits, Stanford Medicine News Centre, 2 October, med.stanford.edu/news/all-news/2017/10/in-patient-injury-cases-offering-apology-does-not-lead-to-lawsuit-increase.html (archived at https://perma.cc/4JD6-C45K) [last accessed 06/02/2019]

32 Ho, B and Liu, E (2019) Does sorry work? The impact of apology laws on medical malpractice, Johnson School Research Paper Series, December, https://papers.ssrn.com/sol3/papers.cfm?abstract_id=1744225 (archived at https://perma.cc/FGK3-X6C9) [last accessed 06/02/2019]

Chapter 18

1 Klein, E (2017) Lyft spent years preparing for Uber's cultural crisis, Vox.com, 21 July, www.vox.com/technology/2017/6/21/15845380/uber-kalanick-resignation-lyft (archived at https://perma.cc/K3NM-8ZKK) [last accessed 26/11/2018]

2 Klein, E (2017) Lyft spent years preparing for Uber's cultural crisis, Vox.com, 21 July, www.vox.com/technology/2017/6/21/15845380/uber-kalanick-resignation-lyft (archived at https://perma.cc/K3NM-8ZKK) [last accessed 26/11/2018]

3 Halperin, B, Ho, B, List, JA and Muir, I (2018) Toward an understanding of the economics of apologies: evidence from a large-scale natural field experiment, September, s3.amazonaws.com/fieldexperiments-papers2/papers/00644.pdf (archived at https://perma.cc/G5MN-JDEN) [last accessed 28/11/2018]

4 Richards, K (2014) Confirmed: companies have been editing Wikipedia pages to make themselves look better, Business Insider, 11 June, www.businessinsider.com/pr-agencies-agree-to-stop-wikipedia-edits-2014-6?r=US&IR=T (archived at https://perma.cc/WS62-RYZN) [last accessed 28/11/2018]

5 Yu, S (2014)'How firms are using 'black PR' to tear down their rivals, *South China Morning Post*, 3 January, www.scmp.com/business/china-business/article/1396461/how-firms-are-using-black-pr-tear-down-their-rivals (archived at https://perma.cc/NC2S-C2NU) [last accessed 28/11/2018]

6 Cox, J (2018) Scammers threaten to review bomb a travel company unless it pays ransom, Motherboard, 28 August, www.vice.com/en_us/article/8xbpdb/scammers-review-bomb-twitter-bots-instagram-fake-reviews-cheapair-std-company (archived at https://perma.cc/YTM9-7SVA) [last accessed 26/11/2018]

7 @Mr_P_pom (2018) Twitter, 18 November, https://twitter.com/Mr_P_pom/status/1064297928326434816 (archived at https://perma.cc/P5EB-Z4WR) [last accessed 26/11/2018]

8 American Airlines (2018) Twitter, 18 November, https://twitter.com/AmericanAir/status/1064299900328910849 (archived at https://perma.cc/B2RK-YLWA)

9 Cox, J (2018) Scammers threaten to review bomb a travel company unless it pays ransom, Motherboard, 28 August, motherboard.vice.com/ (archived at https://perma.cc/FJE8-CBPN) [last accessed 26/11/2018]

10 Association of National Advertisers (2018) Advertisers love influencer marketing: ANA Study, www.ana.net/content/show/id/48437 (archived at https://perma.cc/L8DA-5XBL)

11 Shamsian, J (2018) Beauty brands are reportedly paying $85,000 to influencers who trash their competitors on YouTube, Insider, 30 August, www.thisisinsider.com/brands-reportedly-paying-influencers-to-criticize-makeup-competitors-2018-8 (archived at https://perma.cc/5MU5-DKZY) [last accessed 4/12/2018]

12 Wischhover, C (2018) The shady world of beauty influencers and the brands that pay them, explained, Vox.com, www.vox.com/2018/8/31/17801182/beauty-influencers-pay-negative-reviews (archived at https://perma.cc/X32X-LEET)

13 Stell, M (2018) The (ugly) truth about beauty influencers exposed, Instagram, www.instagram.com/p/BnBcIHngBhy/?hl=en&taken-by=kjbennettbeauty (archived at https://perma.cc/X9HS-JZYV)

14 Shamsian, J (2018) Beauty brands are reportedly paying $85,000 to influencers who trash their competitors on YouTube, Insider, 30 August, www.thisisinsider.com/brands-reportedly-paying-influencers-to-criticize-makeup-competitors-2018-8 (archived at https://perma.cc/5MU5-DKZY) [last accessed 4/12/2018]

15 Prant, D (2018) We wore what is in hot water over allegedly copying jewelry designs, Fashionista, 27 May, https://fashionista.com/2018/05/danielle-bernstein-we-wore-what-jewelry-copy-diet-prada-allegations (archived at https://perma.cc/ZLZ4-PNV9) [last accessed 4/12/2018]

16 Tashjian, R (2018) Can we ever really #cancel Dolce & Gabbana? Garage, 26 November, https://garage.vice.com/en_us/article/d3by7q/dolce-gabbana-diet-prada-cancel (archived at https://perma.cc/BJM7-KXDF) [last accessed 4/12/2018]

17 Harrison, K (2018) Want to try influencer marketing? Be careful, *Forbes*, 22 May, www.forbes.com/sites/kateharrison/2018/05/22/want-to-try-influencer-marketing-be-careful/#2aceac4b4a8b (archived at https://perma.cc/MPU8-GP6F) [last accessed 4/12/2018]

18 Lorenz, T (2018) Rising Instagram stars are posting fake sponsored content, *The Atlantic*, 18 December, www.theatlantic.com/technology/archive/2018/12/influencers-are-faking-brand-deals/578401/ (archived at https://perma.cc/5W9U-LUA4) [last accessed 09/01/2019]

19 Schwartz, B (2013) Google says no comment on why Interflora was penalized, Search Engine Land, https://searchengineland.com/google-says-no-comment-on-why-interflora-was-penalized-149308 (archived at https://perma.cc/MRM7-WJPU)

20 Haynes, M (2014) Negative SEO: Should you be worried? If attacked, what should you do? Moz.com, https://moz.com/blog/preparing-for-negative-seo (archived at https://perma.cc/Q73D-KA9D)

21 Holiday, R (2012) *Trust Me, I'm Lying: Confessions of a media manipulator*, Penguin, London

22 Holiday, R (2012) *Trust Me, I'm Lying: Confessions of a media manipulator*, Penguin, London

Chapter 19

1 Martin, D (2016) Guardian is forced into a humiliating apology for its Corbyn train film report written by a hardline supporter, *Daily Mail*, 8 October, www.dailymail.co.uk/news/article-3827990/Guardian-forced-humiliating-apology-Corbyn-train-film-report-written-hardline-supporter.html (archived at https://perma.cc/R8UT-KCHT) [last accessed 09/02/2019]

2 Shortlist (2019) The Daily Mail forced to issue humiliating apology for misleading Paris article, Shortlist, 7 February, www.shortlist.com/news/daily-mail-apology-misleading-paris-article/379914 (archived at https://perma.cc/YBS7-2QGC) [last accessed 09/02/2019]

3 Johnson, S and Cramb, A (2019) Nicola Sturgeon issues humiliating apology after Alex Salmond wins legal case over sexual harassment inquiry, *Telegraph*, 8 January, www.telegraph.co.uk/politics/2019/01/08/nicola-sturgeon-issues-humiliating-apology-alex-salmond-wins/ (archived at https://perma.cc/Y7ZQ-VANF) [last accessed 09/02/2019]

4 Bucktin, C (2017) America issues humiliating apology to Britain over claims MI6 helped Barack Obama spy on Donald Trump, *Daily Mirror*, 17 March, www.mirror.co.uk/news/world-news/america-issues-humiliating-apology-britain-10048194 (archived at https://perma.cc/3NN4-ZAFJ) [last accessed 09/02/2019]

5 BBC (1998) Japanese Premier apologises to prisoners of war, BBC, 14 January, news.bbc.co.uk/1/hi/47293.stm (archived at https://perma.cc/P5MF-2NWE) [last accessed 27/02/2019]

6 BBC (1998) Japanese Premier apologises to prisoners of war, BBC, 14 January, news.bbc.co.uk/1/hi/47293.stm (archived at https://perma.cc/P5MF-2NWE) [last accessed 27/02/2019]

7 Smith, J (1998) Not so much an apology, more a tabloid PR stunt stunt, *Independent*, 18 January, www.independent.co.uk/voices/not-so-much-an-apology-more-a-tabloid-pr-stunt-stunt-1139299.html (archived at https://perma.cc/Y8V6-N6VV) [last accessed 27/02/2019]

8 Mitchell, D (2012) I'm sorry but this constant demand for public apologies really offends me, *Guardian*, 25 March, www.theguardian.com/commentisfree/2012/mar/25/public-apologies-gingrich-de-niro (archived at https://perma.cc/U6DA-UW9M) [last accessed 17/08/2018]

9 BBC News (2016) Gillian Duffy: 'I don't want to be a European', www.bbc.co.uk/news/av/uk-politics-eu-referendum-36373649/gillian-duffy-i-don-t-want-to-be-a-european (archived at https://perma.cc/LB99-HWDF)

10 Elliott, C (2009) Pushy bloggers to travel industry: Be nice, CNN, http://edition.cnn.com/2009/TRAVEL/traveltips/03/23/blogging.travel.complaints/

11 Lamé, A (2018) Twitter, 16 October, https://twitter.com/amylame/status/1052174601676042240 (archived at https://perma.cc/4DU7-NVL9) [last accessed 4/11/2018]

12 Johnson, J (2018) Waitrose to rename 'sexist' sandwich after protest by feminist campaigner, *The Telegraph,* www.telegraph.co.uk/news/2018/10/17/waitrose-rename-sexist-sandwich-protest-feminist-campaigner/ (archived at https://perma.cc/742A-5JSH)

13 Young, S (2018) Waitrose renames 'sexist' gentlemen's roll after complaints, *Independent,* www.independent.co.uk/life-style/waitrose-gentlemans-roll-sexist-sandwich-kleenex-mansize-name-twitter-a8589466.html (archived at https://perma.cc/EBX4-E9J2)

14 Barnett, H (2018) Waitrose to change sandwich's name after it's branded 'sexist', *Express,* www.express.co.uk/news/uk/1033343/waitrose-sandwich-sexist-heston-blumenthal-causer-sandwich (archived at https://perma.cc/3F6C-H5XA)

15 Bartiromo, M (2018) British supermarket Waitrose changing name of 'Gentleman's' sandwich after controversy, Fox News, www.foxnews.com/food-drink/british-supermarket-waitrose-changing-gentlemans-sandwich-after-controversy (archived at https://perma.cc/XHJ5-K4Y4)

16 Aldersley, M (2018) Waitrose is forced to rename 'sexist' sandwich, *Daily Mail*, www.dailymail.co.uk/news/article-6287773/Waitrose-forced-rename-sexist-sandwich-known-Gentlemans-Roll.html (archived at https://perma.cc/AG7U-RDBN)

17 Young, S (2018) Waitrose renames 'sexist' gentlemen's roll after complaints, *Independent*, www.independent.co.uk/life-style/waitrose-gentlemans-roll-sexist-sandwich-kleenex-mansize-name-twitter-a8589466.html (archived at https://perma.cc/EBX4-E9J2)

18 Griffiths, J (2018) Blum-ing ridiculous: Waitrose has been called out over a 'sexist' SANDWICH... and forced to change its name, *The Sun*, www.thesun.co.uk/fabulous/food/7537736/waitrose-sexist-sandwich-change-name/ (archived at https://perma.cc/EL6N-7PC2)

19 Griffiths, J (2018) Blum-ing ridiculous: Waitrose has been called out over a 'sexist' SANDWICH... and forced to change its name, *The Sun*, www.thesun.co.uk/fabulous/food/7537736/waitrose-sexist-sandwich-change-name/ (archived at https://perma.cc/EL6N-7PC2)

20 Young, S (2018) Waitrose renames 'sexist' gentlemen's roll after complaints, *Independent*, www.independent.co.uk/life-style/waitrose-gentlemans-roll-sexist-sandwich-kleenex-mansize-name-twitter-a8589466.html (archived at https://perma.cc/EBX4-E9J2)

21 Johnson, J (2018) Waitrose to rename 'sexist' sandwich after protest by feminist campaigner, *Telegraph*, www.telegraph.co.uk/news/2018/10/17/waitrose-rename-sexist-sandwich-protest-feminist-campaigner/ (archived at https://perma.cc/742A-5JSH)

22 Nazir, S (2019) Waitrose apologises & pulls 'racist' Easter ducklings from sale, *Retail Gazette*, www.retailgazette.co.uk/blog/2019/04/waitrose-apologises-pulls-racist-easter-ducklings-from-sale/ (archived at https://perma.cc/H9XZ-VCB9)

23 Racine, MD, Wilson, C and Wynes, M (2018) The value of apology: How do corporate apologies moderate the stock market reaction to non-financial corporate crises? *Journal of Business Ethics*, October, www.researchgate.net/publication/328411361_The_Value_of_Apology_How_do_Corporate_Apologies_Moderate_the_Stock_Market_Reaction_to_Non-Financial_Corporate_Crises (archived at https://perma.cc/5PCR-Y68L) [last accessed 06/02/2019]

24 Waterson, J (2018) Waitrose magazine editor quits after joke about killing vegans, *Guardian,* www.theguardian.com/business/2018/oct/31/ waitrose-magazine-editor-william-sitwell-steps-down-over-email-mocking-vegans (archived at https://perma.cc/WE8T-3HWZ)

Chapter 20

1 Siegel, T (2018) Never have to say you're sorry: Meet Japan's apology artist, *Tokyo Weekender*, 20 November, www.tokyoweekender. com/2018/11/never-say-youre-sorry-meet-japans-apology-artist/ (archived at https://perma.cc/F2MZ-M5ZT) [last accessed 27/02/2019]

2 Greenslade, R (2009) Evening Standard launches ad campaign to say sorry to Londoners, *Guardian,* 4 May, www.theguardian.com/media/ greenslade/2009/may/04/london-evening-standard-alexander-lebedev (archived at https://perma.cc/XCQ6-NXA4) [last accessed 27/02/2019]

3 Mueller, J-W (2010) Has Germany really come to terms with its past?, *Guardian*, 21 October, www.theguardian.com/commentisfree/2010/ oct/21/has-germany-come-to-terms-past (archived at https://perma.cc/ R3J3-JSAN) [last accessed 27/02/2019]

4 Qureshi, B (2013) From wrong to right: A US apology for japanese internment, National Public Radio, www.npr.org/sections/ codeswitch/2013/08/09/210138278/japanese-internment-redress (archived at https://perma.cc/GSE7-24A8)

5 Fastenburg, D (2010) American Slavery and Jim Crow, *Time*, http://content.time.com/time/specials/packages/article/0,28804, 1997272_1997273_1997278,00.html (archived at https://perma. cc/28NZ-D63T)

6 Blatz, C, Schumann, K and Ross, M (2009) Government apologies for historical injustices, *Political Psychology,* https://web.stanford. edu/~omidf/KarinaSchumann/KarinaSchumann_Home/Publications_ files/Blatz.Schumann.Ross.PoliticalPsychology.2009.pdf

7 Turtle Island Native Network (2007) Community members said No!, Monthly News Brief, http://webcache.googleusercontent.com/ search?q=cache:H6Z8fa2qlGgJ:www.turtleisland.org/discussion/ viewtopic.php%3Ff%3D23%26t%3D5305+&cd=2&hl=en&ct= clnk&gl=us (archived at https://perma.cc/23ER-PXWX)

8 CBC News (2008) A history of residential schools in Canada, www.cbc.ca/news/canada/a-history-of-residential-schools-in-canada-1.702280 (archived at https://perma.cc/GTG2-AX4G)

9 McKenna, M (1997) Different Perspectives on Black Armband History, Parliament of Australia, Politics and Public Administration Group, www.aph.gov.au/About_Parliament/Parliamentary_Departments/ Parliamentary_Library/pubs/rp/RP9798/98RP05 (archived at https:// perma.cc/F85A-U3ET)

10 Mark, M (2016) Justin Trudeau apologizes for getting physical with lawmakers in a chaotic House of Commons exchange, Business Insider, www.businessinsider.com/justin-trudeau-physical-altercation-house-of-commons-2016-5?r=US&IR=T (archived at https://perma.cc/YAG9-TRXS)

11 Besner, L (2018) Sorry not sorry: is Canada apologising too much?, *Guardian*, 16 May, www.theguardian.com/commentisfree/2018/ may/16/canada-justin-trudeau-apologising-too-much (archived at https://perma.cc/Z6X3-RSJG) [last accessed 27/02/2019]

12 Stewart, JDM (2018) Just in our time, *The Globe and Mail* [letters], www.theglobeandmail.com/opinion/letters/just-in-our-time/ article711341/ (archived at https://perma.cc/H5JT-C7TC)

13 Hargie, O, Stapleton, K and Tourish, D (2010) Interpretations of CEO public apologies for the banking crisis: Attributions of blame and avoidance of responsibility, School of Communication, University of Ulster, 15 June, citeseerx.ist.psu.edu/viewdoc/download?doi= 10.1.1.883.4802&rep=rep1&type=pdf (archived at https://perma. cc/6DHX-VX9C) [last accessed 27/02/2019]

14 Minder, R and Malkin, E (2019) Mexican call for conquest apology ruffles feathers in Spain. And Mexico, *New York Times*, 27 March, www.nytimes.com/2019/03/27/world/americas/mexico-spain-apology. html (archived at https://perma.cc/PY9H-69JG) [last accessed 27/03/2019]

15 Stanley, J (2018) *New York Times*, www.nytimes.com/2018/09/10/ opinion/germanys-nazi-past-is-still-present.html (archived at https:// perma.cc/R8GV-UKFE)

16 Connolly, K (2019) Extreme-right wing of Germany's AfD placed under surveillance, *Guardian*, www.theguardian.com/world/2019/ jan/15/extreme-right-wing-germany-afd-under-surveillance (archived at https://perma.cc/5VMR-HUQU)

17 Huggler, J (2017) AfD politician calls for Germany to stop atoning for Nazi past, *Telegraph*, www.telegraph.co.uk/news/2017/01/18/afd-politician-calls-germany-stop-atoning-nazi-past/ (archived at https://perma.cc/J5ZN-44XD)

18 Nayar, PK (2016) Contrition chic and the politics of public apology, The Wire, 10 May, https://thewire.in/history/contrition-chic-or-the-politics-of-public-apology (archived at https://perma.cc/LJ56-JSPW) [last accessed 27/02/2019]

19 Nayar, PK (2016) Contrition chic and the politics of public apology, The Wire, 10 May, https://thewire.in/history/contrition-chic-or-the-politics-of-public-apology (archived at https://perma.cc/LJ56-JSPW) [last accessed 27/02/2019]

20 Warner, G (nd) The apology broker, National Public Radio, www.npr.org/templates/transcript/transcript.php?storyId=619207707 (archived at https://perma.cc/QU42-JC48)

21 Luh, A and Black, I (2016) Erdoğan has apologised for downing of Russian jet, Kremlin says, *Guardian*, www.theguardian.com/world/2016/jun/27/kremlin-says-erdogan-apologises-russian-jet-turkish (archived at https://perma.cc/TF85-KVJP)

22 Gutman, R and Surk, B (2016) After apparent coup, a crackdown in Turkey, *Politico*, www.politico.eu/article/turkish-military-in-attempted-coup-says-pm/ (archived at https://perma.cc/2QNV-FMUW)

23 Thompson, S (2019) Is Justin Trudeau apologizing for the right reason? *Global News*, https://globalnews.ca/news/4982184/justin-trudeau-jody-wilson-raybould-apology/ (archived at https://perma.cc/BSL6-NKAM)

24 BBC News (2019) Trudeau and Wilson-Raybould: The crisis that could unseat Canada's PM, BBC, www.bbc.co.uk/news/world-us-canada-47408239 (archived at https://perma.cc/87E5-S9QV)

Chapter 21

1 Wheaton, O (2015) 'Yes. We are beach body ready': New advert pokes fun at Protein World poster, *Metro*, https://metro.co.uk/2015/04/30/yes-we-are-beach-body-ready-dove-pokes-fun-at-world-protein-poster-with-new-advert-5175375/ (archived at https://perma.cc/833S-95E4)

2 ASA (2015) ASA adjudication on Protein World Ltd, Advertising Standards Association, www.asa.org.uk/rulings/protein-world-ltd-a15-300099.html (archived at https://perma.cc/MVF2-Y844)

3 Change.org (2015) Apologise for and amend the irresponsible marketing of your new bra range 'body', www.change.org/p/victoriassecret-apologise-for-your-damaging-perfect-body-campaign-iamperfect (archived at https://perma.cc/UF26-C6LA)

4 Fenton, S (2015) Topshop pulls 'ridiculously skinny' mannequins after being shamed by customer on Facebook, *Independent,* www.independent.co.uk/life-style/fashion/news/topshop-pulls-ridiculously-skinny-mannequins-after-being-shamed-by-customer-10420421.html (archived at https://perma.cc/57Y8-9842)

5 Change.org (2015) Apologise for and amend the irresponsible marketing of your new bra range 'body', www.change.org/p/victoriassecret-apologise-for-your-damaging-perfect-body-campaign-iamperfect (archived at https://perma.cc/UF26-C6LA)

6 ASA (2015) ASA adjudication on Protein World Ltd, Advertising Standards Association, www.asa.org.uk/rulings/protein-world-ltd-a15-300099.html (archived at https://perma.cc/MVF2-Y844)

7 Cosslett, RL (20150 Am I beach body ready? Advertisers, that's none of your business, www.theguardian.com/commentisfree/2015/apr/15/beach-body-ready-brands-sexist-advertising-tactics (archived at https://perma.cc/G7A2-UCZX)

8 Wignall, L (2015) 'Beach ready?' posters 'adapted' by campaigners, BBC Newsbeat, 24 April, https://bbc.co.uk/newsbeat/article/32398162/beach-ready-posters-adapted-by-campaigners (archived at https://perma.cc/KA89-7SYF) [last accessed 09/01/2019]

9 Meehan, N (2015) Recently social media's been buzzing with the Protein World advertising campaign story, Brandwatch, www.brandwatch.com/blog/guide-demonstrating-the-value-of-pr-just-got-a-whole-lot-easier/ (archived at https://perma.cc/ARB3-Y872)

10 Brinded, L (2015) Protein World makes £1 million immediately after the 'Beach Body Ready' campaign backlash, Business Insider, www.businessinsider.com/protein-world-makes-1-million-immediately-after-the-beach-body-ready-campaign-backlash-2015-4?r=UK&IR=T (archived at https://perma.cc/QTM5-UUWG)

11 Meehan, N (2015) Recently social media's been buzzing with the Protein World advertising campaign story, Brandwatch, www. brandwatch.com/blog/guide-demonstrating-the-value-of-pr-just-got-a-whole-lot-easier/ (archived at https://perma.cc/ARB3-Y872) [last accessed 09/01/2019]

12 Clarke-Billings, L (2015) Everyone is still really angry about this beach body advert but the diet company says it's just a minority 'making noise', 25 April, www.indy100.com/article/everyone-is-still-really-angry-about-this-beach-body-advert-but-the-diet-company-says-its-just-a-minority-making-noise–lJxMUGbzGeW (archived at https://perma.cc/5TW7-93HJ) [last accessed 13/01/2019]

13 Smith, A (2015) Why Protein World is reaping the rewards from its 'genuine integrity', *Campaign*, 28 April, www.campaignlive.co.uk/article/why-protein-world-reaping-rewards-its-genuine-integrity/1344885 (archived at https://perma.cc/T8NK-79XU) [last accessed 13/01/2019]

14 Mail Online (2015) Hopkins wades in to beach body row, *Daily Mail*, www.dailymail.co.uk/wires/pa/article-3057311/40-000-sign-beach-body-ad-petition.html (archived at https://perma.cc/2RKC-R5RK)

15 Innermedia (2015) Protein World: Brand strategies that sell, www.innermedia.co.uk/protein-world-brand-strategies-that-sell/ (archived at https://perma.cc/MZX9-CRDA)

16 Wassermann, T (2014) Brewer blasts beer censors with 'Sorry not sorry' letter, MashableUK, https://mashable.com/2014/04/28/scottish-brewer-shows-how-to-issue-a-damn-apology/?europe=true (archived at https://perma.cc/Z6KA-Y8KE)

17 Al-Othman, H (2015) Brick Lane Coffee shop comes under fire for 'Sorry, No Poor People' sign after Shoreditch anti-gentrification protests, *Evening Standard*, www.standard.co.uk/news/london/brick-lane-coffee-shop-comes-under-fire-for-sorry-no-poor-people-sign-a3086976.html (archived at https://perma.cc/DV54-4AAX)

18 McCarthy, J (2018) Poundland's naughty elf campaign returns: 'it will be the ASA's worst nightmare', The Drum, www.thedrum.com/news/2018/11/01/poundlands-naughty-elf-campaign-returns-it-will-be-the-asa-s-worst-nightmare (archived at https://perma.cc/H2Q7-GLRR)

19 Buck, K (2018) Poundland being investigated over X-rated adverts which saw an elf 'teabagging' Barbie, *Metro*, 3 January, https://metro. co.uk/2018/01/03/poundland-being-investigated-over-x-rated-adverts-which-saw-an-elf-teabagging-barbie-7200529/ (archived at https:// perma.cc/J5JP-J3U3) [last accessed 13/01/2019]

20 McCarthy, J (2018) Poundland's naughty elf campaign returns: 'it will be the ASA's worst nightmare', The Drum, 01 November, www. thedrum.com/news/2018/11/01/poundlands-naughty-elf-campaign-returns-it-will-be-the-asa-s-worst-nightmare (archived at https://perma. cc/NA85-7EDM) [last accessed 13/01/2019]

21 Buck, K (2018) Poundland being investigated over X-rated adverts which saw an elf 'teabagging' Barbie, *Metro*, 3 January, metro.co.uk (archived at https://perma.cc/NT9N-88S5) [last accessed 13/01/2019]

22 Smith, A (2015) Why Protein World is reaping the rewards from its 'genuine integrity', *Campaign*, 28 April, www.campaignlive.co.uk/ article/why-protein-world-reaping-rewards-its-genuine-integrity/1344885 (archived at https://perma.cc/T8NK-79XU) [last accessed 13/01/2019]

23 Oster, E (2019) Why brands spend $5 million (or more) on a Super Bowl ad to support a cause, *Adweek*, 28 January, www.adweek.com/ brand-marketing/why-cause-related-super-bowl-ads-are-here-to-stay/ (archived at https://perma.cc/C6NF-FG9K) [last accessed 06/02/2019]

24 Peterson, H (2018) Twitter CEO Jack Dorsey forced to apologise for eating Chick-fil-A during Pride Month, Business Insider Australia, www.businessinsider.com.au/twitter-ceo-apology-chick-fil-a-gay-pride-month-2018-6 (archived at https://perma.cc/S63K-S78S)

25 Bergh, C (2018) Ending the gun violence epidemic in America, Levis. com, 4 September, www.levistrauss.com/unzipped-blog/2018/09/04/ ending-gun-violence/ (archived at https://perma.cc/KV5A-YTXY) [last accessed 06/02/2019]

26 Parker, K, Horowitz, JM, Igielnik, R, Oliphant, JB and Brown, A (2017) The demographics of gun ownership, Pew Research Center, www.pewsocialtrends.org/2017/06/22/the-demographics-of-gun-ownership/ (archived at https://perma.cc/3P39-Z4NC)

27 Bain, M (2018) After losing a generation of American jeans-wearers, Levi's is recapturing its cool, Quartzy, 17 May, qz.com/ quartzy/1271588/after-losing-a-generation-of-american-jeans-wearers-

levis-is-recapturing-its-cool/ (archived at https://perma.cc/Z8GY-WKFB) [last accessed 06/02/2019]

28 NRA-ILA (2018) (2018) Levi's teams with billionaire Michael Bloomberg to attack gun rights, National Rifle Association Institute for Legislative Action, 7 September, www.nraila.org/articles/20180907/levi-s-teams-with-billionaire-michael-bloomberg-to-attack-gun-rights (archived at https://perma.cc/7LLD-5GMV) [last accessed 06/02/2019]

29 Oster, E (2018) Majority of consumers want brands to take a stand on social and political issues, according to new study, *Adweek*, 12 January, www.adweek.com/brand-marketing/majority-of-consumers-want-brands-to-take-a-stand-on-social-and-political-issues-according-to-new-study/ (archived at https://perma.cc/747P-TJN9) [last accessed 15/01/2019]

30 Schau, HJ and Gilly, MC (2003)We are what we post? Self-presentation in personal web space, Oxford University Press, 1 December, www.jstor.org/stable/10.1086/378616?seq=1# metadata_info_tab_contents (archived at https://perma.cc/7PJ7-RFKH) [last accessed 28/11/2018]

31 Gilliland, N (2018) Five brand campaigns that took a stand on social issues, eConsultancy, 4 January, econsultancy.com/five-brand-campaigns-that-took-a-stand-on-social-issues/ (archived at https://perma.cc/8L5N-6M9K) [last accessed 15/01/2019]

32 Reyes, L (2018) President Trump: Nike's Colin Kaepernick ad sends 'terrible message', *USA Today,* https://eu.usatoday.com/story/sports/nfl/2018/09/04/nike-colin-kaepernick-president-donald-trump-protest/1196111002/ (archived at https://perma.cc/955A-NX8F)

33 Hudak, J (2018) Big & Rich's John Rich blasts Nike over Colin Kaepernick ad, *Rolling Stone,* www.rollingstone.com/music/music-country/big-richs-john-rich-blasts-nike-over-colin-kaepernick-ad-718648/ (archived at https://perma.cc/6RC9-BVCL)

34 BBC (2018) Colin Kaepernick: Nike suffers #justburnit backlash over advertising campaign, BBC Sport, www.bbc.co.uk/sport/american-football/45407340 (archived at https://perma.cc/Z983-NZ6D)

35 Casey, S (2007) Patagonia: Blueprint for green business, *Fortune,* http://archive.fortune.com/magazines/fortune/fortune_archive/2007/04/02/8403423/index.htm (archived at https://perma.cc/K46D-EYZK)

36 Bergman, S (2019) Piers Morgan almost vomits after tasting Greggs' vegan sausage roll on Good Morning Britain, *Independent*, www.independent.co.uk/life-style/piers-morgan-greggs-vegan-sausage-roll-good-morning-britain-snowflakes-a8716071.html (archived at https://perma.cc/9SHH-JGVW)

37 McCarthy, J (2019) How a bold vegan sausage roll launch left Piers Morgan with Greggs on his face, The Drum, www.thedrum.com/news/2019/01/04/how-bold-vegan-sausage-roll-launch-left-piers-morgan-with-greggs-his-face (archived at https://perma.cc/EV5L-AXC3)

38 Gillette (2019) We believe: The best men can be [video], www.youtube.com/watch?v=koPmuEyP3a0 (archived at https://perma.cc/ZCD9-VUNC)

39 Ostler, J (2019) Gillette me get this ad right, Kantar Insights, 29 January, uk.kantar.com/business/brands/2019/gillette-me-get-this-ad-right/ (archived at https://perma.cc/2H3T-DNLN) [last accessed 09/03/2019]

40 Kemp, N (2019) Pissing off Piers Morgan is a valid marketing strategy for Gillette, *Campaign*, 15 January, www.campaignlive.co.uk/article/pissing-off-piers-morgan-valid-marketing-strategy-gillette/1522940 (archived at https://perma.cc/AYG5-XPCE) [last accessed 15/01/2019]

Chapter 22

1 YouGov (2017) Marks and Spencer is the top brand among women, https://yougov.co.uk/topics/consumer/articles-reports/2017/03/03/marks-and-spencer-top-brand-women (archived at https://perma.cc/495M-7K58)

2 Brinded, L (2018) Marks & Spencer is a decrepit vestige of Britain's class wars, Quartz, 24 May, qz.com/quartz/ [last accessed 21/01/2019]

3 Weaver, M (2018) Marks & Spencer accused of sexism over 'fancy knickers' display, *Guardian*, 12 November, www.theguardian.com/business/2018/nov/21/marks-and-spencer-in-sexism-row-over-fancy-knickers-display (archived at https://perma.cc/6RJZ-J722) [last accessed 29/01/2019]

4 Redman, E (2018) Hi @SofitelBrisbane, your breakfast looks delicious! Hey and just wanted to let you know I'm a woman and I also read the @FinancialReview every day, Twitter, 7 October, https://twitter.com/ elizabethredman/status/1049034184570929154 (archived at https:// perma.cc/95YY-XKKV) [last accessed 29/01/2019]

5 Jackson, K (2018) Breakfast ad leaves Sofitel with egg on its face, Accom News, 10 October, www.accomnews.com.au/2018/10/ breakfast-ad-leaves-sofitel-with-egg-on-its-face/ (archived at https:// perma.cc/59ZQ-UAQU) [last accessed 08/10/2018]

6 Yahoo Finance (2018) Hotel forced to apologise for 'sexist' ad of couple enjoying breakfast in bed, https://finance.yahoo.com/news/ hotel-forced-apologise-sexist-ad-couple-enjoying-breakfast- bed-2-085623770.html (archived at https://perma.cc/RY3Q-7X8L)

7 Sullivan, R (2018) He's reading the AFR, she's reading a Chanel book: Why women are angry about Sofitel hotel ad, News.com.au, www. news.com.au/lifestyle/relationships/dating/hes-reading-afr-shes-reading- a-chanel-book-why-women-are-pissed-off-about-sofitel-hotel-ad/ news-story/6629cbabae416ef71f525fc8040f5c0e (archived at https:// perma.cc/HA6H-7AH9)

8 Griffiths, J (2018) Hotel's 'misguided' ad of couple eating breakfast in bed pulled for angering women, *The Sun,* www.foxnews.com/travel/ hotel-australia-brisbane-breakfast-bed-ad (archived at https://perma.cc/ M2EQ-6PCX)

9 Margan, M and Lackey, B (2018) Turns out this ad ISN'T sexist! *Daily Mail Australia,* www.dailymail.co.uk/news/article-6254945/Sofitel- Brisbane-advert-ISNT-sexist-Daily-Mail-Australia-poll-reveals.html (archived at https://perma.cc/V57C-83JF)

10 *Daily Mirror* (2018) Hotel forced to take down sexist advert, www. mirror.co.uk/news/world-news/hotel-forced-take-down- sexist-13388057 (archived at https://perma.cc/7JRJ-LDFV)

11 Jarram, M (2018) Model pokes fun at M&S window display accused of being sexist, *Nottingham Post,* 21 November, www.nottinghampost. com/news/local-news/model-pokes-fun-ms-window-2245282 (archived at https://perma.cc/QA7N-8GLV) [last accessed 28/11/2018]

12 Weaver, M (2018) Marks & Spencer accused of sexism over 'fancy knickers' display, *Guardian,* 12 November, www.theguardian.com/

business/2018/nov/21/marks-and-spencer-in-sexism-row-over-fancy-knickers-display (archived at https://perma.cc/6RJZ-J722) [last accessed 29/01/2019]

13 Fischer, S (2018) Trust in the media is starting to make a comeback, Axios, 18 December, www.axios.com/trust-in-american-media-still-low-but-improving-bf7842ca-9ddb-4334-a865-6e98f5334db2.html (archived at https://perma.cc/4YS8-9TKW) [last accessed 29/01/2019]

14 *Daily Mirror* (2013) Calls for Marks & Spencer boycott due to toilet roll 'with Allah symbol', www.mirror.co.uk/news/uk-news/calls-marks–spencer-boycott-13895745 (archived at https://perma.cc/T89Q-S8NP)

15 Wright, M (2018) Brewery apologies after use of Hindu symbol on beer bottle sparks protest, *Telegraph,* www.telegraph.co.uk/news/2018/12/28/brewery-apologies-use-hindu-symbol-beer-bottle-sparks-protest/ (archived at https://perma.cc/U7F7-JL3B)

16 Change.org (nd) Remove marks and spencer toilet paper, www.change.org/p/marks-and-spencer-remove-marks-and-spencer-toilet-paper (archived at https://perma.cc/2JS9-28WC)

17 Marks & Spencer (2019) Twitter.com, 19 January, https://twitter.com/marksandspencer/status/1086672109248626688 (archived at https://perma.cc/8NJT-SCE2)

18 Massimo, S, Ferrara, E and De Domenico, M (2018) Bots increase exposure to negative and inflammatory content in online social systems, Proceedings of the National Academy of Sciences of the United States of America, www.pnas.org/content/115/49/12435 (archived at https://perma.cc/SF9H-P7Q9)

19 Fischer, S (2018) Trust in the media is starting to make a comeback, Axios, 18 December, www.axios.com/trust-in-american-media-still-low-but-improving-bf7842ca-9ddb-4334-a865-6e98f5334db2.html (archived at https://perma.cc/4YS8-9TKW) [last accessed 29/01/2019]

20 Google Finance (nd) Marks and spencer share price trend, www.google.com/search?ei=mdpQXPeAF7Oo1fAPj4ad0A0&q=marks+and+spencer+share+price+trend&oq=marks+and+spencer+share+price+tr&gs_l=psy-ab.3.1.35i39j0i22i30l2.6421.7100..8787...0.0..0.200.459.4j0j1......0....1..gws-wiz.......0i71.QqkebRuwXv4 (archived at https://perma.cc/X5UV-6LRP)

21 Taylor, K (2018) Chipotle has rehired the manager that it had fired for refusing to serve customers she suspected of dining and dashing, Business Insider, www.businessinsider.com/chipotle-rehires-manager-dine-and-dash-drama-2018-11?r=US&IR=T (archived at https://perma.cc/4QP5-ZRU3)

Chapter 23

1 McDermott, J (2014) Should brands apologize so much in social media?, Digiday UK, 16 April, digiday.com/marketing/brands-apology-social-media/ (archived at https://perma.cc/4QY5-YQDZ) [last accessed 29/03/2019]

2 Mayhew, F (2017) Daily Mail blames small group of hard left corbynistas for Paperchase ban on promotions in paper, *Press Gazette*, www.pressgazette.co.uk/daily-mail-blames-small-group-of-hard-left-corbynistas-for-paperchase-ban-on-promotions-in-paper/ (archived at https://perma.cc/XW8U-EM47)

3 Racine, MD, Wilson, C and Wynes, M (2018)The value of apology: How do corporate apologies moderate the stock market reaction to non-financial corporate crises? *Journal of Business Ethics*, October, www.researchgate.net/publication/328411361_The_Value_of_Apology_How_do_Corporate_Apologies_Moderate_the_Stock_Market_Reaction_to_Non-Financial_Corporate_Crises (archived at https://perma.cc/5PCR-Y68L) [last accessed 06/02/2019]

4 CBS News (2017) JetBlue refuses to apologize for removing family of five from flight, CBS, www.cbsnews.com/news/jetblue-refuses-to-apologize-for-removing-family-of-five-from-flight/ (archived at https://perma.cc/H8WY-L9ED)

5 Finn, J (2017) Family of five is kicked off a JetBlue flight and banned from the airline after a heated row with a manager because their agitated daughter, one, kicked the seat in front of her, *Daily Mail*, 19 July, www.dailymail.co.uk/news/article-4709046/Family-five-kicked-banned-JetBlue-without-reason.html (archived at https://perma.cc/M9WR-3WYB) [last accessed 27/04/2019]

6 CBS News (2017) JetBlue refuses to apologize for removing family of five from flight, CBS, www.cbsnews.com/news/jetblue-refuses-to-apologize-for-removing-family-of-five-from-flight/ (archived at https://perma.cc/H8WY-L9ED) [last accessed 27/04/2019]

7 ten Brinke, L and Adams, GS () Saving face? When emotion displays during public apologies mitigate damage to organizational performance, *Organizational Behavior and Human Decision Processes*, 1 June, citeseerx.ist.psu.edu/viewdoc/download?doi=10.1.1.706.2307&rep=rep1&type=pdf [last accessed 29/03/2019]

8 Knowledge@Wharton (2012) Tylenol and the Legacy of J&J's James Burke, *Time*, http://business.time.com/2012/10/05/tylenol-and-the-legacy-of-jjs-james-burke/ (archived at https://perma.cc/N2MC-7VU8)

9 *Chicago* (2012) Chicago Tylenol murders: The first domestic terror incident, *Chicago*, www.chicagomag.com/Chicago-Magazine/October-2012/Chicago-Tylenol-Murders-An-Oral-History/index.php?cparticle=5&siarticle=4&requiressl=true (archived at https://perma.cc/HMK6-ABMK)

10 YouTube (nd) James Burke [video] https://youtu.be/N2MSmOqcQb4?t=369 (archived at https://perma.cc/FS3U-AT45)

11 YouTube (nd) James Burke [video] https://youtu.be/N2MSmOqcQb4?t=495 (archived at https://perma.cc/M7YN-89BS)

12 YouTube (2011) James Burke [video] www.youtube.com/watch?v=N2MSmOqcQb4 (archived at https://perma.cc/L49L-2Y6E)

13 Knowledge@Wharton (2012) Tylenol and the Legacy of J&J's James Burke, *Time*, http://business.time.com/2012/10/05/tylenol-and-the-legacy-of-jjs-james-burke/ (archived at https://perma.cc/N2MC-7VU8)

14 Pandya, M, Shell, R, Warner, S, Junnarkar, S and Brown, J (2004) *Nightly business report presents Lasting Leadership: What you can learn from the Top 25 business people of our times*, Wharton, Philadelphia, PA

15 Johnson & Johnson (nd) James Burke: The Johnson & Johnson CEO who earned a presidential Medal of Freedom, www.jnj.com/our-heritage/james-burke-johnson-johnson-ceo-who-earned-presidential-medal-of-freedom (archived at https://perma.cc/B5MA-HQSJ)

16 YouTube (2011) James Burke [video] www.youtube.com/watch?v=N2MSmOqcQb4 (archived at https://perma.cc/L49L-2Y6E)

17 Frantz, CM and Bennigson, C (2005) Better late than early: The influence of timing on apology effectiveness, *Journal of Experimental Social Psychology*, March, www.researchgate.net/publication/ 222331911_Better_Late_Than_Early_The_Influence_of_Timing_on_ Apology_Effectiveness (archived at https://perma.cc/S8XP-ZGWY) [last accessed 29/03/2019]

Index